Segmented work, divided workers

P9-DMM-187

Segmented work, divided workers

The historical transformation of labor in the United States

DAVID M. GORDON
Department of Economics
New School for Social Research

RICHARD EDWARDS
Department of Economics
University of Massachusetts, Amherst

MICHAEL REICH
Department of Economics
University of California, Berkeley

CAMBRIDGE UNIVERSITY PRESS
CAMBRIDGE
LONDON   NEW YORK   NEW ROCHELLE
MELBOURNE   SYDNEY

Published by the Press Syndicate of the University of Cambridge
The Pitt Building, Trumpington Street, Cambridge CB2 1RP
32 East 57th Street, New York, NY 10022, USA
296 Beaconsfield Parade, Middle Park, Melbourne 3206, Australia

© Cambridge University Press 1982

First published 1982
Reprinted 1982, 1983

Printed in the United States of America

Library of Congress Cataloging in Publication Data
Gordon, David M.
Segmented work, divided workers.
Bibliography: p.
Includes index.
1. Labor and laboring classes – United States –
History. 2. Labor supply – United States – History.
3. Capitalism. I. Edwards, Richard.
II. Reich, Michael. III. Title.
HD8066.G65   331'.0973   81–17010
ISBN 0 521 23721 1 hard covers   AACR2
ISBN 0 521 28921 1 paperback

Contents

v

Contents

Tables and figures

Tables

Tables and figures

Figures

Preface

This book grew out of an urgent political concern about persistent political and economic divisions among workers in the United States. These divisions have helped frustrate widespread hopes for a much broader and more dynamic progressive movement in this country. We argue in this book that such disunity persists in large part as a result of historically created objective divisions among workers in their production experiences.

The work leading to this book has passed through several stages. We began, along with others, by helping shape the "dual labor market" hypothesis (see Doeringer and Piore, 1971; and Gordon, 1972a, for a summary of these early efforts). This idea suggested that U.S. workers were located in two qualitatively distinct, nonconvergent labor markets: the *primary* and the *secondary* labor markets. According to the dual labor market hypothesis, the characteristic kinds of jobs in each market created fundamentally different working experiences for "primary" and "secondary" workers.

As originally formulated, the dual labor market hypothesis soon seemed inadequate. It built upon an eclectic theoretical foundation; it had not yet been grounded in a historical analysis of the development of production and labor markets in the United States; and it did not illuminate many of the important dimensions of differentiation among American workers.

We subsequently sought with others to address these weaknesses in dual labor market theory. Papers presented at a conference on labor market segmentation developed some of these concerns. The three of us presented a general historical analysis of the origins of labor market differentiation, and we then formulated a tripartite rather than a dual analysis of divisions among workers. Several others presented specific historical and theoretical analyses of labor market segmentation (see Edwards, Reich, and Gordon, 1975; Piore, 1975; Stone, 1975; and Wachtel, 1975). We had chosen the term "segmentation" in order (1) to suggest that there were more than just two important divisions in the labor market, as the dual labor market view suggested;

ix

(2) to emphasize that labor market divisions are connected by a process through which, to rely on the dictionary, a whole organically "gives origin to one or more new cells by segmentation"; and (3) to distinguish our work from the "social stratification" literature upon which so much of the end-of-ideology analysis depended (see Chapter 1 for a brief review of this literature).

Although most of these early efforts were rather primitive, they nonetheless attracted a certain amount of attention, simply because they represented an interesting alternative view of labor market structure and divisions among workers. (See, in addition to the work just cited, Harrison, 1972; Wachtel and Betsey, 1972; and Bluestone, Murphy, and Stevenson, 1973.) The limitations of this early work generated three main strands of critical response.

First, many Marxist critics questioned the theoretical basis for these early analyses of labor market segmentation. What was the relation between the value-theoretic categories of classical Marxism and the institutional/historical/empirical perceptions that framed the segmentation hypotheses? How could one relate analyses of the mode of production to analyses of segmentation? If tendencies toward the segmentation of labor have recent origins, upon what basis were we arguing that capitalist development "caused" segmentation? Was it not possible that the historical and institutional causes of labor market segmentation were discrete from the dynamics of capitalism?

Second, many neoclassical economists expressed skepticism about the importance and qualitative character of the labor market divisions highlighted by the segmentation analysis. (Cain, 1975, 1976; and Wachter, 1974, present most of these criticisms.) Had we imposed the structural divisions we observed in the data by a priori expectations, or did we provide legitimate tests for structural differentiation? How was it possible to reconcile labor market divergence with the competitive (and homogenizing) mechanisms upon which neoclassical labor market theory rests? Although early tests of the dual labor market and segmentation hypotheses presented evidence supporting hypotheses of behavioral differentiation among segments, could one not easily argue that these tests suffered from incomplete model specification and truncated sample bias?

Third, many historians wondered about the historical accuracy and specificity of our accounts of the origins of segmentation. Was it really possible to distinguish, as our analysis apparently presumed, between historical tendencies promoting job specialization and fragmentation, on the one hand, and those promoting segmentation, on the other? Were our generalizations about the sweep of U.S. labor history obscuring more precise insights available through concrete studies of production and working-class movements?

Many of these criticisms seemed pertinent and appropriate, and they have prompted further efforts to develop analyses of working-class divisions.

Some radical economists have pursued more rigorous theoretical integration of segmentation analysis with classical Marxian value theory and historical materialism. Bowles and Gintis (1977), for example, provide one account of the relationship between heterogeneous labor and the labor theory of value.

Other scholars have pursued cross-sectional empirical specification and analysis of segmentation in production and in labor markets. While many of these empirical studies are beset by data and methodological limitations, the evidence supporting the segmentation perspective continues to mount. (See Edwards, 1979, ch. 9, and Wilkinson, in press, for a review of most of this more recent empirical evidence.)

The historical project has seemed in many ways the least developed. Although U.S. labor historians have opened many new vistas for analyzing and appreciating the history of work and workers in the United States, few have sought to integrate economic analyses of the dynamics of capital accumulation with historical analyses of the complexity, totality, and specificity of working-class experience. The work of David Montgomery (1979, 1980) and his students comes closest, but even their important contributions fall short, in our view, of a systematic account of the connections between capitalist development and working-class life in the United States.

In this book we explore further the historical dimension of labor segmentation analysis. We address two critical questions: Where did labor segmentation come from in the United States? Why did it develop?

We believe that we have made substantial progress on both questions. At the same time, we also recognize that our analysis is ambitious and that our research has opened many more issues than it has closed. We hope this book will stimulate at least some of the additional research that further exploration of our hypotheses requires. We look forward to joining with others in such continuing work.

In preparing this book we have drawn in many ways from the work and suggestions of many of our colleagues and students. To all of them, we offer a collective note of appreciation. Each of us has benefited from the labors of research assistants; we are grateful to Randy Albelda, Joseph Bowring, Bob Cohen, Susan Gabbard, Charles Jeszeck, Paul Ong, and Will Whittemore. We would also like to thank the institutions that have supported some of the research leading to this book: the U.S. Department of Labor, the National Bureau of Economic Research, the Center for Educational Policy Research at Harvard University, the Institute of Industrial Relations at the University of California at Berkeley, and the Institute for Research on Educational Finance and Governance at Stanford University.

We note finally that, in order to emphasize the cooperative character of our work, we have continued our previous policy of rotating the order of our names on the title page.

D.M.G.

R.E.

M.R.

1

The historical transformation of labor: an overview

American capitalism is experiencing a prolonged economic crisis, different in form from but as intractable and profound as the Depression of the 1930s. The manifestations of this crisis surround us. Persistent inflation has reflected a competitive, "zero-sum" scramble to maintain real incomes. Interest rates have fluctuated wildly, at times rising to record levels, increasingly threatening to place home ownership beyond the reach of all but the affluent. Unemployment has stabilized at levels nearly twice those of the mid-1960s, prompting apologetic economists to redefine "full employment." Shortages of basic necessities have recurred. The Social Security system, bedrock of the New Deal effort to protect citizens from economic uncertainty, now seems to rest on shifting sands. Other casualties of the crisis abound: workplace health and safety rules, environmental protection, affirmative action, labor law reform, and more.

Underneath these symptoms lie more threatening portents. The growth of productivity in the U.S. economy has slowed substantially, puzzling nearly everyone who has explored the problem. Whole industries in the United States have flirted with bankruptcy, and the economic crisis has accelerated the devastating process of capital flight and runaway shops. The economy does not seem to work well anymore. Many forecasts for the rest of the 1980s are at least as gloomy as the surprised accounts of the 1970s.

Although the signs of crisis first appeared at the beginning of the 1970s, they were initially misperceived as the reparable consequences of various accidents and exogenous "shocks," such as the legacy of Vietnam or bad harvests or OPEC "piracy." However, the crisis has not only refused to disappear; it has continually deepened, and policy makers have recently begun to suggest major structural reforms, ranging from wholesale dismantling of government programs to "reindustrialization" to controls and economic planning. As the problems have begun to seem both fundamental and chronic, the proposed cures have become progressively more sweeping. Politicians,

1

neoconservative academics, industrialists and bankers, the business press, think tanks – all are getting into the act.

Everyone, indeed, but the one group whose behavior and response will probably be most critical for the direction and effectiveness of economic restructuring: the U.S. working class. Workers and the labor movement in the United States have not yet been able to articulate and advance a program for the resolution of the crisis that defends and furthers not only their own interests but also the general welfare. Why have U.S. workers been so quiescent?

This question raises longer-term issues. Why have unions in the past two decades or more suffered erosion of their relative numbers, cultural image, and political strength? Why have U.S. workers never been able to establish a serious labor-dominated political party? Why, in short, has the achievement of a working-class agenda always remained so distant?

These questions obviously require more than a discussion of the personalities and inclinations of current labor leaders; they require a historical and theoretical analysis of the development of the American working class. Many would agree on one fundamental, although obviously not sufficient, explanation for the relative weakness and taciturnity of U.S. workers. *The American working class is internally divided along many economic, political, and cultural dimensions.* It is critical, therefore, to understand the sources of these sharp and persistent cleavages.

In this book we argue that one cannot understand current divisions in the U.S. working class without tracing the character and effects of *labor segmentation,* of structural and qualitative differences in the jobs and labor markets through which workers secure their livelihood. We develop this argument through an analysis of the historical dynamics of institutional change in American labor-management structures and U.S. labor markets. Our analysis begins with the observation that the present crisis is not the first in our history; U.S. capitalism has experienced at least three prior periods of sustained crisis. We argue that the resolution of these crises resulted in three major structural changes in the organization of work and the structure of labor markets in the United States; labor segmentation represents the third of these three transformations. Each of these qualitative changes was both cause and consequence of larger, macrodynamic changes in the organization of American capitalism.

We propose more specifically that overlapping stages of *initial proletarianization, homogenization,* and *segmentation* have shaped the development of the labor process and labor markets in the United States since the early nineteenth century. Each of these stages crystallized when an economic crisis, not unlike the present crisis, was resolved through the emergence of a new institutional structure that restarted a period of rapid economic growth. The process through which these institutional structures emerged – again, not unlike the process of restructuring that we now see beginning in the current period – involved continuing and intense class conflict. And the manner in which the crisis was resolved led to structural changes that helped shape the American working class.

In the stage of *initial proletarianization,* from the 1820s to the 1890s, a supply of wage workers – producers who must sell their labor power to an employer for a wage or salary – was first created from a previously nonproletarian population. Wage labor became the dominant manner of organizing production. However, although employers hired workers, control over the process of work itself varied considerably among employers. Some employers directly supervised the organization of work while others left such direction to the workers; most typically, the growth of wage labor did not produce fundamental changes in the actual organization of work. The labor market was still rudimentary. Competition played only a small role in determining wages, and older workers passed skills on directly to younger workers.

In the *homogenization* period, from the 1870s to the onset of World War II, the organization of work and the structure of labor markets were profoundly transformed. More and more jobs in the capitalist sector of the economy were reduced to a common, semiskilled operative denominator, and control over the labor process became concentrated among employers and their foremen, who used direct supervision or machine pacing to "drive" their workers. The labor market became increasingly generalized and much more competitive. Skills were much less controlled by workers.

In the *segmentation* period, from the 1920s to the present, political-economic forces produced qualitative differences in the organization of work and three qualitatively distinct labor markets. Although the so-called drive system did not disappear, it was replaced in many sectors by a series of structured rules and incentives, including but not limited to collective bargaining agreements. General skills were increasingly transmitted through the educational system. The segmentation of labor forged and reproduced materially based divisions among U.S. workers that inhibited the growth of a unified working-class movement.

The analysis underlying these arguments requires a major substantive reformulation of the history of labor in the United States. In order to supply readers with a guide to this argument as it unfolds in succeeding chapters, we provide a general overview in this introduc-

3

tory chapter. We first locate our argument in relation to current explanations of working-class divisions, then introduce our analytical framework, and, finally, present a brief schematic summary of our principal hypotheses. Chapter 2 reviews the necessary theoretical foundations and the major implications of these hypotheses. Chapters 3, 4, and 5 develop the content of the historical argument itself. Chapter 6 provides a brief recapitulation of some of the main evidence supporting this argument. In the Epilogue, we trace some of the most important implications of our analysis for the evolution and potential resolution of the current economic crisis in the United States.

Current explanations of working-class divisions

For generations Marxists have frequently forecast that class conflict between workers and capitalists would engulf bourgeois society, eventually displacing or encompassing all other forms of conflict. Twentieth-century capitalist development has confounded that prediction. Particularly in the United States, it has become more and more difficult to recognize or identify the "class struggle" or the "working class." Instead of a spreading, increasingly self-conscious, anticapitalist working-class movement, there are divisions that have persisted and proliferated among people who depend on wage or salary income for their living and who therefore share the common status of "wage worker." Working people identify themselves primarily as blue-collar workers, youth, blacks, students, women, Southerners, Catholics, the poor, consumers, environmentalists, professionals, unionists, or office workers, and rarely as common members of a class defined by its relation to the means of production.

Why has a self-conscious working-class political movement failed to emerge? What forces thwarted its prospective development?

Many explanations of the weakness of working-class and socialist movements in the United States have been proposed (for one attempt at a comprehensive list, see Laslett and Lipset, 1974); these range from general denials of the salience of class in capitalist societies to specific arguments about special characteristics of the United States. Some explanations concern economic factors, such as the historically high levels of prosperity and economic growth in the United States; others examine political factors, such as the early achievement of male suffrage, the subordination of organized labor to the Democratic Party during the New Deal and subsequently, or the two-party winner-take-all electoral system of the United States; still others examine cultural forces, such as the power of the media or the historical prominence of racial, religious, and ethnic factors. Although we are

4

concerned with all these arguments and believe that at least several of them are compelling, in this book we focus on the importance and causes of *divisions within the working class* as a source of its weakness.

Four major explanations of working-class divisions in the United States have dominated the recent literature. We review these explanations briefly as background to a summary of our own argument.[1] Although each explanation contains some insights upon which we try to build, we find none of the four satisfactory by itself.

The first explanation has argued that "postindustrial" tendencies have effectively blurred traditional divisions between capitalists and workers. These tendencies have invalidated, one gathers, the traditional Marxian analysis of the determinant importance of individuals' class-based relation to the means of production. In its original versions, this mode of explanation often referred to the "end of ideology" and the "rise of the meritocracy."[2] Those who promoted it argued that the growing importance of technology and the service sector in advanced industrial societies has placed a rising premium on professional and technical skills. They also argued that entrepreneurial capitalism has given way to a "managerial revolution," that skilled managers have displaced owners as the dominant economic actors in capitalist societies. The end-of-ideologists argued that finely graduated occupational differentiations now provide the most robust guide to divisions and inequalities among different groups in society. People no longer view themselves as capitalists or workers, according to this perspective, but as individuals who belong to their respective status groups, defined primarily by occupational and consumption achievements. (This approach thus resembles the "human capital" school of neoclassical economics.) And because some residual discrimination and precapitalist associations still persist, people also view themselves as white, black, male, female, young, old, belonging to religious and ethnic groups, and so forth.

This explanation has the advantage of openly recognizing and addressing divisions that do persist. It also points to facts that have certainly been prominent in the American experience. However, the postindustrial theory goes too far in denying the utility of class categories. We suspect that working people have more in common than the meritocratic emphasis on occupational divisions implies. Everyone who needs to work for a living and encounters a boss on the job shares a basic powerlessness and dependence that the classical Marxists emphasized as the principal commonality of the working class in capitalist societies.[3] And, most importantly, we believe that the nonclass identifications of many working people can be understood better by building upon rather than rejecting class categories.

5

A second major strand of analysis of working-class divisions was best articulated in the classic work of Harry Braverman (1974). Early Marxist projections had advanced a kind of "wait-and-see" perspective on persistent working-class divisions. Although the working class may seem divided now, the continuing degradation of work under capitalism will inexorably homogenize the conditions that working people confront on the job. Braverman's analysis elevated this perspective to a more coherent and sophisticated plateau. He argued that capitalist dynamics continually transform the labor process, increasingly subjugating workers to their employers and fragmenting their jobs. The occupational divisions that seemed important for many years, Braverman argued, were eroding. Professional, technical, and clerical workers were now suffering the same kinds of degradation that factory operatives had earlier endured. After a long lag, the working class was becoming homogeneous. It would not be long, Braverman's argument seemed to imply, before spreading sectors of the working class would finally recognize the commonalities of their increasingly homogeneous working conditions.

Braverman's work has helped consolidate the fundamental validity of the Marxian emphasis on the capitalist labor process. Nonetheless, his work seems insufficient for understanding the working conditions facing the working class in advanced capitalist societies and the forces affecting working-class consciousness. For example, while Braverman's emphasis on deskilling captures an important feature of the transformation of work, we argue that certain kinds of reskilling have also been significant historically. In general, we argue, while many working people experience mechanization, specialization, and intensive supervisory control on the job, the principal economic forces operating on the U.S. working class in the recent period have not created greater homogeneity, at least in the simple version envisioned by Braverman.[4]

A third strand of analysis has been developed by a new generation of social historians of the working class. This view has been best presented in the United States by Herbert Gutman and his students and is sometimes referred to as the new social history.[5] Pointing to unusual factors in the historical formation of the working class in the United States, these scholars have concluded that American workers have experienced strong forces that have repeatedly fragmented emergent class consciousness. For example, these historians argue that the working class was not created all at once in the United States and that wage workers came from diverse racial, religious, and ethnic backgrounds. A pattern of successive rather than simultaneous periods of immigration resulted in hierarchies and antagonisms

6

among ethnic and religious groups instead of solidaristic responses. Similarly, these scholars suggest, the heritage of racism left by antebellum slavery and postbellum Jim Crow explains the continued salience of race in the United States in general and among working people in particular.

This new social history makes two important advances over the previous historiography of the American labor movement. An earlier literature, pioneered by Selig Perlman (1922), emphasized the significance of the absence of a feudal past, the presence of an open frontier, the early achievement of white male suffrage, and rising earning levels as causes of solidarity-inhibiting social mobility and narrow interest (rather than broad class) consciousness among American workers. Despite its insights, this earlier view of labor history tended, by assuming that unionism would result in conservative outcomes, to obscure rather than clarify the importance and breadth of workers' struggles in U.S. history; in contrast, the new social history focuses on such struggles and examines their outcomes in terms of a complex process that must itself be explained. And by emphasizing the ethnic, religious, and racial diversity in the American working class, the new social history correctly points to an unusual feature that sets the United States off from most other advanced capitalist countries.

This strand of analysis also seems insufficient, however. It does not *by itself* explain why the labor movement in the United States was unable to develop a working-class culture that could overcome racial, religious, and ethnic divisions; other factors, we argue, created the context in which these divisions could remain central. And the social historians fail, in our view, to integrate adequately the analysis of workers' cultural experiences with the evolution of the organization of work and of labor market structure.

A final important strand of analysis has been developed by institutional labor economists. These industrial relations scholars have generally argued that unions and employers in the United States have produced a cooperative and well-working collective bargaining system. In the early 1950s Clark Kerr extended this analysis and observed that a "balkanization" of labor markets between unionized and nonunionized sectors had developed. Kerr and other industrial relations scholars emphasized the importance of custom and tradition in the workings of the labor market and contrasted the structured character of worker–employer relations in the unionized sectors with the unstructured characteristics of nonunion employment relations. In the early 1970s Doeringer and Piore (1971) also theorized that substantially different labor submarkets existed, with different rules of behavior governing each; in their analysis the sources of the dif-

7

ferences lay as much in differing technological and skill characteristics of firms in the two submarkets as in the effects of unionism.[6]

By turning attention to manifold "imperfections" in labor markets, the institutionalist tradition has advanced our understanding of the sources of objective differences among workers' experiences in production, and we draw heavily in this book upon the insights of this literature. These institutionalists also correctly highlight the cooperative aspects of union–management relations in the post–World War II era. However, we also think that the institutional school fails to analyze adequately the determinants of skills, customs, traditions, and rules in the workplace; does not locate the contours of unionism and labor market structure in a sufficient theory of capitalist development; and goes too far in stressing the durability of the postwar labor–capital accord.

Given these dissatisfactions with current explanations of divisions within the U.S. working class, we propose an alternative working hypothesis: The disunity of the U.S. working class persists in large part as a result of objective divisions among workers in their production experiences; these objective divisions constitute both a consequence of continuing capitalist development in the United States and a barrier to a unified anticapitalist working-class movement.

In the remainder of this introductory overview, we first introduce the analytical framework we use to develop our hypotheses about segmented work and divided workers and then preview the historical analysis itself.

Introduction to the analytical framework

In this book we analyze the history of the U.S. working class by examining the interaction among (1) long swings in economic activity, (2) social structures of accumulation, and (3) the organization of work and the structure of labor markets. This interactive framework provides, we believe, a novel and fruitful means of examining and understanding the institutional changes and conflicts that characterize U.S. labor and economic history.

Long swings. By *long swings* we mean alternating periods (of approximately twenty-five years) in the world economy of vigorous and sustained economic activity, followed by equally sustained periods of stagnation. Without yet entering into arguments about their causes, we assert that these long swings are of such fundamental importance that they must inform the historical analysis we attempt in this book.

Table 1.1. *Long swings in the world capitalist economy*

Long swing	Phase	Approximate timing
I	A	1790s to ca. 1820
	B	Ca. 1820 to mid-1840s
II	A	Mid-1840s to ca. 1873
	B	Ca. 1873 to late 1890s
III	A	Late 1890s to World War I
	B	World War I to World War II
IV	A	World War II to early 1970s
	B	Early 1970s to present

Table 1.1 provides an approximate dating for these long swings in the world capitalist economy since the Industrial Revolution. Each swing is identified with a Roman numeral (from I to IV) and the letters A and B, which refer to the successive phases of rapid and slow growth. Chapter 2 presents both a theoretical discussion and some historical evidence that helps justify this focus on long swings.

Social structures of accumulation. By *social structure of accumulation* we mean the specific institutional environment within which the capitalist accumulation process is organized. Such accumulation occurs within concrete historical structures: in firms buying inputs in one set of markets, producing goods and services, and selling those outputs in other markets. These structures are surrounded by others that impinge upon the capitalist accumulation process: the monetary and credit system, the pattern of state involvement in the economy, the character of class conflict, and so forth. We call this collective set of institutions the social structure of accumulation. Our focus on long swings derives in part from a hypothesis that each long swing in capitalist economies is associated with a distinct social structure of accumulation (see Chapter 2 and Gordon, 1980, for development of this argument). These social structures of accumulation define successive *stages* of capitalist development.

We shall propose that long swings and social structures of accumulation are interdependent and mutually determining in capitalist economies. A long period of prosperity is generated by a set of institutions that provides a stable and favorable context for capitalists. This context must provide capitalists with both profitable investment opportunities and a stable societal environment in which to realize them. The boom begins to fade when the profitable opportunities inherent within the existing social structure of accumulation begin to dry up. Although such problems may arise for any of a variety of causes, we shall emphasize the limits posed by the existing institutional structure and the breakup of its cohesion. Long swings are in large part a product of the success or failure of the social structure of accumulation in facilitating capitalist accumulation.

The labor process and labor markets. Two of the constituent institutions of a social structure of accumulation are the organization of work (i.e., the labor process) and the structure of labor markets. In order to understand the historical evolution and transformation of the labor process and labor markets in the United States, we shall trace those institutions through an analysis of long swings and successive social structures of accumulation. An especially important part of this investigation involves the history of work and production relations between capitalists and workers.

Exploration, consolidation, and decay. These initial propositions lead directly to the hypothesis that three qualitative structural changes have affected the labor process and labor markets through the three long swings of U.S. capitalist development. Our analysis also leads us to a further hypothesis about the life cycle of forces shaping the development and transformation of labor in the United States. We propose that each stage shaping the labor process and labor market structure has a lifetime whose adolescence begins in the previous period of economic crisis, whose maturity begins with the construction of a new social structure of accumulation, and whose decline spreads as economic crisis deepens once again.

First, during a preceding period of stagnation, capitalists begin to experiment with new methods of labor management in order to seek solutions to the spreading problems that emergent crisis has imposed and that plague the previous structures shaping the labor process and labor markets. We call this phase the period of *exploration.*

Second, the construction of new institutions features the integration of a new organization of the labor process and a new labor market structure as part of the new social structure of accumulation. These new features help provide the foundation for rapid capital accumulation and relatively high rates of profit during phase A of each stage of accumulation. Although workers respond to and resist capitalists' explorations, the most promising forays, shaped by the impact of workers' struggles, are gradually consolidated. We refer to this phase as the period of *consolidation*.

Third, spreading stagnation, crisis, and workers' struggles begin to undermine the existing structures of the labor process and labor markets. Consequently, the effective force of the institutions that had dominated during phase A begins to diminish. We refer to this phase as the period of *decay*.

We combine this life-cycle hypothesis with our more general propositions about long swings and the forces successively shaping the labor process and labor markets. Table 1.2 summarizes our proposed hypotheses by locating each tendency shaping labor, with its three life-cycle phases, in the context of the long swings framing U.S. capitalist development since the nineteenth century.

Innovations necessary for consolidation. One final set of hypotheses completes the framework within which we develop our historical analysis of the transformation of labor in the United States. We suggest that the consolidation of each tendency shaping the labor process and labor markets depends on important institutional innovations that resolve the problems revealed by initial explorations. In each successive period of crisis and exploration, capitalist experiments with new systems of labor management initially generate worker resistance. The consolidation of the new structure of labor management does not occur until that conflict is resolved through institutional innovations that either overwhelm or integrate the mode of worker resistance to the new structure.

This observation grows out of specific hypotheses about the institutional innovations necessary for consolidation in each of the three main periods of our analysis. Initial proletarianization depended, we shall suggest, upon the creation of a mechanism ensuring an ample excess supply of wage workers. After the mid-1840s, this mechanism increasingly involved the generation of continuous immigration from abroad as well as the continuous erosion of independent farmers' and artisans' economic bases. Homogenization depended, we shall argue, both upon new techniques of production that helped break skilled workers' control over the labor process and also upon the discovery and application of a variety of techniques that rendered ineffectual the unified workers' opposition that homogenization had tended to generate. And segmentation depended, we shall propose, upon the successful integration of the strong national industrial unions of the 1930s into a cooperative collective bargaining system, limiting the

11

Table 1.2. *Long swings and forces shaping labor in the United States*

Long swings and phases	Approximate timing	Initial proletarianization	Homogenization	Segmentation
IA	1790s to ca. 1820			
B	Ca. 1820 to mid-1840s	Exploration		
IIA	Mid-1840s to ca. 1873	Consolidation		
B	Ca. 1873 to late 1890s	Decay	Exploration	
IIIA	Late 1890s to World War I		Consolidation	
B	World War I to World War II		Decay	Exploration
IVA	World War II to early 1970s			Consolidation
B	Early 1970s to present			Decay

further impact of the union movement and initiating a period of labor peace between employers and workers.

It is important to stress at this point that the historical analysis in this book should be understood as an analysis of labor in capitalist production and not of all labor or work performed in the economy. We pay very little attention to household labor, for example, even though we recognize its critical historical importance. We have chosen to concentrate on work within the capitalist wage-labor system precisely in order to sharpen our focus and to emphasize the evident centrality of our subject.

Preview of the historical analysis

This set of propositions, further elaborated in Chapter 2, summarizes the theoretical framework within which we develop our historical analysis of the evolution and transformation of labor in the United States. As a final guide to the detailed historical analysis of Chapters 3, 4, and 5, we preview the principal strands of our analysis in the following paragraphs.

The initial proletarianization of labor

We argue that the process of initial proletarianization accompanied the first phase of capitalist development in the United States from the slowdown of the 1820s and 1830s through the late nineteenth century. Both Marxist and mainstream historians have noted that initial proletarianization in the United States featured certain unusual characteristics: It took place in a country relatively free from feudal traditions and with a large supply of fertile and available agricultural land. Our analysis of initial proletarianizaiton further specifies this general view.

In the United States the development of a wage-labor system initially faced a series of obstacles. The lack of a feudal heritage and the availability of land kept down the number of landless individuals potentially available for capitalist factories. Because of this scarcity of wage labor, employers were forced to explore and eventually rely on four diverse and initially quite different sources of wage labor: native white male agricultural workers, young native women and children, immigrants, and artisans. As these supplies developed, in varying proportions over time, a wage-labor market gradually emerged, facilitating the growth of capitalist production.

Innovations extending the flow of immigration helped consolidate the initial process of proletarianization by the early 1850s. Even after consolidation, however, the capitalists had not yet truly transformed the labor process. While external labor market competition helped enforce some discipline of workers on the job, the diversity of sources of labor supply and the continuing power of many workers to control their own labor processes ensured that the organization of work remained relatively unstandardized. Throughout the period of rapid growth from the 1850s through the early 1870s, several relatively diverse internal systems of "labor control" in production coexisted, corresponding at least in part to the respective characteristics of the sources of labor supply. As a result, the labor market continued to be divided into distinct pockets; a single, generalized, homogeneous, and universally competitive arena for the exchange of labor power did not yet exist.

As capital accumulation slowed and economic crisis spread after the early 1870s, the underdevelopment and diversity of mechanisms for labor control hampered capitalists. Employers were constrained by the continuing control of skilled labor over production methods. While falling prices and mounting labor protest combined to squeeze enterprise profits, the untransformed and therefore uncontrollable structure of the labor process and labor markets limited the levers available to employers in their quest for protection from competition and for greater labor control. These difficulties became more and more evident as the crisis of the eighties and early nineties deepened.[7]

The homogenization of labor

We argue that the process of homogenization of labor became more and more dominant in the United States from the late nineteenth century through the 1920s and 1930s. The emergence and trajectory of this tendency toward homogenization closely followed the rhythms of the long swings through which the U.S. economy was passing during those years.

Employers responded to their problems of labor productivity in the late nineteenth century with mechanization, greater use of foremen to supervise workers, and decreasing reliance on skilled labor. Contemporary observers aptly referred to the results of this homogenizing development as the *drive system*. The early effects of the homogenization period included increasing capital–labor ratios and plant size, transformed labor processes with an increase in the proportion of operatives, a slight decrease in skill differentials, the spread of a national labor market, and most important, a vastly expanded effective labor supply. But the early explorations with the drive system also contributed to spreading labor unrest as the turn of the century approached. The consolidation of homogenization required some further institutional reforms.

Consolidation was quickened by the merger movement at the turn of the century and the huge "consolidated" firms that resulted. These larger firms were able both to pursue homogenization more rapidly than smaller firms and to pioneer the new policies that corporations implemented to undercut unified worker opposition. These innovations included the development of centralized personnel departments, cooperation with and cooptation of craft unions, and manipulation of ethnic differences among industrial workers.

The interdependence between corporate consolidation and innovation in the labor process and labor markets meant that the consolidation of the process of homogenization took time. The system of homogenization was not fully established until the end of World War I.

Despite most corporations' successes in weakening the labor movement in the early 1920s, some problems of the drive system began to appear. In particular, the rigors of the drive system and increasingly severe external labor market competition, both joint products of homogenization, resulted in rising labor turnover among production workers and the restriction of effort even by unorganized workers. Consequently, many large and "forward-looking" corporations began to experiment during and after World War I with further changes in the labor process in order to reduce their vulnerability to the contradictions of the drive system.

The major decay of the drive system took place with the Depression. But the drive system and the early additional experiments from World War I through the 1920s provided the context within which the Depression affected the labor process and labor markets and generated the focus of increasingly militant and widespread labor protest after 1934. By the late 1930s, it was impossible to deny the decay of the reigning system of labor control.

The segmentation of labor

We argue, finally, that the segmentation of labor accompanied and helped facilitate the period of rapid capital accumulation in the United States after World War II. As with our earlier analysis of initial proletarianization and homogenization, we suggest that the process of segmentation has experienced a life-cycle conditioned by the rhythm of the most recent long swing in the United States.

Large corporations initiated the period of segmentation in the 1920s and early 1930s when they began to explore new mechanisms for more effective and reliable labor control. In the mid-1930s workers in mass-production industries revolted on an unprecedented scale, highlighted by the massive sitdown strikes of 1936–1937, and succeeded in gaining recognition for industrial unions. The consolidation of the segmentation process was achieved only after this extended industrial conflict in the 1930s had been moderated by the labor peace constructed in the late 1940s and early 1950s. This capital–labor accord required a set of social and governmental arrangements; a crucial part of these arrangements included employer recognition of unions, grievance procedures, and seniority rules for layoffs and promotions; in return, employers gained discretion over changes in the organization of work, provided that increases in wages were granted in return for increases in productivity. Similar arrangements were worked out in large nonunion firms, although without jointly determined grievance procedures.

Once consolidated, segmentation contained two important dimensions. One dimension involved the growing divergence between *primary* and *secondary* jobs. As a result of the combined impact of corporate experiments and union struggle, many large corporations adopted structured internal systems of labor management. At the same time, most smaller firms were constrained to retain the more primitive drive system of labor control. The second dimension of segmentation resulted from corporate efforts to establish new systems for generating and deploying general skills among workers. These systems were necessary to replace the craft method of skill generation upon which corporations had formerly relied and to gain greater control over the parts of the labor process that skilled workers had formerly dominated. These new mechanisms led, in turn, to a growing divergence within the primary segment between *independent primary* and *subordinate primary* jobs.

These two segmentation processes eventually dominated the development of the labor process and labor markets during the 1950s and 1960s. Segmentation also played a major role in channeling the effects of past and present race and sex discrimination. Consequently, segmentation also established the context within which corporations and workers began to respond to and seek leverage over the economic crisis of the 1970s and early 1980s.

The chapters that follow develop these arguments in detail. Even before that detailed elaboration, however, the principal implications of our argument should already be clear.

Previous analyses of the history of labor have failed to integrate critical and complex connections among macrodynamics, institutional structures, the organization of work, and the character of the working-class movement. Our analysis suggests that these connections have produced a sequence of qualitative transformations in the structure of the labor process and labor markets in U.S. capitalism. It also leads us to suspect that we are currently witnessing the throes of a fourth structural transformation, another qualitatively new system shaping work and labor markets in the United States. We attempt in this book to illuminate the general contours of these successive transformations; the specific character of the process of segmentation that has dominated the recent stage of capitalist development; and the effects of segmentation on the relative power and unity of the U.S. working class. We hope that our analysis sheds new light on this history. We also hope that this historical analysis will help us all recognize the political contingency of past and present structural change. Too often, we tend to view changes in the organization of work as technically determined or historically predestined. Our analysis suggests an alternative view: If people and classes have influenced the transformation of labor in the past, we should be able to influence its reconstruction in the present and future.

2

Long swings and stages of capitalism

We locate our analysis of labor segmentation within a historical materialist model for studying capitalism. That framework provides a coherent set of propositions about capital accumulation and class relations in capitalist societies. And yet, our argument suggests that there have been several decisive qualitative transformations *within* the capitalist epoch. Are we suggesting that the character of capitalism has changed? Has capitalism passed through successive stages of development? How does our analysis differ from traditional mainstream and Marxist accounts?

This chapter outlines the principal theoretical foundations and implications of our historical analysis. The first section reviews the elements of the theoretical perspective that we presuppose in our analysis and also discusses some of the weaknesses of traditional Marxian analyses that prompt us to emphasize institutional transformations within the capitalist epoch. The second section develops our theoretical perspective on long swings and social structures of accumulation; this perspective is critical for our proposed reformulation of the history of labor in the United States. The final section highlights some of the principal implications of both our theoretical perspective and the historical analysis toward which it points.

The dynamics of capitalist development

Capitalism can be defined as a wage-labor system of commodity production for profit. The owners of the means of production (capitalists) employ the immediate producers (workers). Employers pay workers wages, keeping the fruits of the labor process for vending on the market at a profit (or loss).

Given these defining characteristics, several conditions must be satisfied for the existence and reproduction of capitalist economies. The legal system must recognize and protect rights of private property. There must be a substantial supply of wage workers. Capitalists must be able to generate profits in production, requiring reliable and reproducible mechanisms of labor management. At least some basic decisions about production and distribution must be mediated by markets, requiring money as a medium of exchange and a measure of exchange value. Both the household and the state must serve some critical supportive functions, providing steady and continued access to wage labor, shaping the political space within which capitalists can enjoy and command whatever profits they achieve, and contributing to cultural and ideological perceptions that reinforce individualism.[1]

Even if these conditions are met, capitalist economies do not stand still. As the historical materialist perspective suggests, capitalist economies continually change and develop, driven constantly by the dual dynamic forces of intercapitalist competition and capital–labor conflict. Indeed, a principal strength of the historical materialist framework has been its ability to illuminate some of the most important historical developments in capitalist societies. More specifically, the version of the historical materialist perspective that we use illuminates five principal tendencies that have dominated the trajectory of capitalist development.[2] These tendencies have operated in the United States and provide a background to our own analysis of the history of labor.

1. Capitalist accumulation continually attempts to *expand* the boundaries of the capitalist system. Seeking to increase their sales and profits, capitalists continually seek to expand the geographical limits of their markets and try to transform more areas of social life into profit-making activities. This expanding nature results both from the necessity for each capitalist to meet the competition of other capitalists and from the cost pressures created by worker–capitalist conflict.

2. Capitalist accumulation persistently increases the size of large corporations and *concentrates* the control and ownership of capital in proportionately fewer hands. This tendency is also produced by competition among capitalists and by capital–labor conflict. Bigger firms are better able to capture economies of scale, where present. Large firms are also better able to find new supplies of labor and to develop successful means of labor management; the cost of these activities gives large firms definite advantages over smaller ones.

3. The accumulation of capital *spreads wage labor* as the prevalent system of production, draws a larger proportion of the population into wage-labor status, and *replenishes the reserve pool of labor*. The expansion of large-scale capital continually drives out small businesses (including merchants, professionals, and farmers); these previously independent groups must then work for another capitalist. The continuing quest for new supplies of labor brings additional workers into the labor market from outside the traditional boundaries of the

capitalist economy, while labor-saving innovations replenish the supply of labor from inside the wage-labor economy. The relative power of capitalists and workers is mediated by the rate at which this replenishment proceeds.[3]

4. Capitalist accumulation continually *changes the labor process,* both through employers' introduction of improved technologies and new machines and through the imposition of increasingly intensive labor-management systems upon workers. A replenished reserve pool of labor – tendency (3) above – simply ensures that capitalists can find workers who are required to submit to capitalist authority in the workplace. The extraction of effort from the workers does not necessarily follow; it requires the development of labor-management techniques. These techniques have become more complex as firms have grown larger and as worker organizations have gained in power.

5. In order to defend themselves against the effects of capitalist accumulation, workers have responded with their own activities and struggles. Atomized through labor market competition and faced with the continual threat of surplus labor supplies, workers are driven to strengthen their connections with other workers in order to protect their wages, jobs, and working conditions and in order to advance their own interests. This tendency toward *collective working-class activity* leads not only to labor unions but also to informal resistance on the job and more organized forms of political activity and self-defense off the job. Consequently, capitalist development has led to the progressive development of more formal, better organized, and more extensive expressions of collective working-class strength.[4]

Each of these five tendencies has developed unevenly, and it would take us too far afield to recount the details for each case. To give one example, the tendency toward concentration of capital may be periodically arrested and even turned back by the appearance of new technologies, the opening of new markets or sources of raw materials supply, or the entrance of new firms seeking to expand from successful operations in other industries. The pace of concentration may also vary considerably among economic sectors. Yet, for the economy as a whole over long time periods, capitalist development has produced the domination of the economy by progressively larger corporations.

These five dynamic tendencies, framed even within a relatively traditional Marxian analysis, account for a great deal of the concrete history of capitalist societies. However, several considerations have led us and many others to move beyond this perspective in order to correct some of its weaknesses and to add additional tools with which to understand the history of capitalist development.

First, many traditional Marxists have used this dynamic analysis to generate mechanical theories of historical inevitability in which the emergence of a class-conscious proletariat always lurks around the next corner. In recent decades many Marxists have corrected this mechanical determinism by adding to the traditional analysis a variety of complicating factors and insights. This recent literature has featured the role of intermediate strata and classes and the resulting variety of possible multiclass alliances, the relative autonomy of political and ideological forces, an emphasis on human agency rather than abstract laws in historical change, an emphasis on the influence of production relations upon the evolution of production forces, the importance of historical contingency in shaping the responses of different groups to capitalist development, and the diverse spatial and temporal paths of capitalist development. These additions permit a more creative approach to the study of historical change, moving beyond kismetic views of inevitable historical evolution (see, for example, Marglin, 1974; Laclau, 1977; Tabb and Sawers, 1978; Wright, 1978; Thompson, 1979; Gintis, 1980; and Plotke, 1981).

Second, the Marxian analysis of capitalist dynamics, no matter how subtly one pursues its modern reformulation, remains indeterminate when it is pursued *only* on this abstract level. For our purposes here, the most important instance of this indeterminacy arises in the analysis of the labor process and labor markets.

While the dynamic tendencies outlined above help shape the organization of capitalist production in general, the specific evolution of production relations also depends on the changing relative power of the opposing classes and their respective instruments of struggle. These depend most importantly, but not exclusively, on the character of the production relations. This interdependence between production organization and the shape of the capital–labor conflict means that a final specification of the character of production at any point and time cannot depend solely on analysis at an abstract level but must also focus on more concrete determinations.

Similar caution should inform analyses of the labor market. Here, employers and workers bargain over the effective wage rate, the hours of work, and other elements of the wage-labor contract. The outcome of this bargaining reflects an extraordinarily wide range of forces: the extent to which workers are unified or divided, the intervention of the state, the ability of capitalists to develop new wage-laboring populations, the availability of new labor-saving technologies, the elements of race and ethnicity, the pace of accumulation and hence the strength of the macroeconomy. Noting the extent of development of the five major dynamic tendencies of capitalist economies is not sufficient.

To overcome these limitations, many historians, following the lead of E. P. Thompson in Britain and Herbert Gutman in the United States, have placed virtually singular emphasis on concrete and specific analyses of the daily lives of workers and employers in particular periods and locations. Although extremely valuable, these studies are usually quite divorced, especially in the United States, from more abstract theoretical formulations; consequently, their broader meaning remains ambiguous (for useful reviews, see *Radical History Review*, 1978–79; Brody, 1979; Davis, 1980; and Montgomery, 1980).

We propose that an intermediate level of analysis, focusing on the logic of long swings and stages of capitalism, is necessary for an understanding of capitalist development. This intermediate analysis is intended to complement both the traditional and abstract Marxian approach to capitalist development and the more recent concrete analyses of everyday life. In the next section we present the elements of such an intermediate analysis: a theory of stages of capitalism that we then apply in our historical analysis of the labor process and labor markets in the United States.

Long swings and stages of capitalism

The abstract analysis outlined above must be complemented, we argue, by an analysis of long swings and stages of capitalism. In this section we review the most important theoretical building blocks for this theory of stages of capitalism. We begin with a review of the requirements of capital accumulation, turn next to an analysis of the relation between long swings and social structures of accumulation, and close with a more formal theoretical discussion of this view of institutional change.[5]

The social structure of accumulation

Many scholars within the Marxian tradition have argued the importance of uneven development and stages of capitalism (see Mandel, 1975, chs. 2 and 4, for some suggestions and review). These analyses have often led theorists to posit stages of "competitive" and "monopoly" capitalism, focusing on the transformation of the conditions of product market competition. In our view, writers in this theoretical tradition (including ourselves, in our early work) fail to capture the breadth and complexity of the process of capital accumulation. Our analysis of this process has led us to develop a concept of the *social structure of accumulation* for the purposes of historical analyses of capitalist development.

22

Our development of this concept begins with a simple proposition: The accumulation of capital through capitalist production cannot take place either in a vacuum or in chaos. Capitalists cannot and will not invest in production unless they are able to make reasonably determinate calculations about their expected rates of return. Both the Marxian and mainstream traditions of economics have recognized this relation between investment and expectations.[6] Unfortunately, however, both traditions have tended either to elide the importance of the external environment in the formation of expectations about the rate of profit or to fail to provide a substantive account of that environment. Although many economists may recognize the importance of external factors, most have nonetheless left the investigation of those factors to sociologists and political scientists.

We argue, in sharp contrast, that macrodynamic analyses should begin with the political–economic environment affecting individual capitalists' possibilities for capital accumulation. Without a stable and favorable external environment, capitalist investment in production will not proceed. We refer to this external environment as the social structure of accumulation. Its elements derive from the specific set of requirements, neither unlimited nor indeterminate, that must be satisfied for capital accumulation to take place. We derive this finite set of requirements from the Marxian analysis of the process of capital accumulation.[7]

The process of capital accumulation contains three major steps. Capitalists, in business to make profits, begin by investing their funds (money capital) in the raw materials, labor power, machinery, buildings, and other commodities needed for production. Next, they organize the labor process, whereby the constituents of production are set in motion to produce useful products or services – the input commodities are transmuted through production into output commodities. Finally, by selling the products of labor, capitalists reconvert their property back to money capital. These funds then become the basis for the next round of capital accumulation.

The social structure of accumulation consists of all the institutions that impinge upon the accumulation process. Some institutions have a general impact; others relate primarily to one specific step in the process. We discuss each in turn.

As capitalists push their capital through each step of the accumulation process, they are touched by some general institutional features of their environment. Among the most important institutions are the system ensuring money and credit, the pattern of state involvement in the economy, and the structure of class struggle. Money and credit are essential at every step because money is required for exchange or credit is needed until the exchange can take place. The pattern of state involvement in the economy likewise affects all the steps of capital accumulation because the state can enhance the profitability of investment (through subsidies, enforcement of regulations, greater commodity purchases, and so forth) or diminish it (through taxation, regulation, legitimizing unions, and so forth). Finally, the structure of class struggle, whether conducted through unions, in political parties, sporadically by spontaneous outburst, or through the electoral system, conditions the expectations of capitalists at every stage.

The first step in the capital accumulation process, the collection of the necessary inputs, relies more particularly on systems of natural resource supply, intermediate (produced goods) supply, and labor supply. The structure of natural supply will determine the extent to which capitalists can secure access to needed quantities of raw materials and energy at predictable prices. The supply of intermediate goods determines access to produced goods used in production. Labor supply, the most problematical of the three, involves both the structure of the labor market, determining the immediate supply of labor, and the social institutions (family, schools, etc.) that reproduce the labor force generationally.

The process of production, the second step in the capital accumulation process, takes place inside the capitalist enterprise itself, an institution under the capitalist's own control. The enterprise consists of two related parts; the top management structure and the organization of the actual labor process.

The final step in capital accumulation, the selling process, involves at least three institutional features. First, the capitalists' success in realizing their profits depends upon the structure of final demand, including consumer purchases, government expenditures, export markets, and so forth. Second, the pace of capital accumulation is conditioned by the structure of intercapitalist competition, namely, the degree to which elements of competition and monopoly are present and the various forms of that competition. Third, this step relies upon sales and marketing systems, including distribution networks and advertising.

The construct of the social structure of accumulation, comprising a specific set of institutions, has both an inner and an outer boundary.[8] Its inner boundary demarcates the institutional environment for capital accumulation (that is, the "social structure") from the capital accumulation process itself. Its outer boundary distinguishes this social structure from other social structures in the rest of a society.

24

We understand the capital accumulation process to be the microeconomic activity of profit making and reinvestment. This activity is carried on by individual capitalists (or firms) employing specific workforces and operating within a given institutional environment. We wish to separate that process from its environment. This separation is obvious in the case of such institutions as markets, including labor markets, since they exist externally to the firm.

The separation between capital accumulation and its institutional environment is less obvious but no less important in the case of our other main focus of interest, the organization of the labor process. Here, how each individual capitalist goes about organizing the labor process in his or her firm is properly considered an aspect of the accumulation process itself. However, each capitalist organizes the labor process within a specific social context, which contains a socially "representative," customary, or expected organization of the labor process. We stipulate that this latter element in the organization of the labor process constitutes a component of the social structure of accumulation.

The inner boundary of the social structure of accumulation, then, divides the capital accumulation process itself (the profit-making activities of individual capitalists) from the institutional (social, political, legal, cultural, and market) context within which it occurs.

In the other direction we specify the outer boundary so that the social structure of accumulation is not simply a shorthand for "the rest of a society." We do not deny that *any* aspect or relationship in society potentially and perhaps actually impinges to *some* degree upon the accumulation process; nonetheless, it is not unreasonable to distinguish between those institutions that directly and demonstrably condition capital accumulation and those that touch it only tangentially. Thus, for example, the financial system bears a direct relation whereas the character of sports activity does not.

In our judgment, the imprecise and hence inevitably arguable nature of this outer boundary does not reduce the usefulness of the concept of a social structure of accumulation. Moreover, we recognize that different social structures of accumulation may incorporate (or exclude) differing sets of social institutions. Indeed, it would be possible to argue (although we have not done so below) that successive social structures of accumulation have incorporated increasing aspects of social life, thus making, for example, the post-1945 structure the most complex and societally far-reaching.

Based on this analysis of the process of capitalist accumulation, we further propose that a social structure of accumulation alternately stimulates and constrains the pace of capital accumulation. If the constituent institutions of the social structure of accumulation are stable, working smoothly and without challenge, capitalists are likely to feel secure about investing in the expansion of productive capacity. But if the social structure of accumulation begins to become shaky, if class conflict or past capital accumulation have pressed the institutions to their limits and they begin to lose their legitimacy, capitalists will be more disposed to put their money in financial rather than direct investments, earning a financial rate of return whose security compensates for its lower average expected levels.[9]

Because capital accumulation depends on disconnected investment decisions by individual firms, it appears that one can understand those decisions through models of individual behavior. Investment in capitalist economies is mediated fundamentally by social (or institutional) forces, however – that is, by factors external to individual capitalists that are determined by collective social activities. Macrodynamic analyses of growth and disequilibria must take the structure and contradictions of this conditioning environment into account. The social structure of accumulation, in short, is external to the decisions of individual capitalists, but it is internal to the macrodynamics of capitalist economies.

Long swings and social structures of accumulation

Both mainstream and Marxist economists have tended to agree that capitalist economies are likely to experience periodic short-term and self-correcting business cycles. Many economists within both traditions have also suggested that capitalist economies may be prone to disequilibria, leading at least potentially to crisis tendencies or stagnation from which the economy is incapable of recovering without external assistance. Our model of stages of capitalism goes beyond both traditions, suggesting not only that capitalist economies are prone to longer-term fluctuations in the pace of capital accumulation but also that these fluctuations are mediated by a determinate institutional structure, the social structure of accumulation, which cannot be analyzed separately from (and therefore is not exogenous to) the capitalist economy itself.

Our analysis builds upon a series of propositions about the connections between social structures of accumulation and long swings in world capitalist economic activity. In Chapter 1 we already noted the existence of such long swings in the world capitalist economy since the Industrial Revolution. This section explores the connections between the institutional environment within which capital accumulation takes place and the alternating rhythms of the pace of economic activity.

26

The scholarly literature has long debated both the existence of long swings and their causes and significance (Mandel, 1975, 1980; Rostow, 1978, part 3; and Barr, 1979, provide recent surveys). Our position is that long-swing arguments are plausible and warrant serious attention. We do not believe that the existence of long swings has been "proved," since the interpretation of the data involves judgment rather than the administration of a universally accepted existence test. More to the point, we find the notion of long swings extremely useful in helping to illuminate the institutional macrodynamics we are studying. In the appendix to this chapter we review some of the evidence that leads us to this position.

The most interesting issues concern the causes and significance of long swings. Economists have attributed long swings to the effects of uneven spurts in the rate of technical change, to long-term trends in population growth and movement, to the effects of financial institutions, and to changes in patterns of consumption, relative prices of raw materials, and international capital mobility, with differences in emphasis on the relative weight of each of these factors and on their causal interrelations. A related debate has focused on the endogeneity or exogeneity of the causes of long swings. If they are endogenous, the theory emphasizes automatically repeating long cycles. If the swings are prompted by exogenous forces, recoveries from stagnation and the periodicity of long swings result from a succession of unique historical factors or accidents.

In our view these debates suffer from two misperceptions. First, they tend toward *single-factor* theories of long swings; our emphasis on the importance of social structures of accumulation leads us to emphasize the *multidimensional* character of the capitalist accumulation process and the macrodynamics that it generates. Second, these debates tend to define the internal–external boundary with respect to the individual entrepreneur; our attention to social structures of accumulation leads us to shift that boundary and to refocus the question of internal and external elements.

We propose an alternative model that views long swings as in large part the product of the success or failure of successive social structures of accumulation in facilitating capital accumulation. Although we do not wish to deny the important consequences of largely exogenous events in producing long swings, we note that such forces as demographic trends and technological innovation are heavily influenced by endogenous economic conditions, particularly when we concentrate on the world (as opposed to national or regional) capitalist system. Our institutional analysis suggests that the conditions creating a period of prosperity contain endogenous contradic-

27

tions that ultimately bring the prosperity to an end. But the manner in which the ensuing crisis is resolved is not fully endogenous, for the crisis exacerbates conflict over the structural reforms that are necessary for a recovery, and the resolution of this conflict involves unpredictable political elements. The periods of boom and stagnation alternate, then, partly in response to exogenous events but more importantly in response to endogenous changes in the institutional context (see Gordon, 1980, and Weisskopf, 1981, for related treatments).

We develop our model here by tracing the connections between the social structure of accumulation and the pace of accumulation through a single stage of capitalist development. We then consider some theoretical issues that arise in this model.

Our scenario begins at the onset of a period of expansion in a capitalist economy (such as the late 1840s, late 1890s, or early 1940s in the United States). We have already noted that rapid economic growth depends upon the existence of a favorable social structure of accumulation. We are therefore presupposing that a previous crisis has somehow been resolved through the construction of a new social structure of accumulation. In particular, given the importance of production for capital accumulation, we are specifically presupposing a stabilization of conditions of production and, therefore, a moderation of whatever class struggle has intensified during the previous period of crisis.

Once begun, the expansion is likely for several reasons to continue for many years. First, the previous crisis is likely to have restored many of the conditions of profitability in the economy, for example, through depreciation or abandonment of less productive capital or through the stimulation of new technological and managerial innovations. Second, the initial investments necessary to form the social structure of accumulation are likely to provide a large (multiplier/ accelerator) stimulus at the beginning of this period of expansion. Most importantly, the boom period is long because favorable conditions for capital accumulation have become institutionalized. In other words, these conditions become established not just as the current policy of the current dominant political party; rather, they become embedded in the society's institutional structure.

It seems just as likely, however, that the expansion will not continue at a rapid pace indefinitely. (We discuss this problem more formally in the following section.) First, as we have already noted, the growth process in capitalist economies is prone to a variety of disequilibria that can choke the boom; the Great Depression of the 1930s was set off by such a development. Second, and more important for our purposes, the expansion itself is likely to set off forces that undermine

28

the institutional basis of the expansion. At first, short-term business cycles appear and act as self-correcting economic adjustment mechanisms. Such corrections take place within the context of the established institutions, which are slow to change and remain relatively unaffected by the short-term cyclical fluctuations. But at some point barriers to accumulation begin to appear that persist through the short-term business cycle.

These barriers develop because successful capital accumulation ultimately either runs up against limits imposed by the existing institutional structure or begins to destabilize that structure. In the first case, the institutions themselves produce the constraints; in the second case, the disruption of the institutions produces the constraints. In either case, further rapid capital accumulation becomes more problematic within the existing set of institutions.

Although the development of these barriers in each of our three periods is discussed in detail in subsequent chapters, it will be useful to provide some illustrations here. The initial proletarianization and the homogenization periods provide examples of how the prevalent organization of work could begin to limit the profitability of production. In the late-nineteenth century the artisans' control over the production process limited further advances in productivity in many industries. In the 1930s the homogenization of labor produced the conditions under which mass-production workers could successfully organize unions, thereby undermining the profitability of the homogenization system. The segmentation period provides an example of how a long boom period can upset its own institutional bases. The prosperity of the 1960s undermined the postwar capital–labor accord by giving labor and other noncapitalist groups greater economic and political power, thereby destabilizing one of the principal institutional arrangements that had made the long boom possible. In each case, prevailing institutions no longer worked favorably for rapid capital accumulation.

As the economy begins to stagnate, the institutions of the social structure of accumulation are further disrupted, complicating the process of recovery. Institutional destabilization may occur either because the resources that are required for the maintenance of the institutions themselves are becoming scarcer or because those institutions presuppose a smoothly functioning economy. Class conflict may intensify during this phase, as it did in the 1870s or 1890s and again in the 1930s. Given the stagnation, there is less chance for a labor peace purchased out of the (reduced) growth dividend.

Individual capitalists are then unlikely to engage in productive investment until a new and reliable environment emerges. Consequently, the resolution of a period of economic instability will depend upon the reconstruction of a social structure of accumulation. Indeed, we can define an economic crisis as a period of economic instability that requires institutional reconstruction for renewed stability and growth. For capitalists seeking such reconstruction the process is difficult and unpredictable, because it requires some collective action and the creation of a political consensus. Individual capitalists acting in isolation cannot restore prosperity.

As economic crisis deepens and the social structure of accumulation begins to become unfavorable, capitalists are in ever greater need of collective strategies capable of restoring the rate of profit. At first they may not engage in self-conscious collective action, for the early phases of crisis are likely to generate virulent intercapitalist competition. In those instances reforms may be forced upon them by the state or by noncapitalist groups. Even if capitalists are able to overcome their differences, their collective actions are likely to coexist with efforts by other classes and groups that seek to protect their working and living conditions. As a result, the resolution of an economic crisis is likely to be shaped by the relative power and the respective objectives of capitalists, workers, and other economic groups.

This point is illustrated in the United States by the responses to the economic crises of the late-nineteenth century and the 1930s. In each case, major structural changes were required to create the basis for a subsequent long swing of prosperity; but the character of the outcomes differed substantially in the two cases.

The economic crisis at the end of the nineteenth century was resolved by institutional changes in the form of intercapitalist competition, in the role of government, and in the organization of the labor process. The merger movement produced oligopolies in most major industries, but a split between small and large capitalists prevented the immediate consolidation of a new social structure. Only the war provided the context for building a political constituency that could stifle antibusiness reform and establish a favorable regime. By the 1920s large capitalists were relatively united and labor had been defeated. Management had succeeded in capturing greater control over the organization of work and in reducing the effectiveness of labor resistance (see Edwards, 1979).

The crisis of the 1930s was also ultimately resolved on the basis of a greater role for the state, this time involving Keynesian demand management and changes in capital–labor relations. The state now regulated capital–labor relations directly, both at the workplace (through the machinery set up by the Wagner Act and its successors) and through the provision of a variety of social welfare programs. Although employers were relatively divided during this period, workers were better organized, and they were able to influence the outcome on terms that were substantially more favorable than in the previous crisis period.

Both of these examples indicate that the onset of a stagnation phase marks the beginning of increasing pressure on all classes to maintain their positions. As stagnation tips into crisis, all classes must maneuver to restructure economic relations so as to protect and advance their own interests – some, of course, with more power and self-consciousness than others. Although there is no guarantee that a successful new social structure will emerge, if one does it will reflect the alignment of class forces (and other social influences) that produce it. Thus, the rise of a new social structure of accumulation depends upon the previous downswing and more specifically on the concrete historical conditions that the period of the downswing bequeathes to the major classes.

In this respect, "exogenous" forces may be very important. For example, the war devastation elsewhere in the world during World War II left the United States in an overwhelmingly powerful economic and political position, and the nuclear monopoly created an awesome military advantage, all of which may be considered at least partly exogenous. In this context, it was possible to create a new social structure of accumulation based in part on steadily rising real wages for American workers.

Regardless of the importance of exogenous forces, it is significant that the old institutions are not restored intact once the crisis has been resolved. This pattern results from systematic factors. Because collective actors are seeking solutions to their problems within a context of institutional instability, their struggles during crisis are likely to make problematic the reestablishment of the previously existing social structure of accumulation. For example, after U.S. workers had organized industrial unions in the late 1930s, it was virtually inconceivable that a resolution of the economic crisis of the 1930s could build upon old labor process and labor market structures from the 1910s and 1920s. The restoration of favorable conditions for capital accumulation after an economic crisis usually requires the shaping of a *new* social structure of accumulation, whose character is formed in large part by the nature of capitalists' and workers' collective struggles during the previous period of economic crisis.

We thus have the likelihood of a *succession* of social structures of accumulation within the capitalist epoch. We refer to the periods

31

featuring these respective social structures of accumulation as *stages of capitalism*.[10]

This scenario, focusing on the connections between long swings and social structures of accumulation, can be summarized in a series of discrete propositions:

1. A period of expansion is built upon the construction and stabilization of a favorable social structure of accumulation.

2. The favorable institutional context for capital accumulation generates a boom of investment and rapid economic activity.

3. The success of the capital accumulation process pushes investment to the limits that are possible within the social structure of accumulation. Continued rapid capital accumulation requires (among other changes) either a reproduction of the conditions existing at the beginning of the boom or a transition to a new organization of the labor process and labor markets. The initial conditions are difficult to reproduce, and needed reforms are not easily achieved.

4. Accumulation slows and the period of stagnation is entered. Attempts to alter the institutional structure are met with opposition, especially in a stagnationary context.

5. Economic stagnation promotes the further dissolution of the existing social structure of accumulation.

6. The restoration of the possibility of rapid capital accumulation during an economic crisis depends on the construction of a new institutional structure.

7. The internal content of this institutional structure is profoundly but not exclusively shaped by the character of the class struggle during the preceding period of economic crisis.

8. The new social structure of accumulation is virtually certain to differ from its predecessor, thereby generating a succession of stages of capitalism.

9. Each stage of capitalism is likely to feature a long period of expansion, then a subsequent long period of stagnation.

In presenting this theoretical approach to long swings and stages of capitalism, we do not mean to imply that this dynamic constitutes the only structural and conflictual force affecting social and economic change in capitalist societies. Structural conflicts arising from relations among races, genders, and nations, for example, are also likely to have their own relatively independent logic and dynamics. Such forces are not unimportant or even necessarily less important than those that we address in our analysis. We have simply concentrated on one important dimension of our social and economic history; these other critical dimensions are not our main focus in this work.

Problems in long-swing theory

We have proposed that capital accumulation takes place only within the context of a social structure of accumulation. If this proposition is correct, it is not logically possible to develop formal models of capitalist growth and instability without simultaneously developing models of social structures of accumulation. However much it may challenge several traditions of economic analysis, we are suggesting both that macrodynamic behavior depends upon the environmental conditions necessary for capital accumulation and that instability in that environment is likely. To develop a theory of *long* swings from these propositions, however, one must also account for the duration of the different moments of instability. In this section we discuss the duration issue more explicitly and attempt to clarify three important theoretical questions that a long-swing theory must address:

1. Why do the expansions that are stimulated by new social structures of accumulation last longer than short-term business cycle expansions?

2. Why are these longer periods of expansion limited in duration, and how does the concept of the social structure of accumulation contribute to our understanding of the causes of the length of the expansion as well as the eventual stagnation?

3. Why is a slowdown of accumulation (conditioned by the social structure of accumulation) not self-correcting? likely to push the economy from stagnation and instability to crisis? likely to create a long period of contraction before recovery once again becomes possible?

These are difficult questions, to which we do not have complete answers. We outline here the directions in which our analysis leans.

First, the expansion phase of a long swing spans several short-term business cycles because the institutions composing the social structure of accumulation are durable and remain favorable to capital accumulation. These advantages continue to accrue even during short-term cyclical contractions, enhance the profitability of individual investments, and help speed recovery.

For example, the postwar accord between capital and labor provided a stable and cooperative collective bargaining system, permitting employers to institute productivity-enhancing innovations in technology and the organization of work. In return, workers received regular increases in wages as well as expanding social welfare benefits provided by the government. Employers could count on the stability of this system for some time, and it worked quite well to generate an underlying favorable context for capital accumulation.

33

The social structure of accumulation can be conceptualized as a durable investment that, once installed, pays off over a long period of time. It is durable because much investment has gone into its institutionalization; and it is successful because it results from the distillation of a long period of experimentation.[11]

Second, at the same time, the institutions of a social structure of accumulation themselves are likely to limit the potential for indefinite expansion. The end of the boom begins when successful capital accumulation creates obstacles that stand in the way of continued accumulation. Such problems may appear in any of a variety of the constituent institutions of the social structure of accumulation: Output markets may become saturated; important inputs (for example, labor or energy supplies) may become exhausted as sources of continued growth; accumulation may change the relative strengths of classes, weakening some and strengthening others and disrupting the old patterns of class relations.

Thus the postwar capital–labor accord institutionalized expectations of continuing increases in real wages as well as rising benefits from social welfare programs. Although these expectations fueled a rising rate of inflation by the 1970s, they could not be dampened within existing institutions. The structure of the capital–labor accord now blocked rapid capital accumulation. Or, to take another example from the postwar period, U.S. growth was built, among other factors, upon the expansion of U.S. corporations in European markets and upon the international economic relations established at Bretton Woods in 1944. Yet it was essentially inevitable that the growth of European firms would ultimately eliminate the initial advantages of U.S. corporations and that the recovery of Europe (and Japan) would strain and break up the Bretton Woods system.

These examples suggest that the limits imposed on an expansion are specific to the particular institutions of the existing social structure of accumulation. This hypothesis is analogous to traditional economic hypotheses about eventually diminishing returns to scale *within* a fixed productive environment. If one keeps the same capital equipment, returns to labor are likely to diminish at some point as one reaches the capacity of labor or capital or both. Similarly, an economy that expands *within* the same social structure of accumulation is likely to encounter diminishing returns to continual expansion; as the "capacity" of that institutional structure is approached, its effectiveness in promoting accumulation is diminished.

Third, why does a capitalist economy retain the *same* social structure of accumulation once it has begun to display diminishing returns? The answer to this question arises from the relatively disconnected and unplanned character of the decisions of individual units of capital accumulation in a capitalist economy. Although individual capitalists depend upon their social environment, they retain relative autonomy in their individual enterprises. Individual capitalists are jealous of their individual prerogatives. Even if state planners begin to recognize some of the increasing friction or inefficiency of an existing social structure of accumulation, capitalists and others with perceived vested interests in the old order are unlikely to welcome changes in that environment. Thus, individuals in a class may block the reforms that would advance the general interest of the class (see Block, 1977, for some related comments).

These remarks must be amplified in order to provide better support for our contention that the economy must plunge into crisis before individuals and groups will achieve the institutional adjustments necessary for renewed growth. Why is gradual change in the social structure of accumulation unlikely? Why is abrupt structural change such a recurring feature of the long-swing dynamic of capitalist economies?

A kind of negative answer is provided by those neoclassical economists who have recently extended optimization analysis to the study of macroinstitutional change. (We refer to a tradition initially stimulated by Coase, 1937, and best exemplified in recent years by North and Thomas, 1973. Davis and North, 1973, and Higgs, 1980, also apply some of these insights to issues related to this study.) Confronted with our argument thus far, this group of economists would probably argue that individuals can continuously calculate the costs and benefits of potential institutional change and build the least costly coalition necessary to change institutions in desired directions. These neoclassical economists would therefore argue that social structures of accumulation are likely to experience a continuing process of marginal institutional adjustment and that the costs of institutional frictions would rarely get out of line.

Our answer is substantially different. To begin with, it is extremely unlikely that many individuals will have perfect information or foresight about the benefits or costs of present or prospective institutional arrangements. Habits formed by ideology and the traditions of cultural practice during the boom are likely to impose blinders on individuals' perceptions and calculations, lending a conservative bias to their evaluation of the relative merits of prevailing and potential institutional structures. Consequently, the desirability of serious institutional change will be underestimated.

Moreover, the multidimensionality of social structures of accumulation makes coalition-building extremely complicated. Some interest

35

groups, defined with respect to their interests in one set of institutions, may prefer movement in a particular direction of change, whereas some other interest groups, defined by their relationship to other institutions, may prefer potentially inconsistent directions of change. And since sharp group conflicts about the distribution of the relative costs and benefits of alternative paths of institutional change are likely to emerge, some resolution of these conflicts must be achieved. These considerations do not mean that successful coalition-building is impossible, but they do suggest that the process of constructing coalitions of sufficient scope and strength to forge new social structures of accumulation is likely to prove complex and time-consuming.

In short, social structures of accumulation will exhibit considerable inertia, and coalitions aiming to change those institutions will emerge only slowly. As a result, capital accumulation within a given social structure of accumulation is likely to encounter diminishing returns to continuing capital investment, and this deceleration is likely to intensify until substantial adjustments in the social structure of accumulation can be made. But these adjustments are not likely to occur for some time.

We thus provide an answer to the third question about the duration and persistence of contraction and crisis. The length of phase B of a long swing results from the long lag before individual actors can mobilize collectively *and* from the long lag before collective struggle reaches the point of compromise or clear-cut victory that permits construction of a new social structure of accumulation.

This consideration leads us to suggest that long-swing contractions cannot be self-correcting and that a recovery cannot begin unless and until individual actors are able to mobilize coherent and collective forces which – either through some kind of social "compromise" or, alternatively, through decisive class victory – effect the necessary structural adjustments in the social structure of accumulation. Until this happens, initial stagnation is likely progressively to erode the stability of the reigning social structure of accumulation, leading to deepening economic crisis. Within this context, it would be surprising if crises were resolved in anything shorter than a long period of complex political struggle and conflict among capitalists, workers, and other groups.

This brings us to another common question about long-swing analysis: Why do each of the phases of a long swing regularly last for twenty-five years? Our institutional analysis does not suggest that the expansion and contraction phases of a long swing will last any specific number of years and certainly does not indicate that each long swing will have the same duration. On the contrary, we expect that the duration of each phase of a long swing is best understood within the specific context of each stage of capitalism.

Indeed, we suspect that much of the previous literature on long swings has exaggerated their symmetrical periodicity. We can take the United States during the past three long swings for an example. Even if one believed in the precision of a dating exercise, which we do not, one does not find regular periodicity. In Table 2.1, in the appendix to this chapter, the expansions and contractions of the long swing are dated from trough to trough of a business cycle. If one accepts that relatively arbitrary yet consistent dating, one finds that the five successive A and B phases of the last two and a half long swings have lasted thirty-two, sixteen, twenty, twenty-four, and thirty-two years, respectively. This pattern hardly indicates perfectly symmetrical cycles.

Several additional considerations should guide the application of this framework of long swings and stages of capitalism.

To begin with, it is important to emphasize that the analysis of stages of capitalism derives from propositions about the operation of the *world* capitalist system. Since capitalism operates on a world scale, one should analyze its contradictions and social structures of accumulation on a world scale. Hence, evidence of long swings should be organized, as much as possible, for the world capitalist economy as a whole (see the appendix to this chapter). At the same time, the analysis must also focus on the structure and contradictions of the social structure of accumulation within specific nations. While international factors provide pressures on national institutions, the content of the social structure of accumulation may vary significantly from one country to another, and many institutions are determined primarily by domestic forces.

As a related issue, we suspect that the relative synchronization of long swings among individual national economies within the world capitalist economy as a whole depends upon the character of the respective stages of capitalist development. In both the 1840s-to-1890s stage and the post–World War II stage one group of national capitalists, first the British and then the Americans, dominated the world capitalist economy. In each case the hegemonic power was able to create a relatively stable international environment, and the rhythms of many countries closely followed the rhythm of the dominant power. In contrast, in the first four decades of the twentieth century, intercapitalist competition among nations generated a much more unstable international environment, and individual countries' growth rates were less influenced by a single national power. As Ap-

37

pendix Table 2.1 suggests, for example, the A phases of the stages featuring British and American hegemony were relatively long – thirty-one and thirty years respectively, according to this particular dating scheme – whereas the A phase of the stage featuring a less stable international environment lasted only about twenty years. Although we do not want to make too much out of the specific dates involved, these differences among stages do illustrate the importance of analyzing the international contexts within which successive long swings unfold.

We have further suggested that the construction of a social structure of accumulation requires explicit and self-conscious actions by leading political actors. By emphasizing these conscious acts we do not intend to suggest a purely conspiratorial, behind-the-scenes process that is hidden from the public's view until it is unveiled as an accomplished fact. Instead, we see this process as occurring quite openly and as involving first the development and then the mobilization of a consensus supporting the new institutional structure.

It is also important to emphasize that the stages-of-capitalism analysis is fundamentally qualitative in nature, based on propositions about the social relations necessary for continued capital accumulation. The stages of capitalism that emerge historically cannot be characterized by a single dimension of institutional transformation. As we have already noted, the social structure of accumulation comprises a fairly long list of institutions. Each one is necessary if rapid capital accumulation is to proceed, and each may therefore require reconstruction during and after an economic crisis. Consequently, the institutional transformation from one stage to the next has a multidimensional character. Therefore, studies of and evidence about long swings should build as much as possible upon qualitative institutional analysis and should not be reduced exclusively to the study of a series of quantitative indices of economic variables.

Finally, we emphasize that our stages should not be distinguished by single-point dating schemes. Rather, they should be conceived of as overlapping institutional distributions, with the end of one stage coinciding through several years with the beginning of the next. The complexity of the process of construction and consolidation of a new social structure of accumulation precludes narrow dating. As we have argued, this process does not happen overnight. It is likely to take many years, beginning long before the end of a crisis and continuing substantially into the period of the new stage of capitalism. As a result, it is difficult to determine the precise moment when a given historical tendency becomes dominant; one can find events that support or fail

38

to support a particular narrow dating scheme. For this reason, the historical analysis in the chapters that follow pays more attention to the differing developmental characteristics that distinguish one period from the next and less attention to issues of specific dating and time.

Concluding comments

We devote each of the three following chapters to an elaboration of the logic and dynamics of three successive stages shaping the labor process and labor markets. Given this introduction to the general logic of our historical analysis, it seems important to make some concluding comments of clarification and qualification.

We want to underscore our treatment of this historical argument as a connected set of detailed historical *hypotheses*. Given the scope of the historical argument, our essay cannot provide the kind of rigorous detail that would be necessary to establish sufficient tests of every hypothesis; that would require several volumes. Each of the three succeeding chapters does provide a considerable body of historical evidence that supports the general argument we have sketched in this chapter. This evidence demonstrates, we believe, the plausibility of our set of hypotheses. We hope that our elaboration of these hypotheses will be sufficiently compelling to stimulate further historical research along the lines we suggest in this work.

We also want to warn readers against the direct superimposition of our analysis onto the history of the labor process and labor markets in other capitalist countries. We have presented specific historical hypotheses about the structures of labor processes and labor markets for U.S. capitalism. We do not suggest that these hypotheses constitute general hypotheses about those structures for all capitalist countries for each of the stages of capitalism that we analyze. For example, the dates of the initial proletarianization stage will vary considerably among capitalist countries. And, to make another kind of point, it is not clear that the labor process and labor markets would pass through the stages of both homogenization and segmentation, in that order, in all capitalist countries. As transnational corporations have come to dominate the world capitalist economy, it is possible that countries beginning capitalist development after the 1920s or after World War II would never experience a stage of homogenization of labor and would pass directly to a stage dominated by segmentation or its appropriate historical equivalent. Much more work on international comparisons must be done before our analysis can provide a useful historical guide to the analysis of labor history in other countries.

Historical contributions. We want to close by mentioning briefly a few of the important features that distinguish our work from other historical writing in this area. This summary should help alert the reader to these points in the detailed argument that follows.

First, our analysis suggests that the development of the labor process and labor markets and, by extension, the formation of the working class in the United States have passed through several discontinuous stages. This approach contrasts with the more continuous, more evolutionary emphasis of many historical accounts. Consider some of the institutionalist labor economists' arguments about the development of trade unions for a different kind of argument (see, for instance, Lester, 1958, and Ulman, 1955). Or, consider the emphasis in much of the "new economic history" on the continuities of American development (see, for instance, Lee and Passell, 1979). We think that the historical account afforded by our analytic framework is much more illuminating and accurate than the evolutionary version.

Second, many historians' accounts of labor history focus almost exclusively on workers' efforts to organize on their own behalf. Many Marxist accounts of capitalist development focus almost exclusively on the logic of competition or the effectiveness of capitalists' efforts to shape the labor process (as in studies of Taylorism or Fordism). Our account places central theoretical and historical emphasis on the *combined* effect of both capitalists' and workers' activities within the broader context of the contours of capital accumulation.

Third, our historical analysis of the labor process, labor markets, and the working class in the United States makes possible a systematic effort to explore the connections between the process of capital accumulation and the history of workers' struggles. We have found that almost all concrete analyses of U.S. labor history pay far too little attention to the influence of the dynamics of capital accumulation on the limits, objectives, and instruments of workers' struggles.[12]

Fourth, our analysis leads directly to some implications about the changing mechanisms for transmission of skills. One crucial aspect of a successful social structure of accumulation is the arrangement by which new cohorts of workers are trained in the skills necessary to run the productive apparatus. Such a mechanism must be provided if capital accumulation is to occur, and the distribution of *control* over the mechanism that transmits skills has substantial implications for the balance of power between classes. Since we have not systematically elaborated this point in the historical analysis of Chapters 3, 4, and 5, we include in a note to this paragraph a brief summary of our suggestions about the relationship between phases in the transformation of labor and corresponding changes in the mechanisms that transmit skills.[13]

Fifth, early analyses of dual labor markets and labor market segmentation developed through cross-sectional analyses of labor markets and microsample data. This led to an exaggerated focus on the characteristics of individual workers and a reified analysis of the boundaries dividing segments. Our historical analysis aims at providing a much more dynamic account of the processes generating the segmentation of labor in the hopes of placing more emphasis on the structures that generate segmentation and the historical contingency of both these postwar structures and the resulting segmentation.

Sixth, institutionalist analyses of labor market divisions and segmentation have placed primary emphasis on historically specific institutional features giving rise to those divisions, such as union bargaining, job-specific skills, secondary workers' attitudes, and the demand curves of peripheral industries. Our analysis places much greater emphasis on the process through which the dynamics of capitalist development led to and provided the context for the development of segmentation. Many economists talk about the possibility of "upgrading" the jobs of low-skilled secondary workers, increasing their wage levels, and improving their working conditions. Our alternative explanation of the skill structure of jobs indicates that such reforms could not take place without profound challenges to the present structure of the capitalist economy.

Finally, earlier analyses of segmentation, including our own, overemphasized the importance of corporate planning. Workers are not passive pawns in the hands of omnipotent corporate planners, nor are they subject to inexorable laws of capitalist development. The analysis we present in this book aims to redress the imbalance of these earlier treatments, viewing the dynamics of accumulation and the transformations from one stage of capitalism to the next as products of a two-sided class struggle. This emphasis has important implications. If worker and union practice played an instrumental role in shaping the structures of segmentation, then it seems likely that worker and union actions can similarly play an instrumental role in shaping the institutions that will emerge from the present structural crisis of capitalism.

Appendix: The evidence for long swings

Many scholars continue to doubt the plausibility of the long-swing hypothesis. Because this proposition plays such an important role in our analytic framework, we review in this appendix some of the evidence that leads us at least provisionally to accept the existence of long swings.

The most important indicators, as we argue in Chapter 2, are periodic instances of qualitative institutional change. In Chapters 3, 4, and 5 we concentrate on precisely these kinds of indicators for the United States. As a result, we shall not review here the general qualitative evidence of alternating periods of stability and instability in the world capitalist system. Although our historical analysis does not "prove" the existence of long swings, it at least serves to illustrate the kind of qualitative analysis that is, from our perspective, most pertinent to "tests" of the long-swing hypothesis.

We turn here to the quantitative evidence about which many economists have remained relatively skeptical since the 1940s and 1950s.[14] Although economists accept that prices in capitalist economies have moved through long swings, many have tended to doubt that other quantitative indicators confirm the long-swing hypothesis. Despite these doubts, however, the record provides considerably more support for the existence of long swings than this traditional skepticism would warrant.

Based on the framework for analyzing stages of capitalism and long swings that we have outlined in Chapter 2, we would expect both rates of growth in real output and rates of profit on real investment to provide the most illuminating quantitative indicators of long swings. Historical data on rates of profit are problematic and unavailable on a consistent and continuous basis over a sufficiently long period. In recent years, in contrast, reasonably consistent data on output since the 1840s and 1850s have become available for several of the advanced capitalist countries. For the United States, in particular, the effects of the long swing on output can be tested by measures of changes in the rate of growth of real aggregate output, or Gross National Product (GNP). Alternatively, because we are interested primarily in the capitalist sector and because agriculture has until recently been dominated by slave, sharecropping, and independent family production, we sometimes refer in our specific historical chapters to the rate of growth of industrial output.

Table 2.1 summarizes the evidence on rates of growth in real output in four major capitalist economies – the United Kingdom, the United States, Germany, and France – from the middle of the nineteenth century. (We exclude Japan in order to permit consistent comparisons with the same set of countries throughout the period.) In order to track the systemic movement of the world capitalist economy as a whole, we compute a weighted average of the four growth rates for each period. This weighted average growth rate is higher in each A phase than in the succeeding (or preceding) B phase. The same general pattern appears for each of the individual economies. Because the figures presented in the table are compounded (exponential) growth rates, even small differences in the calculated rate of growth reflect significant (compounded) differences in trends of actual output.

This uniformity appears greater in swings II and IV than in swing III. In the A phase of II the world capitalist economy was dominated by the United Kingdom; in the A phase of IV the United States was the leading capitalist nation. Hence, the expansion phase of III is unusual because of the absence of a hegemonic economic power, permitting a greater variation in individual country experiences. For example, the differences in growth rates between

Table 2.1. *Growth of real output over the long swing*

Long swing	Years[b]	Average annual percentage growth in real output[a]				
		United States	United Kingdom	Germany	France	Weighted average[c]
IIA	1846–1878[d]	4.2	2.2	2.5	1.3	2.8
B	1878–1894	3.7	1.7	2.3	0.9	2.6
IIIA	1894–1914	3.8	2.1	2.5	1.5	3.0
B	1914–1938	2.1	1.1	2.9	1.0	2.0
IVA	1938–1970	4.0	2.4	3.8	3.7	3.8

[a]The growth rates presented in the table are the average annual exponential (compound) rates of increase in an index of real output, with 1913 = 100.

[b]The dates for these comparisons were selected in the following manner: We assumed on the basis of qualitative historical evidence that the boom of stage II began in roughly 1845 and lasted until 1873; that the boom of stage III began after the collapse of 1893 and continued until 1913; and that the boom of stage IV began after the downturn of 1937–8. We then selected the next trough (in the short-term business cycle) following those key dates as the dating point for the respective phases of the long swing. (We chose to make trough-to-trough comparisons of output growth rates in order to avoid overstating the growth in boom periods by measuring to an artificially high peak before the crash. For example, one would overstate the boom in France, Germany, and the United States if one measured to the peak of 1913; the vulnerability of those economies is reflected by the depth of the recession from 1913 to 1914.) The specific trough dates varied slightly among countries from 1848 to 1894; we calculated growth rates with respect to the separate and specific trough for each country, while the dates presented in the second column of the table are the respective dates for the United States.

[c]The four-country averages are weighted by their respective shares of world trade, since the long swing reflects a world capitalist effect mediated through international exchange. The series reported in the table were calculated with ex post weights in order to capture the emergent dynamics of each period.

[d]The figures in this row are approximate since the specific output data had to be interpolated between decennial figures for 1840 and 1850. We interpolated on the basis of average exponential growth over those ten years, with a business-cycle adjustment based on the average amplitude of trend-to-trough fluctuation for the respective countries during the first period when annual data become available.

Sources: Output data from Maddison (1977, table A-5, pp. 128–131). Dating of business-cycle troughs from Burns and Mitchell (1946, pp. 78–79); for 1970 from Center for International Business Cycle Research (1981). Shares of world trade from Rostow (1978, table II-2, pp. 52–53).

phase IIB and phase IIIA are not always large. The differences are most pronounced for the United Kingdom and France, whose economic fortunes were relatively declining in phases IIB and IIIA, and least obvious for the United States and Germany, whose economies were boosted during the 1870s and 1880s by their growing relative power in the world economy.[15] (This also explains the relatively small difference in the weighted growth rates between phase IIA and phase IIB.)

Table 2.1 also indicates that Germany grew more rapidly in phase IIIB than in phase IIIA. But this exception does not jeopardize the general conclusion, for the German experience was unusual in both the 1920s and the 1930s. During the Weimar period the inflationary frenzy generated an artificial boom, and during the Depression German prosperity was fueled by Hitler's Nazi expansionism. Apart from these exceptions, the differences in growth rates indicate alternating long swings of expansion and stagnation in the main capitalist economies.[16]

In addition to differences in real growth rates, one would also expect that phases of stagnation in the long swing would involve relatively greater vulnerability to cyclical economic downturns than would phases of long expansion.[17] This suggests two hypotheses: (1) Economies would spend relatively more time in business-cycle upturns during long-swing expansions and relatively more time in business-cycle recessions during long-swing contractions; and (2) because of their greater vulnerability during long-swing contractions, economies would experience relatively sharper business-cycle downturns during the B phase of the long swing than during the A phase.

Table 2.2 presents evidence that appears to support the first hypothesis about the shape of short-term business cycles over the long swing. This table shows the ratio of duration (in months) of upswings to duration of downswings over each phase of the long swings since the middle of the nineteenth century. As Table 2.2 shows, all three economies experienced relatively longer periods of expansion during the upswing of stage II than during its period of contraction. Between the 1890s and World War II, the picture is a little more mixed. The United States shows the same pattern as for the previous long swing. The United Kingdom has a higher expansion/contraction ratio for the boom than for the bust, but the "bust" ratio is above 1.00. (In the underlying data this exception reflects the long period of "recovery" during the Great Depression from the 1932 trough to the 1937 "peak.") In Germany, the relationship is reversed; the expansion/contraction ratio is higher for the interwar period than for the prewar boom. This reversal reflects the special experiences of the German economy noted in the previous paragraphs.

The second hypothesis is somewhat more difficult to test because annual data on output are available only intermittently before 1870. The hypothesis is nonetheless confirmed for stages III and IV. For the four principal capitalist countries, the average (unweighted) change in total output during the recessions of stage III expansion, from 1894 to 1914, was −2.0 percent per year. During the stage III contraction, from 1914, through 1938, the average annual decline during recessions was −3.8 percent per year, almost twice as sharp an amplitude. If we included the 1914 recession in phase B rather than phase A, moreover, the figures would provide even stronger support: The average phase A amplitude would then be −1.2 per-

Table 2.2. *Expansion and contraction over the long swing*

Long swing	Years	Expansion/contraction ratio (months)		
		United States	United Kingdom	Germany
IIA	1848–1873	1.80	2.71	1.61
B	1873–1895	0.86	0.76	0.79
IIIA	1895–1913	1.14	1.62	1.33
B	1919–1940	0.67	1.36	1.82
IVA	1948–1971	1.95	n.a.	n.a.

Sources: Gordon (1978a, p. 26) for long swings II and III. The U.S. figure for phase IVA is based on the periodization in Center for International Business Cycle Research (1981). The ratio for England and Germany is not computed for phase IVA because the postwar cycle dating provided by the Center for International Business Cycle Research only begins with the mid-1950s.

cent per year and the average phase B amplitude would increase to −4.0 percent per year.

We are more familiar with the evidence for stage IV. For the United States, for example, the average annual change in total output during the recessions of phase A from 1947 to 1967 was +1.1 percent per year. During the two completed recessions of phase B, the average annual decline in output was −0.9 percent per year.

Another dimension of the long-swing analysis focuses on its international dimensions. If there have been long swings of alternating expansion and stagnation, we would expect those swings to affect the channels of foreign trade and the international transmission of macroeconomic instability. Table 2.3 traces an index of total world trade (in constant prices) through the successive long swings since the mid-nineteenth century. Although the data are often imperfect, they show clear alternations in the rate of growth of world trade. Rapid expansions of world trade occur during the A phases, and much slower growth occurs during the B phases of the long swings.

There is also some corroborating evidence about the transmission of economic instability. Maddison (1977, p. 112) tabulates the number of instances in which total annual real output actually declined in the sixteen major capitalist countries since 1870. Table 2.4 summarizes those results from phase IIB (sufficient data are not available for phase IIA) through phase IVA. The summary table indicates that many more countries experience not only slower growth but also actual contraction during a long-swing stagnation than during its expansion.

One final potential indicator of long swings involves evidence on the rate and composition of investment and technical innovation. Principally following the lead of Schumpeter (1939), several economists have hypothesized that technological innovation would cluster, out of necessity, late in the long-

Table 2.3. *Growth in world trade over the long swing*

Long swing	Years	Average annual percentage change in world trade
IIA	1850 to 1876–80	+7.04
B	1876–80 to 1891–5	3.75
IIIA	1891–5 to 1913	5.42
B	1913 to 1936–8	0.26
IVA	1936–8 to 1970	10.98

Source: Calculated from data in Rostow (1978, table B-3, p. 669). Dates for this table are dictated by data presented by Rostow. Data based on an index of the volume of trade in constant prices.

Table 2.4. *Frequency of output declines in the world capitalist economy*

Long swing	Years[a]	Average annual frequency of output declines, 16 capitalist economies
IIB	1873–1892	2.3
IIIA	1893–1913	1.7
B	1914–1937	4.4
IVA	1948–1969	0.6

[a]The dating of phases begins with a business-cycle peak, in order to include the first recession of each phase within that phase. Just as phase IVA begins after World War II for these calculations, the phase IIIB figure excludes 1915–1918 in order to eliminate the unusual effects of World War I.
Sources: Calculated from Maddison (1977, table 5, p. 112). Business-cycle reference dates from Burns and Mitchell (1946, pp. 78–79).

period stagnation and that infrastructural investment would be particularly likely to bunch in the long downswing or, in our terms, at the beginning of the construction of the new social structure of accumulation.

Data on technological innovation and the composition of real investment are notoriously difficult to marshal on a sustained quantitative basis for sufficiently long time periods. Hartman and Wheeler (1979) have nonetheless provided some interesting exploratory evidence that seems at least partially to support these hypotheses. They find that growth-theoretic measures of technological innovation, based on the residuals from time-series estimation of aggregate production functions, are substantially higher during long downswings than during upswings and that some fragmentary measures of infrastructural investment indicate that downswings have "been marked by disproportionate levels of infrastructure expansion" (1979, p. 66).

None of these quantitative comparisons are conclusive, but they provide enough support for the long-swing hypothesis, even on the quantitative terrain, to suggest its plausibility. We make use of the long-swing framework, in this tentative spirit, to help organize our historical analysis of the labor process and labor markets in the United States.

3

Initial proletarianization:
1820s to 1890s

We label the period from roughly the early 1820s to the mid-1890s as the stage of *initial proletarianization*. In these years wage labor was decisively installed as the central condition of the labor force; although wage labor was not yet dominant numerically, the momentum established during this period made it certain to become so. Proletarianization did not end with the slump of the 1890s, and indeed continues to the present; however, it was during the stage of initial proletarianization that wage labor came to be the "normal" condition of producers in the United States. Subsequent conflict would focus mostly on the conditions of wage labor and only rarely on the fundamental issue of its merits as a system.

In this chapter we trace the exploration, consolidation, and decay of the social structure of accumulation based on initial proletarianization. Since this system provided the first successful basis for extensive capitalist production in the United States, its rise and consolidation cannot be separated historically from the emergence of capitalism itself. From cross-national comparison, however, we know that capitalism can develop in a variety of ways, and analytically we can see that the particular institutions that emerged were not historically inevitable. We would argue for the United States that the emergence of this particular set of institutions did follow an underlying logic, derived from the particular constellation of class forces and other influences operating at the time. The first social structure of accumulation, like those that followed it, was a product of the particular and historically contingent class struggle and social context from which it emerged.

With the decay of this social structure of accumulation and the exploration, as we see in Chapter 4, of a new social structure of accumulation, the distinction between the particular stage of capitalism and capitalism in general becomes much more visible.

48

Growth and stagnation in the world economy

As we argue throughout this book, the U.S. (and world) economy has passed through several long swings, with each swing being characterized by a phase of rapid accumulation (the A phase) and a phase of stagnation (the B phase). Underlying these long waves a secular development process brings both quantitative growth and qualitative change. Both the continuing development process and the uneven pace of accumulation shape the organization of the labor process and the structure of labor markets.

To understand American capitalism, which developed somewhat later than its British counterpart, it is sufficient to begin with the B, or stagnation, phase of the first (world) long swing. Nonetheless, we might note beforehand that the preceding years had been prosperous even for the United States. The war in Europe generated substantial demand for foodstuffs and war material, and American merchants cashed in on the carrying trade, serving as well-paid go-betweens among the various belligerents and between them and their own (and often each other's) colonies. Derivatively, American farmers and plantation owners saw the prices of their crops rise, and throughout the 1790s the international terms of trade moved consistently in favor of the United States (North, 1961, p. 31). During this period new banks and insurance companies came to line State Street in Boston, and all the nation's major ports rapidly increased their trade and populations. Yet the boom, supported by expansion in the international economy but vastly inflated by the United States' peculiar (and profitable) position in the war, quickly deflated when political events undermined its foundations. The Embargo Act, the British blockade, the collapse of war demand with the post-Waterloo peace, and perhaps most devastatingly, the release of pent-up inventories of British manufactured goods ended the prosperity.

U.S. industry experienced the British-led stagnation in the early decades of the nineteenth century, certainly after 1810 or 1812 and extending through the 1820s; the recovery did not really get under way until roughly 1843. This period in the United States reflected the uneven and ambiguous nature of the long-wave stagnation. On the one hand, old lines of profitable investment petered out. The carrying trade, which had provided such great and enduring returns in the earlier period, never recovered after 1808 (North, 1961, p. 61). Similarly, the huge slaveholder investments in tobacco and rice production earned little return with the decline and closing of European markets. At the same time, population increased relatively rapidly, based al-

49

most entirely on natural increase rather than immigration (Davis et al., 1972, table 5.1). These elements would account for the often hypothesized (but also disputed) decline in real per capita income thought to have been experienced in the period from roughly 1810 to 1840 (David, 1967). On balance, economic growth in these years occurred relatively slowly, probably on the order of 3 or 3.5 percent per year (see Taylor, 1964; North, 1966; David, 1967; Davis et al., 1972, tables 2.2 and 2.3; and Gallman, 1975).

On the other hand, the slow rate of growth was neither uniformly slow nor devoid of new opportunities. The expansion of the late 1810s and the boom of the early 1830s contrasted sharply with the slow pace of the 1820s. Then, too, the boom in world (primarily British) demand for cotton opened the final and profitable chapter in the history of slave production. With hard times for New England farmers came new opportunities for migrants to the Ohio Valley. Even for the big merchants, new investment possibilities emerged, as we shall see in the section "The period of exploration" in this chapter. Both the general austerity of the times and the new opportunities played a part in the proletarianization process.

After the early 1840s the accumulation process again speeded up, moving into the second long swing, from the stagnation to the expansion phase. We need not accept a mechanical notion of this growth spurt – Rostow's "take-off" being the most notorious – to recognize that for a period of some thirty years, say from 1843 to 1873, the U.S. economy and especially the expanding industrial sector in the North showed rapid and more or less continuous growth. Net national product, for example, appears to have grown by roughly 4 percent or more per year over this period, a significant speedup from the pre-1840 rate, and industrial output spurted to over 6 percent (see Table 3.1).[1] Although other quantitative evidence is largely lacking, the impression of rapid growth, especially for the northeastern and north-central states, has not been challenged (see also Easterlin, 1961).

Population increased rapidly during this period, averaging over 3 percent per year in the 1840s and 1850s. Massive migrations of English craftsmen, Irish peasants, and German artisans and workers offset the slight decline in fertility among the resident population. The Civil War tended to deflect the trend, but here national averages are somewhat misleading, especially for this period. For example, even during the 1860s, while aggregate population growth slowed more substantially, the northeastern and north-central states experienced a population growth rate of nearly 2.5 percent (*Historical Statistics*, 1975, series A-2, A-172).

The expansion was built in part upon a wide variety of economic

Table 3.1. *Average percentage annual rates of growth in real output in the United States*

Long swing	Years	Growth in net national product	Growth in industrial output
IB	1810s to 1840s	3.3–4.5	4.3–5.6
IIA	1840s to 1870s	4.0	6.5
IIB	1870s to 1890s	3.5	5.5

Source: The data cover different time periods and reflect diverse estimating procedures. Figures for phase IB are taken from David (1967) and Gallman (1975) and refer to 1800–1840. NNP figures for IIA and IIB are calculated from Gallman (1966) and Davis et al. (1972, Table 2.9) and refer to 1840–1870 and 1880–1900. Industrial output figures are calculated from Gallman (1960) and refer to 1839–1874 and 1874–1899. All of these estimates are subject to substantial error, revision, and controversy, and they should be interpreted with extreme caution to reflect orders of magnitude only. (For example, the range for IB reflects the differences between David and Gallman.) The NNP numbers for phases IIA and IIB are essentially comparable to the figures we present in Table 2.1 (4.2 and 3.7 percent, respectively). The marginal differences in magnitude reflect our effort to interpolate between the decennial censuses of 1840 and 1850 in order to make consistent trough-to-trough comparisons. The numbers reported here, taken directly from Gallman (1966), are not based on trough-to-trough or other business-cycle adjustments. As in Table 2.1, all figures are compounded rates of growth.

and political factors beyond our present focus: the continuing strong world demand for cotton, the gold discoveries, the first of the big nineteenth-century migrations, the opening of new western territories, the Civil War. These were not independent forces, as each was itself shaped by the expansion; for example, Irish and German immigrants came to the United States in part because of increasing opportunities here (Davis et al., 1972, ch. 5). These various factors in turn contributed to the boom.

Similarly, as we shall see, this boom both increased the pressure for proletarianization – good investment opportunities pressed capitalists to find new ways to profit from them – and came in turn to depend on proletarianization, as employers collectively contributed to the boom by reinvesting their profits.

The expansion phase, like the stagnation before it, showed neither a smooth nor always an unambiguous trend. Yet, with but minor breaks in each decade, Northern industrialists found an expanding domestic market for their wares and brilliant new possibilities for investment – in railroads, textiles, boots and shoes, arms, farm implements, and a host of other industries. Southern slaveholders saw a different story, of course, suffering periodic sharp breaks in the antebellum world cotton price and destruction of their investments in the war and its immediate aftermath. Yet in terms of the expanding capitalist sector, the slaveholders' demise caused hardly a ripple and in many cases opened new opportunities.

The growth of both GNP and industrial output during the 1860s was, of course, greatly influenced by the war. On the one hand, the war stimulated northern industry dramatically, and the emergence of many "war millionaires" indicated the possibilities for highly profitable business. On the other hand, the war also disrupted and destroyed; whole regions and industries in the war zone were reduced to shambles. National estimates of the growth of industrial output and GNP reflect this effect of war as well, and the high growth rates sustained in spite of this unique (for the United States) economic devastation indicate the underlying force of the rapid accumulation (Davis et al., 1972, ch. 2).

The long boom (in the North and West) came to an end with the hard times of the mid-1870s. Starting with the panic in 1873, continuing for more than twenty years, and ending with the "Great Depression" of the 1890s, the U.S. economy experienced the much weaker accumulation possibilities of the new stagnation.

The downturn was felt much more sharply in the world economy, as especially British (and to a lesser extent, French and German) industry began a phase of slow growth. In part, the reduced investment opportunities abroad ameliorated the U.S. situation, since British, French, and German resources flowed to the United States. It is well known that investors responded with massive movements of capital; for example, it is estimated that as much as one-third of the huge railroad investment of the period derived from foreign sources (Ripley, 1915, pp. 4-8; Davis et al., 1972, p. 507). This capital influx contributed greatly to the substantial capital formation of the period (Kuznets, 1961a). Similarly, working people responded to the hard times by emigrating in greater numbers (Thomas, 1954).

Still, in the United States net national product grew by an estimated 3.5 percent per year (see Table 3.1), a substantial rate but noticeably less than that of the preceding decades. Population growth slowed considerably, to slightly over 2 percent between 1875 and 1898. (The slow population growth did allow per capita income to increase from about $170 in the early 1870s to $210 in 1898, which, when adjusted for the deflation, amounted to a real average annual increase of around 2.4 percent [calculated from *Historical Statistics*, 1975, series A-7, F 1-5]).

Other indicators suggest that while the United States escaped the worst of this late-nineteenth-century stagnation, systemic problems persisted. Business bankruptcies were high; profit margins seem to have fallen greatly; and all three decades, especially the 1870s and 1890s, witnessed sharp, severe, and prolonged business cycle depressions. (Some of these effects are traced in greater detail in the corresponding section of Chapter 4.)

This stagnation period differed from the earlier period of slow accumulation in one important respect. The secular development process itself had changed the character of the economy. As we argue later, by the last decades of the nineteenth century, wage labor had been installed as the established system of labor relations. Even more to the point, at least half the labor force now depended upon wage employment. Hard times at the beginning of the century had meant bankruptcies for some merchants, but for most people they implied only a time of austerity and greater debts; being self-employed, most of the free labor force continued to farm or carry on their trades. The hardships should not be underestimated – witness the marginal farmers who lost their farms or the famous "Yankee farm girls," who were driven to factory employment. Nonetheless, the self-employed status of most workers meant that they had some resources and flexibility in meeting the hard times.

By the end of the century, however, depression brought a whole new problem: unemployment. The slump of the 1870s, for instance, created for the first time a national specter of huge groups of workers deprived of their means of livelihood (Davis et al., 1972, ch. 6). The secular development of capitalism now intersected with the long-wave downturn in a brutally new fashion.

Once again, factors beyond our present focus played a part: the slowdown (or "climacteric") in British growth, the stagnation in the cotton trade, the reduced opportunities for further profitable railroad investment, and the vicissitudes of American farmers increasingly dependent upon an unstable world food market. Yet here too, as we shall see in the section "The period of decay" in this chapter, the overall pace of capital accumulation reflected as well as provided a context for the development of a proletariat; just as the capitalists' success in discovering new sources of wage labor had fueled the earlier expansion, so now their difficulties in managing their workers placed obstacles in their path.

Thus, the period dominated by a social structure of accumulation founded on initial proletarianization began in the long-swing stagnation of the 1820s and 1830s, spanned the expansion stage of the forties through the mid-seventies, and can be said to have decayed during the stagnation of the 1870s through the 1890s. We must note that we use the term *decay* in a limited sense, to signify that the main forces of development and the principal conflicts between capitalists and workers no longer centered on whether wage labor would exist but centered instead on the conditions of wage labor. For individual employers these long swings in economic activity (and the shorter-run business cycles) constituted the context within which they set their efforts to fashion profitable uses of wage labor. For the capitalist sector as a whole (and derivatively, for the entire economy), the successes and failures of these capitalists represented a major force in creating the boom and stagnation phases.

Initial proletarianization

With the overall pace of capitalist accumulation as background, we turn to a more detailed investigation of the exploration, consolidation, and decay of the stage of initial proletarianization, examining in detail the changes it brought for the working population.

American society before capitalism

The United States was born as a child of emergent British capitalism, yet its parentage did not immediately stamp it as capitalist itself. Indeed, at the beginning of the nineteenth century the capitalist organization of production – that is to say, production carried on for profit by means of wage labor – constituted an insignificant proportion of the total economic life of the nation. The United States *developed* into a capitalist country; it was not born as such.

In North America, as elsewhere in the empire, the imperial needs of British capitalism had spawned nearly all modes of production except the capitalist mode. After independence as well as before it, agriculture was the predominant sector of production (and remained so throughout the nineteenth century), and wage labor was little used anywhere in farming. Slaves produced the most important crops, tobacco being in decline but cotton ascendant. Among the free labor force, independent farmers constituted by far the largest group. The arrangement closest to wage labor was bonded labor, a condition in which people were bound for a period of some years in repayment of a trans-Atlantic passage or other debt; in practice, however, the redemptioners moved on to independent farming, rarely accepting permanent wage-labor status (Morris, 1946).

Even in the small nonagricultural sectors, use of wage labor was spotty and irregular. Most craft and artisan production was carried on by independent producers, perhaps with the aid of family members, apprentices, and others, including journeymen sharing in the proceeds. Most of the textile products and even many other manufactured goods that found their way into the domestic and export trade were in fact produced on the farm; household manufacturing supplied country folk with employment during slack seasons, and some family members, especially adolescent girls, worked their spinning wheels and looms pretty much throughout the year, providing the family with hard-earned money income for their essential purchases (Tryon, 1917). Part-time manufacture blended gradually into full-time cottage industry, as some families specialized – at least to the extent of making their gardens, livestock, fishing, and other sources of income secondary. In the cities, the extensive commercial and trading activities tended to be conducted by family businesses, and the porters, clerks, and others who worked for wages supplemented rather than supplanted this principal labor force. These diverse alternatives to wage work created the widely observed "scarcity of labor" in the colonies and young nation (Lebergott, 1964).

Wage workers found their employment primarily in the major cities, where port activities drew most workers. David Montgomery has provided the most insightful view of the early nineteenth-century urban working classes, and he reports that "it was the demand for seamen, longshoremen, carters, and domestic servants which absorbed unskilled wage laborers already in the eighteenth century" (Montgomery, 1968, p. 15). By the 1820s and 1830s, two other sources of demand opened up: work building the roads and canals and work in the construction trades (including shipbuilding) within the cities.

Yet even as these activities came to depend upon wage employment, workers in these areas still constituted a tiny fraction of the productive labor force. Statistics on this point are virtually nonexistent, but perhaps the orders of magnitude can be suggested by the following. In 1800, Stanley Lebergott estimates, wage earners in cotton textiles and iron manufacture amounted to a mere 2,000 persons, between 0.1 and 0.2 percent of the nonslave labor force (Lebergott, 1964, p. 510). Michael Reich, lumping together indentured servants with wage workers, suggests that such labor in all occupations accounted for not more than 20 percent of the nonslave workforce in 1780 (Reich, 1978, table 1).

Thus, although wage labor was not unknown, it was far from being a prevalent or even common way of organizing production. Slave production, independent farming, craft and artisan production, household manufacture, trade and commerce, indentured servitude, family work, petty commodity production – these were the chief relations of production within which the early-nineteenth-century labor

55

force operated. Although they lived in a capitalist world, productive Americans were not for the most part themselves subjected to capitalist relations of production. Capitalism was a revolution yet to come.

The period of exploration: 1820s to 1840s

The construction of this first social structure of capitalist accumulation in the United States can be understood without much simplification as a process dependent upon the creation of a wage-labor supply. Other elements were also involved, to be sure: the property issues resolved in the Constitution, the establishment of the Bank of the United States as the basis for a credit and monetary system, tariff protection from British goods, and the extension of political sovereignty in the West, among others.[2]

With these developments as background, we are concerned with two great changes that transformed the American labor force between the 1820s and the 1890s.

First, the release of the slaves from their servitude freed them legally to choose any economic pursuits they wished. But before blacks entered the wage-labor force, they had to pass through several decades of brutality and poverty in the quasi-feudal system of sharecropping or tenant farming. Finally, having survived this system and been driven from it, they began, some fifty years after their emancipation, to "choose" wage labor. The integration of blacks into the modern working class, made possible by the demise of chattel slavery in the nineteenth century, thus properly belongs to the history of the twentieth century.[3]

The other great transformation also involved an emancipation, a "freeing," but it effected a different change in economic relations as it proceeded. Out of the diverse working population of noncapitalist production – that is to say, out of the independent craftsmen, farmers, household producers, and others who constituted the precapitalist population – a working class of laborers dependent upon their wages for survival was created. The process by which this came about, despite all of its enormous diversity in detail, was in essence uniformly simple. Those who became wage workers had first been stripped of their means of production – freed or deprived, that is, of all alternate ways of supporting themselves. They were driven to wage labor.

This process involved much more than slowly adding to the pool of available wage workers; wage labor, as we have already seen, can be traced to the earliest settlers. (By the end of the eighteenth century, it was possible to point to the young women in the Boston sail duck factory visited by George Washington in 1789; to the forge workers, at least those who were not slaves, at the Baltimore Iron Works; to the carters and stevedores on the Philadelphia and New York docks; to the families employed by General Humphrey, Moses Brown, and other pioneer mill owners; and to others who had become entirely dependent on wages.) More fundamentally, the new groups that entered the labor force after the turn of the century, and especially in the 1820s and 1830s, came to constitute the first phalanx of a permanent and sizable working class. Whereas the earlier wage workers had been exceptional, noteworthy for their very peculiarity, the new groups of wage workers soon made wage labor legitimate.

Capitalists, the eventual employers of these new workers, provided the chief dynamic force, their goods competing with, eroding, undermining, pushing in at the boundaries of traditional production until it was finally overwhelmed. At each small advance, some producers rooted in and sustained by a precapitalist mode of production suffered a loss, either being entirely "released" from such production to find their duty in wage labor or, at a minimum, discovering a heightened dependence upon that portion of their activitites that involved a capitalist as middleman or part-time employer. This competition between emergent capitalist and stagnant noncapitalist production operated all the way up from the village level, where "capitalist" master shoemakers hired more than their share of *jours* (or journeymen) and extended their operations at the expense of the independent cordwainers, to the international level, where the new spinning and weaving mills in Lancashire displaced both British cottage weavers and spinners on New England farms. In this important sense capitalism developed from the bottom up, following Marx's "really revolutionary road," and constituted an impersonal social force, a revolutionary movement nearly without names or leaders or important personages except those humble entrepreneurs who saved and reinvested and saw their businesses grow (Clark 1929, vol. 1; Dawley, 1976; Hirsch, 1978).

Capitalist producers put their products into direct competition with the handiwork of craftsmen, and here they had certain inherent advantages. Unlike the conservative, slow-to-change craftsmen, the new capitalists were intent upon exploiting the possibilities opened up by social change. They tended to be oriented more to the developing market, in the case of the merchants qua capitalists, because their previous experience was in marketing and because, having been relieved of the necessity of devoting full attention to production (they hired workers to produce), they could turn their energies in part to working the market. For example, in shoemaking, it was the capitalists who saw the possibilities in producing heavy boots for the western miners and cheaper shoes for the Southern market, and their control over these markets gave them much leverage to force journeymen shoemakers to accept their terms (Dawley, 1976).

The capitalists also introduced technical change in the production process, although here, except for textiles, their advantage did not lie primarily in making use of "modern" technology (that came somewhat later, and is discussed in Chapter 4). Their edge here resulted from their willingness to ignore the craft traditions. The crafts, organized to protect the collective interests of its members, stressed control of supply and quality of workmanship. But the capitalists cared little for either, and although they by necessity adopted the technology of the crafts, they soon introduced changes: They were less finicky about standards, and they used cheaper labor – poorly trained jours or would-be apprentices – wherever possible.

The biggest advantage enjoyed by the capitalists, however, was the cheapening and regularizing of production they could achieve through control of the labor process. Blanche Hazard's observation (see below under "The period of consolidation") in this chapter about the making of boots and shoes was also true for weaving, cooperage, and the other crafts: The factory was profitable because it permitted effective supervision. The workers, brought together under the foreman's watchful eye, had to work steadily and submit to the discipline of an industrial rhythm. Craftsmen had been accustomed to following their own work patterns, working hard during some parts of the day and easing up during other times, observing "Blue Monday" but banging away the rest of the week, keeping up the pace during some seasons and slacking off in others. Then, too, when every shoemaker worked in his own "ten-footer"or a weaver kept his own loom, each could knock off when the garden needed tending or the fishing was good or a neighbor needed help in building a fence. Such casualness gave the craftsmen much freedom, but it understandably did not provide for regular or stable production. It also made it difficult to expand production when new markets opened (Hazard, 1921, p. 100).

When capitalists stepped in to hire the jours themselves, they began to organize the production process directly. They could now require steady work and put overseers on the job to ensure that the production pace was maintained. As Moses Brown, of the firm of Almy and Brown, put it, "We have 100 people now at weaving, but 100 looms in families will not weave so much cloth as 30, at least, constantly employed under the immediate inspection of a workman" (quoted in Clark, 1929, vol. 1, p. 432). Such supervision did not change the production technique at all, but it certainly reduced production costs. Wastage and spoilage were reduced, product uniformity improved, and the effective labor input of the workforce vastly increased. Although craftsmen did not quickly yield either their casual pace or their old work habits, they were now literally forced to defend themselves, as Herbert Gutman (1973) has so convincingly argued, on the capitalists' turf rather than on their own. Eventually this change would spell the demise of the crafts, as, for example, when Andrew Carnegie and the other steel masters waged their epic battle later in the century with the iron crafts for exactly the reasons cited by Moses Brown (Chapter 4, under "The period of exploration"; Brody, 1960; Stone, 1975). Yet even in the more immediate situation, control over the labor process benefited capitalist producers in their struggle with the independent craftsmen. Thus, in addition to having a more acute sense of the market, the capitalists brought to market goods that were cheaper in quality and almost always cheaper in price. When it came to relatively unfettered market competition, they simply outclassed the craftsmen.

Yet the social context within which these pioneer capitalists had to operate was usually ungiving and sometimes openly hostile to their efforts. Labor – that is, workers for hire more or less permanently on a full-time, year-round basis – was scarce, costly, and in many cases just unavailable. Traditional society resented and often resisted the investors' efforts to create a labor supply. In this sense, initial proletarianization required more than the independent and uncoordinated actions of humble entrepreneurs; it required more dedicated and class-conscious action to establish a social structure of accumulation. Whole populations rooted in noncapitalist ways of producing were released from traditional employments through this broader process.

The story is complicated in another sense by the qualifications necessarily introduced through the special circumstances surrounding U.S. proletarianization. Throughout most of the proletarianization phase, for example, farmland at the frontier could be obtained by adventurous and optimistic souls. Those willing to settle – the people who moved to the railroad lands were a case in point – could usually obtain some credit, so even the start-up costs did not need to be accumulated in full beforehand. But if land was available, how is it possible to say that alternate means of survival were unavailable? Here we must rely on less than absolutes. As the century wore on, of course, the frontier moved west, and the costs of getting to the frontier, not to mention land and equipment costs, increased. Although mortgages were available, loans for equipment and seed were more difficult to obtain.

Moreover, the farmers' periodic protests throughout the century reinforced the easterner's well-founded suspicion that making a go of farming was more difficult than simply moving to the frontier (Shannon, 1945).

In addition, farming required certain skills and even an agricultural temperament, and many ruined craftsmen or destitute immigrants undoubtedly (and no doubt correctly) perceived that they would make poor farmers. Knowledge of when and what to plant, how to handle livestock, what to do about drought or plant disease or pests, and how to market a crop eluded many workers not brought up in farm families. And of course, women, especially single women, who were most in need of an income, were essentially precluded from the chance to set up as independent farmers in the West.

Thus, though land was theoretically available (and a real avenue of escape for many who did have some resources), it was of little practical significance to the people most threatened by the advance of capitalism. Moving west to farm was costly, risky, full of unknown dangers, and often impossible. Young men without families could take the chance, just as they could scramble for gold in California, but for most people the great escape valve was shut.[4]

So, as conditions in their traditional callings deteriorated, usually as a result of competition from capitalists entering the same line of endeavor, these household producers and craftsmen and others suffered real declines in their living standards. When their situations became desperate, they saw little alternative. Freed of their traditional livelihoods, they "chose" wage labor.

The story was also complicated because people in very different circumstances came to be freed for wage labor, and their stories are not the same. In what follows, we describe the four main groups who entered wage employment in the early- and mid-nineteenth century: native-born white males, craftworkers, native-born white women and children, and immigrants. These overlapping groups held distinctive places in the precapitalist systems of production, and the burgeoning capitalist sector touched each of them in diverse ways.

Native-born (white) males. The biggest source of wage labor consisted of native-born males, overwhelmingly whites but with a slight sprinkling of free blacks, who were pushed off or attracted from the farms, from the rural landless, and from the growing propertyless class in the towns and cities. We leave for discussion below the craft workers, whether native-born or foreign-born, who came to constitute a second flow of labor into the waged sector, and here we concentrate on those new workers who brought little experience and craft tradition to their employment.

As a demographic group, native-born white males tended to be highly overrepresented in farming, shopkeeping, the professions, independent craft work, and other alternatives to wage labor. Moreover, young men in this group tended to be the most likely to exercise the options of going to sea, moving west, essaying the goldfields, and so forth. Yet, despite their relatively lower rate of proletarianization, their very predominance in the labor force made them an important labor supply.[5]

Native-born males without extensive craft backgrounds provided the major supply of labor, especially before mid-century, in virtually every industry except the needle trades and New England textiles, where females predominated, and specialized crafts, like carpet-weaving and pottery-making, where foreign-born (and usually foreign-trained) craftsmen established new industries.[6] In industries like iron production, printing, foundry work, food refining, lumber and wood, fuel, chemicals, and brewing they filled most of the jobs, providing general labor, with only the highly skilled workers like typesetters or brew-masters coming up through the crafts. Elsewhere they served as helpers, sometimes with the expectation of mobility that was associated with real apprenticeships, but more frequently with informal arrangements that guaranteed no such pattern. Even in the New England textile mills (discussed under "Females and children") the jobs in machine shops and other activities not utilizing operatives were mostly filled by such males, and they sometimes accounted for a quarter or a third of the entire labor force (Copeland, 1912, ch. 11).

Evidence concerning the origins of this early labor force is scanty, depending mostly on the examination of raw census returns, but it confirms this description. The most useful work is undoubtedly John Modell's (1971) fascinating and detailed analysis of a working-class ward in the emerging industrial city of Reading, Pennsylvania. Because Modell is able to go beyond the native-born versus foreign-born breakdown, he can tell us much about the patterns of internal migration. This happy circumstance derives, as Modell (1971, p. 78) puts it, "from the overzealousness of the census enumerator," one Charles Neidly, who recorded, in much greater detail than he was instructed to, the birthplaces of people in Spruce Ward.

Reading provides a useful case study because it represented the kind of middle-sized city (population 15,000 in 1850), like Holyoke or Syracuse or Trenton, within which so much of emerging American

Table 3.2. *Work force in Spruce Ward, Reading, Pennsylvania, 1850*

Occupation	Nativity of workers (%)						Total no. of workers
	Reading	Other Berks county	Contiguous counties	Rest of United States	Foreign	Total	
Construction, transportation workers	25	28	20	13	15	100	151
Artisans	23	27	14	11	25	100	113
Operatives	16	12	20	19	34	100	135
Laborers	16	37	11	6	30	100	217
Apprentices, assistants, helpers	31	17	20	7	25	100	60

Source: John Modell, private communication, based on Modell (1971).

industry was located (Montgomery, 1967, ch. 1; Gordon, 1978b). Spruce Ward's foreign-born population (12.9 percent) was quite representative of Pennsylvania (13.1 percent), though higher than the national figure (9.7 percent). Moreover, Spruce Ward was a working-class area, housing diverse workshops and factories ranging from small artisan shops to the large Seyfert and McManns nailery and tube works, which used steam power and employed two-hundred workers in 1850.

Of the more than five hundred artisans, operatives, laborers, helpers, assistants, and apprentices employed in Spruce Ward in that year, over 70 percent were native-born (see Table 3.2). Moreover, the birthplace data reveal a striking migration pattern: Native-born workers who came to make up Reading's emerging industrial labor force had migrated largely from the surrounding countryside. As Modell (1971, p. 82) puts it: "Those who contributed most heavily (in proportional terms, and in this case absolutely as well) to the laborers, the *lumpen proletariat*, those with minimal skills and meager security, were not the foreigners but those from the immediate country around – probably displaced agriculturists and sons of agriculturists."

Much the same picture – native-born craft, artisan, or agricultural producers, scattered throughout hamlets and rural areas and reliant upon independent production, flowing to wage labor in the growing industrial towns – emerges from Alan Dawley's (1976) important study of nineteenth-century Lynn, Massachusetts, shoemakers. Dawley has carefully examined the census records to report on the origins and movement of Lynn's industrial labor force. His results (see Table 3.3) for 2,435 male shoe-factory workers demonstrate the overwhelming preponderance of domestic sources of labor "freed" from other livelihoods. As Dawley (1976, pp. 135–136) concludes:

> In both numerical and cultural terms, the most significant segment of mobile recruits were the former outworkers of the New England shoe industry. As the central shops evolved into factories, causing the collapse of the outwork system, people whose well-being once depended on what the freighter brought [i.e., outwork] each month were sent reeling about in search of work. Large numbers found their way to Lynn.

Thus, what we find for Reading, Pennsylvania, and Lynn, Massachusetts, and appears to be true as well for Philadelphia, Syracuse, and elsewhere (see Modell, 1978; Laurie, Hershberg, and Alter, 1977; and Laurie, 1980), is that pressure on the land and domestic production generated a surplus population and, mixed with emerging employment opportunities in the cities, stimulated an extensive migra-

Table 3.3. *Nativity of shoemakers employed in Lynn,*
Massachusetts, factories, 1870

Nativity	Percent
Massachusetts natives	56
Other New England	23
Other United States	2
Foreign-born	19

Source: Dawley (1976, p. 136).

tion to towns and cities that established the basis for an effective labor supply. Later, the migration from farm to town would become a torrent, involving millions of persons, but by mid-century the movement was already substantial.[7]

Craftsmen. The demise of craft production carried another great wave of displaced producers into the wage-labor pool. In activities like shoemaking, chandlery, printing, carpet-making, fine goods weaving, hatmaking, and cabinetry, immigrant craftsmen or their native-born sons had by 1800 established the American version of craft production. A curious brew concocted of European traditions and American conditions, this system maintained the forms and aspirations of the European guilds, seeking careful control over price, supply, training of labor, and work standards. But traditions were shallower and the restrictions harder to enforce. The crafts constantly had to fight against the predations of masters who took on too many apprentices, apprentices who moved on to journeyman status (often by migration) before the requisite years in training, journeymen who worked for less and produced cheaper goods than the standards allowed. All of these difficulties were symptomatic, of course, of the incompletely established power of the crafts, and were compounded by the difficulties imposed by a steady immigration of craft workers fleeing the deteriorating conditions facing their crafts in England and elsewhere.

The eventual outcome of the competition between craft and capitalist organization was perhaps never in doubt. But it was this context – craft organization inherently weakened by a shorter, fainter tradition and by substantial social flux – that permitted the intrusion of the capitalists to create such devastation in the crafts within the span of a few short decades. By the 1840s and 1850s, the system of independent craft production was in total disarray and retreat.

Capitalist organization penetrated the crafts from two directions.

Neither attack brought such bold, immediate change as had the textile capitalists (who encountered mostly household, not craft, production), but both fundamentally transformed productive relations nonetheless. On the one hand, masters and even journeymen rose from the ranks to become employers, eventually transmuting craft production from within. On the other hand, merchants seeking goods to trade sometimes invested backwards, inserting themselves into the production process itself and thereby revolutionizing relations. In both cases, the careful, measured hierarchy of apprentice, jour, and master, in which most apprentices were not too far off the mark in dreaming of their futures as masters, gave way to the simpler and more demeaning structure of boss and worker.

The first path, that of capitalist rising from the ranks, can be seen in the Massachusetts boot and shoe industry. In the important manufacturing town of Randolph, for example, boots and shoes had been produced by local craftsmen since colonial times. In the first half of the nineteenth century, Randolph merchants "put out" materials to shoemakers; although their capital provided the leather and other inputs, the merchants exercised little control over the production process itself. The shoes were either sold locally or marketed through Boston wholesalers. Beginning in the 1840s, however, boot and shoe manufacturers began to emerge from among the more successful craftsmen, employers of labor who now pioneered factory production and sold their goods directly to the Boston wholesale houses. Of the eighty-three boot and shoe manufacturers operating in Randolph in 1850, fully fifty-two had either been shoemakers themselves or were sons of shoemakers (Weiss, 1976, table 3 and passim). Use of wage labor became more extensive and more permanent.

Brewing is another industry that illustrates this up-from-the-craft phenomenon. In the mid-nineteenth century some thirty-five hundred breweries, all small and mostly owned and operated by a brew-master, served local markets. The Best family, German brewers who migrated to Milwaukee, opened their brewery (later to become the Pabst Company) in the 1840s. Although their labor force initially consisted almost entirely of family members, their business soon passed through the craft stage as they established themselves as brewery capitalists (Cochran, 1948). Hirsch (1978) tells a similar story for the artisans of Newark, New Jersey.

The second path, that of merchant capitalist entering the sphere of production, was also widespread. The most prominent case was, of course, the textile industry, where merchants, from Providence's firm of Almy and Brown to the famous Boston Associates, provided the chief entrepreneurial drive. Especially in the weaving operations their entrance displaced independent craftsmen who had operated looms at home for full-time or at least seasonally important employment. The carpet-weavers, for example, organized initially "upon a small-shop and household basis" (Clark, 1929, vol. 1, p. 569), soon faced competition from and eventually employment in the big merchant-financed mills at New Haven, Lowell, Thompsonville, and elsewhere (Cole and Williamson, 1941). So, too, the big mills, started with merchant capital and using power looms to weave cloth goods, put the independent hand-weavers out of business. Victor Clark (1929, vol. 1, p. 430) notes that hand-weaving, except of carpets and occasional household fabrics, disappeared in New England between 1830 and 1840 and in Philadelphia by 1860. Here also competition between craft and capitalist production degraded and displaced craft producers.

The competition operated on an international scale as well, with foreign, especially British, manufactures disrupting traditional patterns of production. In some cases British goods directly displaced American craftsmen. In other cases, it was British craftsmen who were uprooted and who then migrated to the United States. The demise of British weavers before the onslaught of English capital, and their subsequent migration to the United States in large numbers, is well known (Ware, 1931, pp. 205–207; Berthoff, 1953). Similarly, periodic unemployment in the English pottery manufacture prompted the exodus of many craftsmen from Staffordshire; the successful migrants were not the masters but the journeymen who found employment in the United States (Thistlewaite, 1958). In these and numerous other industries, the advance of British capitalism generated a flow of labor to and a redundancy of craftsmen in the United States, overpopulating many trades.

Regardless of whether the capitalists grew out of the crafts or entered through the merchandising of the product, their effect on the independent craftsmen who remained in the trade was everywhere depressingly similar. "Prices" – that is to say, the craftsman's piece rate – fell in real terms. Pressure to increase output and cut corners in production increased. The independent producers and small shops had difficulty keeping afloat. Pauperism spread, and the specter of poverty confronted tradesmen who lost their means of support. Craft workers organized to oppose the competition and maintain their position, but they were fighting a rearguard action (Hazard, 1921; N. Ware, 1964; Weiss, 1976; Hirsch, 1978).

Norman Ware (1964, ch. 4) provides the most detailed examination of this "degradation of the worker." The business depressions at the end of the 1830s left the already overpopulated crafts in a destitute and desperate state. Ware notes the decline in prices (wages) in the iron industry after 1837; the erosion of independence and living standards among Lynn shoemakers; the introduction of wholesale work and cheap German labor in cabinetmaking, which left craftsmen lowly paid or unemployed altogether; and the increasing unemployment of compositors and other printing tradesmen when, "as early as 1836 the transfer of control that reduced the printers from men with a profession to wage-earners was well advanced" (p. 55).

Craft relations underwent continuous change during these years, as the jours and apprentices became increasingly subject to capitalist relations. What was intended by the jours to be temporary employment stretched into long years; what was meant to be a necessary compromise in standards during hard times became impossible to escape even in good ones. "Prices" gave way to "wages," a term, Norman Ware (1964) reminds us, that had previously applied only to day labor. As a result, craft workers no longer organized their own work; capitalists now did. Despite their skills and extensive control over the immediate processes of production, both of which the craft workers had brought with them into the new relations of production, they were now wage workers.

Females and children. Females, especially women who were unmarried, widowed, divorced, or whose husbands were "off traveling" in the informal divorce of the day, came to constitute a third source of labor largely distinct from the craft workers. Occupational statistics for this period are scanty and unreliable, but it seems probable that by the end of the eighteenth century only a tiny fraction of the adult female population worked outside the home, although a substantial number were probably engaged in domestic manufacture through the putting-out system, especially around Philadelphia and Boston. Over the following two or three decades the employment of women expanded slowly, most of the growth occurring in the needle trades and in those textile mills based on the "family system" of labor.[8] Still, the number of women engaged in producing commodities for exchange remained strictly limited.

Although women in domestic industry almost certainly represented the quantitatively most important female labor force until well into the nineteenth century, the famous Lowell mill girls more clearly reveal the efforts that employers made during this exploration phase to create an effective labor supply. Employers refused to wait for the glacial improvement in labor scarcity that derived from the "natural progress" of society in the years after 1800; instead, they actively intervened.

The distress of New England agriculture coupled with the patriarchal nature of farm households brought numerous "Yankee farm girls" into the wage-labor pool. More localized in New England than the process that dispossessed craftmen, this new labor force responded to the call of rich Boston merchants, the Appletons, Lowells, Lawrences, and other big Boston traders. These merchants had reaped huge profits in the wartime carrying trade; with its demise, they looked elsewhere for investment opportunities. Land speculation, banking, insurance, the China trade, all offered possibilities; but these merchants were understandably also drawn to textiles, already the basis of a number of fabulous British fortunes (Clark, 1929, vol. 1, pp. 367–368; Ware, 1931).

Female labor was often linked with the employment of children of both sexes. Indeed, the "Yankee farm girls" were often young women in their early or mid teens. The connections between female and child labor sometimes went deeper.

The earliest mills had depended on a system, sometimes called the "Rhode Island system," although it really derived from English practice, that recruited entire families - husband, wife, and children - for factory labor. This made feasible the employment of married women (alongside their husbands); but even more, employing the mother permitted hiring the children as well, and child labor was important in these enterprises. In some mills children represented the bulk of the force. One survey estimated that in 1820 children made up 45 percent of the total number of workers employed in cotton mills in Massachusetss, 55 percent in Rhode Island, and 54 percent in Connecticut (cited in Ware, 1931, p. 210).

Children were sometimes recruited from the poorhouses and orphanages, but a more dependable supply could be obtained by employing the whole family. Caroline Ware (1931, p. 199) cites the 1816 work force at the Slater mill as typical: one family with eight members working, one family with seven members working, two families each with five members working, four families each with four members working, five families each with three members working, eight single men, and four single women. The two biggest families by themselves accounted for nearly a quarter of the sixty-eight-person work force. Since the pay under the family wage system was substantially less for children than adults (and for women than men), it is little wonder that employers seeking new hands tried to attract big families; the seventeen mills advertising in the *Massachusetts Spy* between 1816 and 1836, for example, called for big families, "of five or six children each" (Ware, 1931, pp. 199–200).

Whereas the family system proved adequate for small mills, which could recruit mainly from surrounding communities, it failed when employers tried to concentrate larger masses of labor. The difficulties could be seen in the greater energies that even owners of small mills were forced to devote to recruiting, including extensive newspaper advertisements. When the Boston merchants began considering big textile investments, they realized that they needed a new labor supply. Although the family system probably remained predominate, in the sense that a majority of those working in all cotton and woolen mills came to their employment in family units, the real stringency of the family labor supply caused the big capitalists to look elsewhere (Ware, 1931, ch. 8; McGouldrick, 1968, pp. 34–38).

These investors, the so-called Boston Associates, pioneered what came to be known as the Waltham System in the factories they opened in the mill towns spreading north and west from Boston, towns like Waltham, Lowell, Lawrence, Holyoke, and Chicopee. As Victor Clark (1929, vol. 1, pp. 547, 450) concludes in his exhaustive history of American manufacturing:

> They expressed the type of industrial organization that eventually was to prevail in America ... [The factory] differed from previous establishments of equal size, either here or abroad, in performing all operations of cloth-making by power at a central plant. Labor was specialized and workers were organized by departments ... In a word, the commercial, technical, and operative elements of a factory were brought together in accordance with an intelligent plan and so coordinated as to make a more efficient producing unit than had hitherto existed in this country. Manufacturing was specialized completely and no longer retained even subordinate relations with household industry or general merchandising. The idea of the factory, as we know it, was conceived and demonstrated so that its application at other places and to other industries was a mere matter of adjustment.

What mattered most, for our purposes, about this new idea of the factory was not the technology it housed, but the organizational principles by which its labor process was established. Most importantly, capitalists hired workers to carry out production activities that they (the capitalists) had organized. Unlike the case of the crafts, where capitalists simply took over the preexisting technique, with its limitations, here the capitalists began afresh. They had no old system to smash, and they organized production to suit their needs. Employers and their foremen supervised individual workers, maintaining discipline and seeking to regulate the latter's pace.

At the beginning, the Boston manufacturers faced two principal labor problems. First, workers were difficult to obtain, since a working class, dependent for its livelihood upon the sale of its labor power, had not yet developed on any extensive scale. The specialization of labor embedded in the technical organization of the factory required relatively large numbers of low-skilled workers. But few people wanted to work permanently in the New England factories, and those who did take a job were likely to leave the factory as soon as they had accumulated enough savings for a farm (Montgomery, 1968). The expansion of factory production therefore required the development and recruitment of a new labor force.

Second, many Americans were already familiar with the growth of the factory towns and of the factory proletariat in the Manchesters of England during the first two decades of the nineteenth century. They feared similar developments in the United States, and public opinion weighed against the recruitment and use of wage workers who would be subjected to oppressive tasks in the factories.[9]

The solution was the famous "Yankee farm girl" experiment. In 1827, of the 1,200 workers in Lowell, 90 percent were female (Baker, 1964, p. 11). According to Norman Ware (1964, p. 71), "A new labor force was available in the women and girls of New England, once their initial aversion to the factory discipline could be broken down." The Boston manufacturers established "such arrangements as seemed good to them to attract the New England women into the mills and guard them from immoral influences as best they could" (p. 72).

Young unmarried women were recruited from their family farms. Special dormitories were erected to protect them physically. Religious and cultural activities intended to provide spiritual and moral education began and ended the working day. The work itself was to teach the virtues of discipline in industry. The wages saved by the young women were to supply the essentials of a household when they left the factory to get married. As Hannah Josephson (1949, p. 67) says:

> After a period of adjustment, the new girl found living and working conditions at Lowell quite tolerable, at least in the early stages of its development, the mills being distinctly superior to those in other industries and the boarding houses comparing very favorably with the standards of lower and middle-class homes.

The girls "flocked eagerly to the mills and boarding houses," Josephson concludes, converging on the factory towns "in a constant stream" (p. 65). The stream flowed in both directions, of course, for the young women did not expect and were not expected to stay long;

median tenure was probably between two and three years. As long as the flow into the mills was sufficient to staff the machines, the rapid turnover was an integral part of the solution. H. M. Gitelman (1967, p. 235) writes: "The significance of the high turnover is that it resolved a basic fear about the factory system; it insured against the development of a permanent factory population subject to dependence upon and possible exploitation by employers."

That the new labor force consisted of single females reflected more than the dynamics of emergent capitalism; it derived as well from the patriarchal system of production in New England households, and particularly from the role of girls and single women within that system. As Edith Abbott (1924, p. 47) emphasized, "the earliest factories did not open any new occupations to women ... work which women had been doing in the home could be done more efficiently outside the home, but women were carrying on the same processes in the making of yarn or cloth." Thus, no preexisting craft protections hindered establishing the mills, and the earliest manufacturers did draw upon those – mainly girls and single women – who were assigned the spinning and (to a lesser extent) the weaving within New England households. In this sense, the Waltham system can be interpreted as a method of attracting women in domestic manufacture into capitalist workplaces. From the perspective of generating a labor supply, the system did not so much compete with domestic manufacture as complete it, marking the last step in the logic of commodity production.

But the links to patriarchal production went far beyond just the similarity of tasks. As Nancy Folbre (1979) has persuasively argued, the whole logic of household production was involved. For one thing, the textile products that were made, first yarns and later woven cloths, replaced precisely the articles that farm daughters had produced at home; thus, when Almy and Brown and the other early merchants began marketing the products of English factories and the first American mills, they made the household's single women the most expendable part of the family's labor force.

Then, too, sons and daughters continued to be obligated to support the household until they could establish households of their own. For sons this typically meant working until they inherited land, often a long wait because the fathers benefited from sons' labor while the sons remained at home, and the fathers therefore had an incentive to delay parcellation. Many young men ran off to the sea or the West or the city, of course; yet, if they remained within the family orbit, their labor was needed on the farm. For daughters, especially those past "marriageable age," the obligations were as real but the means of fulfilling them within the home less obvious, and they became more problematical as outside commodities substituted for the goods the daughters had produced. Thus, as employers searched out a new labor force, the Yankee farm girls, feeling the necessity, as Sarah Bagley put it, of "a father's debts . . . to be paid, an aged mother to be supported, a brother's ambition to be aided" (quoted in Foner, 1978, p. 160), took up work in the factory.

There was another push, that of the tyranny of patriarchal authority within the home, which many of the women must have been pleased to escape (Ware, 1931, pp. 215-225; Folbre, 1979). The irony, of course, was that they escaped to the carefully controlled patriarchal world of the employers' dormitories, where their parents could be assured that they were being properly supervised and isolated from "immoral influences." Nonetheless, the sense of independence, the exhilaration of being out in the world, the pride at having their own savings accounts comes through in the women's writings in the *Lowell Offering* and elsewhere (*Lowell Offering*, passim; Ware, 1931, pp. 215-225). The extent to which poverty forced the women into the mills is disputed; but it seems certain that for many families, the mill jobs represented for the daughters the sort of escape that the sea or the goldfields provided for the sons.

In these boarding mills, women provided the bulk of the labor – estimates suggest about 75 percent overall, higher in the mills producing just cotton – and they were paid the least. They were subject to supervision by the male foremen, surrogate fathers, as it were, who continued patriarchal authority (Ware, 1964, p. 111; Folbre, 1979, ch. 8).

While the system seemed to generate high profits for the employers and provide real opportunities to the operatives in the 1820s and 1830s, the iron discipline of capitalist competition changed the balance in the late 1830s.[10] As a result of increasing competition from British producers employing lower-wage labor and the general depression beginning in 1837, textile company profits fell sharply.[11] Company managers faced increasing pressures to cut labor costs, virtually their only manipulable costs. The hours of work apparently increased substantially in the 1820s, and did not decline until the late 1840s. Not blessed with any new technical inventions that might have increased labor productivity, employers turned to their one alternative – speedup and/or the intensification of labor.[12] Vera Shlakman (1934, p. 98) writes that, after 1840, "factory operatives were seldom free from the fear and pressure of reductions of wages and the speed-up of machinery." Wages were reduced and the speed of the looms themselves was increased.[13] Many operatives were assigned three or four looms to operate, rather than one or two. The "premium system" was instituted, providing financial incentives to overseers to get more work out of the operatives. Hannah Josephson (1949, p. 220) concludes that "this completely altered the relationship between the girls and their immediate supervisors."

The factory women resisted this deterioration in their working conditions, but they were unable to have significant impact. The Lowell operatives struck – "turned out" to demonstrate, really, rather than withdrawing their labor – in 1834 and 1836, and there were similar turnouts at Dover, Chicopee, and elsewhere (Josephson, 1949, ch. 11). Throughout the 1840s the women supported great petition drives to limit the hours of work, but this effort, too, mostly failed.

The achievements of the mill magnates were not slight. Although their operations had begun in the absence of any widespread wage-labor system, they succeeded in establishing an industrial labor market. When the family system proved itself unable to provide an adequate labor supply, the employers had generated new sources of labor. Finally, consistent with the expectations and moral strictures of early-nineteenth-century New England society, the capitalists had based their factory recruitment on a system of benevolent paternalism, under which cultural activities, the moral education of the factory girls, a shared civic or community life, and capitalist production were all supposed to flourish. That this system, too, would soon prove inadequate and its peculiar distinguishing features be abandoned was beside the point; they had established the basis for an effective labor supply.

Unskilled immigrant labor. The final source of wage labor, different from either native-born males or craft workers or females drawn from domestic manufacture, was the influx of unskilled immigrants.

During the period of exploration of the new social structure of accumulation, that is, up until the early 1840s, unskilled immigrants provided a portentous but quantitatively insignificant labor supply. The overall proportion of foreign-born residents in the U.S. population remained low, and not all migration is properly included in this category. The migrants included large numbers of British artisans and other skilled workers. Indeed, it appears likely that there was a substantial trans-Atlantic circulation of craft workers rather than simply a one-way flow (Thistlewaite, 1960). In any event, these producers largely shared language, craft traditions, religion, culture, and material interests with other craft workers. Although the heavy immigration placed great pressure on the crafts, the proletarianization of the craft workers followed the same lines discussed above, whether the workers were native-born or not.

The early noncraft migrants, and the masses of non-British immigrants who followed them later in the century, established new patterns. They differed sharply from the native-born stock in terms of religion (heavily Catholic or Jewish rather than Protestant), language, culture, and even race. They also differed sharply from one another, of course, and so they introduced a degree of heterogeneity in the working class that was unusual in the capitalist world.

The bewildering diversity of forces that set these various peoples in motion is beyond the scope of this discussion, except for this point: in general, people migrated when forced to, when conditions facing them in their homelands had deteriorated to such an extent that they perceived their futures as bleak and intolerable, and when, in consequence, they had few resources (Thistlewaite, 1960; Handlin, 1970). Even then, only the young and able-bodied were likely to migrate, and they frequently saw their migration as temporary, an expedient by which to recoup their devasted lives "at home." Indeed, the very high return rates indicate that many made good on this promise to themselves.

In a movement of peoples as vast as the one being considered here, exceptions to the above generalization abound. Historians of the trans-Atlantic migration have pointed to the extensive circulation of workers, with unknown numbers of "repeaters" who remigrated seasonally or cyclically (Thistlewaite, 1960). Swedes and Norwegians tended more than others not to wait to migrate until they were destitute. Jews fleeing the pogroms and poverty of Russia and Poland demonstrated little desire to return. Professional people, even people of substantial property, appear to have migrated from all parts of Europe.

Yet even the exceptions are instructive. The Swedes and Norwegians tended to use their superior resources to avoid wage labor, establishing themselves instead in relatively greater numbers as midwestern farmers. The Jews, undoubtedly in part because they focused less on going back to Europe, tended to be more disposed toward joining unions and fighting for better conditions in America.

Even considering all the necessary qualifications and anomalies, however, the general point stands. The masses of immigrant labor arrived with few resources; that is, they had effectively been proletarianized *before* they migrated, and once in the United States, they moved directly into the wage-labor force.

Many immigrants, and not just those British craftsmen who migrated early in the century, came with highly developed skills; but still they tended mainly to expand the ranks of those doing unskilled work. The reason for this paradox is simple: Large numbers of mi-

74

grants failed to find work that used their skills. Hence, the long debate over whether the earlier migrants from northwestern Europe
had more skills than the later arrivals from southern and eastern
Europe (eventually stalemated by the conclusion that they had different skills) was essentially beside the point; the occupations in which
the foreign-born found themselves once in the United States bore
little correspondence to the skills they had developed in the old country. Language barriers, antiforeign prejudice, lack of licensing, different production techniques, and the personal strain of the adjustment all conspired to limit the immigrants' occupational choices
(Hutchinson, 1956; Spengler, 1958; Medoff, 1971). As one study put
it (Bloch, 1920, p. 762):

> The available statistics . . . seem to show definitely that on the
> whole neither immigrant agricultural workers nor the immi-
> grant skilled workers follow their former occupations . . . The
> fact that many occupations show an increase of foreign born
> entirely disproportionate to the number of immigrants of the
> same occupation who came into the country indicates that
> immigrants choose an occupation without much regard to
> their previous training experience.

Or, more simply, as a review of this literature concluded, "immigrants
added more to the supply of unskilled and semiskilled than of skilled
labor" (Eckler and Zlotnick, 1949, p. 99).

The earliest unskilled immigrants, largely Irish and German,
landed in the port cities but seem to have passed through them to
find employment in the road- and canal-building projects of the West
(Montgomery, 1968). Yet already there were reports of less than fully
trained labor being used in some of the crafts (cabinetmaking and
shoemaking, for example) and in new lines of industry, such as
sugar-refining, where no substantial craft tradition existed.

The first immigrant wave to provide substantial factory recruits
came with the Irish migration at mid-century. Although Irish immigration had begun earlier, the Irish began to appear in large numbers
in the textile factories by the early 1840s. Composing less than 20
percent of the factory work force before 1850, Irish women made up
half or slightly more of the industry's work force by 1855. Before long,
at least by the beginning of the Civil War, Irish boys and men began to
join them and soon became a fifth of the factory work force (Copeland, 1912; Cole, 1926, vol. 2, ch. 26; Gitelman, 1967).

The employers apparently did not intentionally set out to replace
the Yankee girls with the Irish. For instance, exploring company records, Gitelman (1967, p. 242) concludes that the Irish were not

brought into the mills explicitly as strikebreakers. The Irish were simply there, having fled the famine and "settled on their arrival in the filthy cellars of the seaboard cities" (Ware, 1964, p. 36), and they offered their labor to the manufacturers as the turnover of the Yankee girls increased.[14]

With the changing source of labor, the peculiar features of the Waltham experiment tended to fall away, but the basic conditions of production in the textile factories did not change. Wages were not increased nor was speedup reduced. According to recent studies, productivity in the mills continued to rise as a result of the speedup, despite the shift in personnel.[15] Minor changes in the technology continued to be made, but neither more nor less rapidly than in the earlier period.

Despite the similar experiences inside the factories, an important difference distinguished the Yankee and Irish operatives, and that difference alone clarifies the significance of the change in personnel. Unlike the early Yankee farm girls, the Irish had nowhere to go when they quit or were dismissed from the factories. Lacking alternative means of supporting themselves, they were fully proletarian, entirely dependent upon selling their labor power. One worker tried to explain the increasing preference of the employers for the Irish in the 1850s as follows (quoted in Gutman, 1973, p. 545): "Not coming from country homes, but living as the Irish do, in the town, they . . . can be relied on at the mill all year around." When wages dropped, Gitelman (1967, p. 244) adds, the Yankee girls left the mills. When wages continued to drop in the 1850s, "the Irish responded to the low wages . . . by sending their children into the mill."

Yet the Yankee "girls" – in the early days the appelation had not been entirely inappropriate, since many were indeed in their late teens – had also changed. Increasingly, the female operatives were no longer girls, but older women who had spent many years in the mills and who no longer had parents or marriage prospects to "return" to when they tired of life in the factory. They, too, had been proletarianized.

The dependence of the Irish and increasingly the Yankee women on factory employment fundamentally strengthened the capitalists' power over their workers. Gitelman (1967, p. 237) notes that "virtually all studies conclude that by the 1850s . . . wages and working conditions had become exploitive." Handlin (1970, p. 91) notes that "it was the vital function of the Irish to thaw out the rigidity of the system. Capitalists readily admitted that they could not [quoting one employer] 'obtain good interest for their money,' were they deprived of this constant influx of foreign labor."

76

These early efforts exploring the use of largely unskilled immigrant labor pioneered business practices that would become crucial during the long boom of the 1840s through the 1870s. The immigrants continued to come, in increasing numbers, throughout the century and beyond. But the later groups confronted an expanding industrial system, an established set of wage relations into which they were funneled. Further development would proceed within the capitalist mode.

By the early 1840s, then, when business activity began slowly recovering from the severe depression of the preceding few years, employers had experimented with and explored these four pools of wage labor. They had tested the water and found that while it was chilly, it was by no means unbearable. To an extent that would have seemed unbelievable to even a perceptive observer like Tench Coxe (1965) a generation earlier, the dearth and dearness of American labor no longer presented an insurmountable obstacle to a growing capitalist sector. No more was an employer restricted to hiring apprentices and journeymen, with their cantankerous and contentious craft demands, or widows, orphans, and poorhouse inmates, with their own peculiar liabilities. Employers too had been "freed," or had freed themselves, to exploit the possibilities inherent in social production and wage labor on a mass scale.

As these accounts indicate, the labor force recruited in the nineteenth century was marked by great diversity. There was, first of all, the division between the artisans and skilled workers and the unskilled. Although both were now subject to the discipline of the capitalist, they brought to that relationship very different expectations and traditions. For the craft workers, capitalist rule in the workplace seemed demeaning and illegitimate, a usurpation of the craft workers' rightful prerogative to work for themselves. They opposed any further intrusions, especially when the bosses sought to reorder the labor process itself, and they used the control inherent in their skills to defend their privileges.

The unskilled workers, and especially the Irish and other foreign-born, had, by contrast, little conception of an alternate organization of production, little relevant experience to draw upon, and little power to bargain with or resist the capitalists. They were more helpless in the face of the forces swirling around them. They did not come unmarked by their pasts, as though they were clean slates for the capitalists to draw upon. With their primarily rural origins they, too, were unused to the rhythms and disciplines of capitalist production;

77

and for some, like the Irish, religious and ethnic allegiances provided a source of identity that they used to resist the capitalists' efforts to remold them. Still, their position was weaker, which showed in how little they could wring from the system (see Gutman, 1973).

Then there was the sexual and age division, between men in most lines of work and women and children concentrated in the textile industry and parts of the needle trades. Women workers were like the unskilled in that they had no useful tradition of an alternate production system – the patriarchal relations within the household could hardly serve. On the other hand, their class origins were mostly different from those of the unskilled, and in this respect they were more like the craft workers. But mainly the women workers were just different – different from men, to whom the patriarchal society delegated the task of providing for their families, and different even from most women, who remained in the home (as wife, spinster in-law, domestic servant, daughter, or whatever). Few male workers and even few of the female workers themselves – if we can accept the evidence of such sources as Harriet Martineau (1837) and the *Lowell Offering* or the staunchly prolabor *Voice of Industry* – accepted that they, as wage workers, shared much with other workers.

Then there were the ethnic divisions – "ethnic" standing as shorthand for that whole complex of religious, cultural, psychological, familial, and other differences that marked the way men and women went about their work, built their communities, lived and died and even sent off their dead. Scottish weavers, German tradesmen, Jewish tailors, Italian, Irish, and Lettish peasants, Poles, Dalmatians, Greeks, French-Canadians, and Bohemians all brought distinct traditions and attempted to adjust to their new circumstances in unique ways.

Little wonder, then, that the American working class would have so little conception of itself *as a class*. Indeed, David Montgomery (1967) reminds us that contemporary accounts were accurate when they almost invariably spoke of the working *classes*. Change had come quickly, in the span of one or two generations, and the differences between workers loomed larger than their commonalities. This is not to say that they never took joint action; occasionally they did, as, for example, when Philadelphia workers staged a general strike in the mid-1830s or when both men (mainly mechanics) and women (mainly textile operatives) joined in the 1840s to press for the ten-hour day. Still, though capitalist organization had subjected them all to the insecurity of the labor market and to the discipline of the workplace boss, and in this sense had brought them objectively to wage-labor status, it remained for subsequent capitalist development to bring their common status to the fore.

The period of consolidation: 1840s to 1870s

The new labor situation provided the basis for a highly successful social structure of accumulation and hence for the long boom that extended from the 1840s until the mid-1870s. Other elements within the institutional environment – notably political support for roads, canals, and other internal improvements; the rapidly developing domestic market based on shipping goods to the South and West; and, of course, the tremendous boost to industry from the Civil War – all contributed to facilitating the accumulation process. There can be little doubt, however, that the solution of the labor problem provided the key to the construction of a viable social structure of accumulation.

This "solution" contained limits and constraints, and the limits helped shape the kind of development that would take place. (Moreover, while capitalists would reap big profits within the system, they would ultimately run up against the constraints as well.) Most fundamentally, capital accumulation was to be based on proletarianized but largely *untransformed* labor. Capitalists hired labor but relied on traditional techniques of production. They organized the production process in the social sense, gathering together labor, materials, tools, and other essential ingredients of production and disposing of the output. Yet, except where there was no preexisting organization of production to draw upon, they did not organize or transform the labor process in detail. Instead, they adopted existing (precapitalist) methods, including major reliance on the workers' own knowledge of production. Although producers lost their tools and independence when they became wage workers, large numbers of them retained their skills and control over their work processes.

The use of proletarianized but untransformed labor implied two important consequences for the succeeding decades of development. First, it meant that the capital accumulation process would be marked by tremendous diversity, as the array of noncapitalist methods of production were transferred wholesale into the capitalist sector and these, plus some new ones introduced by the capitalists, were operated side by side. Later in the century (as we see in Chapter 4), the pressure of intense competition would begin to generate an evenness, pushing all producers to adopt the same techniques, as the slackness that permitted alternate methods was wrung out of the system. But here, in the middle decades of the century, diversity prevailed.

Second, development and growth in the labor process itself came primarily in the form of extension rather than qualitative change. Operations grew bigger, employment increased, capitalization soared, and output steadily mounted, but the nature of the production process itself changed slowly. Even where change was the most impressive, where new machinery and new power sources necessarily disrupted old ways, they tended to be used to extend and multiply traditional techniques rather than introduce qualitatively new methods.

Both of these points, the second one especially, run counter to much received wisdom among economic historians, and we must be clear not to weaken the argument by overstatement.[16] In some whole industries and in some operations within other industries, particularly in those lines of production for which the antecedents were limited or lacking altogether, qualitatively new methods appeared. This, too, was part of the diversity of development. Yet it would be a mistake to characterize the period as an industrial revolution in which technical change provided the overpowering catalytic impetus to growth. Capitalist accumulation required a new social organization of producers: proletarianized but not necessarily transformed labor. Within this cleared field, technical change could be harnessed and made to work for employers, improving the harvest, but hardly causing it.

The rapid development made possible by the new social structure of accumulation was apparent throughout the emerging industrial economy. Real output and employment increased dramatically in all the leading industries (see Table 3.4). In cotton goods, which had already achieved substantial growth by 1840, real output more than tripled and employment doubled by 1870. In boot and shoe manufacture, real output nearly quadrupled, and the 1870 labor force was five times the size of the 1840 staff. And although capitalist production expanded most dramatically in manufacturing, the highly favorable accumulation context was evident elsewhere as well. In railroads, employment (not counting clerks and officials) had jumped from a few thousand in 1840 to 154,000 in 1870, and throughout the transportation, communications, and extraction sectors, employment soared. Even in agriculture, particularly in the harvesting of the corn and wheat crops in the midwestern farm belt, wage labor became an increasingly important feature of farm operations.

One clear indication of the boom in capitalist industry appears in the change in the sectoral composition of the economy. In 1820, only about 11.5 percent of the employed labor force worked in the sectors most directly affected by the capitalist revolution – manufacturing, construction, and mining. By 1870, with the institutionalization of a new wage-labor system, the percentage employed in manufacturing, construction, and mining had increased to 26.5, a level of concentration in these sectors which remained roughly constant for the next century.[17] (See Table 6.1 for subsequent history of this variable.)

Yet this rapid growth of capitalist production was marked and shaped by the possibilities and limits imposed by a proletarianized but untransformed labor force. The generalized and vague picture of U.S. development drawn by conventional economic historians emphasizes the powerful impact of technology as bigger, more modern, and more "efficient" factories are asserted to have gradually replaced smaller workshops. But this picture is sustained only as long as it remains vague, and it is almost surely incorrect for the period we are considering here. The consensus view, confusing the time a new technique is invented with when it is actually put into practice on the shop floor, and having a studied ignorance of the social relations of production, overlooks the crucial role of what we have termed the social structure of accumulation.[18]

Part of the needed revision is suggested by the continuing importance and status of craftsmen in large factories. One study (Laurie, Hershberg, and Alter, 1977) found, for example, that skilled craft workers in Philadelphia in 1880 earned higher wages in virtually every trade when employed in big plants (over fifty workers) than in small ones – testament, apparently, to their continuing critical roles in the production process.

A much more important revision of the conventional view comes from a careful look at the sources of output growth during this period of rapid expansion. The consensus has traditionally implied that technical innovation and factory economies of scale provided a massive boost to the output of the new industrial system. We argue, in contrast, that there was little technical innovation during this period and that capitalists adapted existing techniques to their new wage-labor system. This argument implies, in turn, that the principal source of output expansion lay in extensive rather than intensive growth, in the simple expansion of employment rather than in rising productivity per worker employed.

An interesting variety of evidence supports our view for this period of prosperity from the mid-1840s to the early 1870s. One simple measure comes from aggregate data for manufacturing output and employment. Inasmuch as the decennial censuses provide some reasonable measures of both output and employment, one can compare the rate of growth in output and employment from 1840 to 1870. Our own analysis of this period would lead us to expect employment expansion, a simple reproduction of existing operations, to account for the lion's share of output growth.

Table 3.4 presents both aggregate and disaggregated data for manufacturing between 1840 and 1870. The first row presents a range of estimates for the percentage of aggregate output growth in

Table 3.4. *Percentage change in output and employment for industries, 1840–1870*

Industry[a]	(1) Percentage change in real output	(2) Percentage change in employment	(3) Percentage change in output per worker	(4) Percentage output change accounted for by employment change[b]	
				E_1	E_2
All manufacturing	846	497	59	59	93
Cotton goods	255	101	76	40	70
Boots and shoes	295	435	(−26)	147	109
Machinery	438	538	(−16)	123	104
Woolens	424	281	38	66	91
Carriages and wagons	329	155	68	47	79
Hats	97	(−15)	135	n.a.	(−39)
Sugar and candy	3,046	3,200	(−5)	105	100
Bricks and lime	168	117	24	70	86
Paper	510	280	62	55	88
Glass	346	433	(−19)	125	105
Furniture	507	194	108	38	79
Hardware and cutlery	229	280	(−12)	122	105
Precious metals (gold, silver, jewelry)	280	500	(−37)	179	113
Various metals (lead, tin, copper)	435	314	28	72	94
Granite, marble, etc.	956	375	121	39	87
Potteries (stoneware, earthenware)	322	200	33	62	90

Cordage	50	50	0	0	0
Musical instruments	885	43	600	68	95
Tobacco	745	42	500	67	94
Drugs, medicines, paints	956	91	450	47	90

[a]Industries selected include all those listed in the 1840 Census for which value of output and employment are given and for which comparable data could be obtained for 1870. Those 1840 industries excluded from the table are "silk" and "flax," for which finished goods are excluded in 1840 but included in 1870; "mixed" manufacture, for which no 1870 counterpart exists; "mills," which in 1840 includes both flour mills and saw mills but apparently not lumber mills (no 1870 counterpart could be constructed); "houses," for which no comparable 1870 data could be obtained. The percentage change in value of output has been calculated on the basis of prices adjusted to reflect inflation, taken to be approximately 42 percent of 1870 prices over 1840 prices. See *Historical Statistics of the United States*, 1975, series E-52.

[b]The two figures given in column 4 can be interpreted as lower and upper bounds. Let Q = total output, N = employment, and $AP = Q/N$; then

$$\Delta Q = Q_{1870} - Q_{1840} = (N_{1840}) (\Delta AP) + (\Delta N) (AP_{1840}) + (\Delta N) (\Delta AP)$$

The first term on the right represents the change in total output due to increased productivity; the second term represents the effect of increased employment; the third represents the interaction effect of both changes. The two figures in column 4 are, respectively, the estimates:

$$E_1 = \frac{\Delta N(AP_{1840})}{\Delta Q} = \frac{\text{column 2}}{\text{column 1}}$$

$$E_2 = \frac{\Delta Q - (N_{1840}) (\Delta AP)}{\Delta Q} = 1 - \frac{\text{column 3}}{\text{column 1}}$$

Thus E_1 excludes the interaction effect, while E_2 includes it. E_1 comprises the lower bound estimate, except when the interaction effect has a negative sign. When employment change was itself negative the formula for E_1 is not meaningful and we have marked it as "n.a."

In industries where the estimates exceed 100 percent, productivity growth was negative.

Sources: Data for 1840 taken from U.S. Department of State, 1841, pp. 354–361. Data for 1870 taken from U.S. Department of Interior, 1871, pp. 394–398.

manufacturing which can be attributed to the expansion of employment (see table notes for explanation of the computations and the
reasons for presenting a range of estimates). As column 4 shows,
employment growth accounts for between three-fifths and nine-
tenths of output growth in all manufacturing, leaving a minority
share for all other causes of growth.[19] Other causes include increasing
capital per worker, better management, more efficient allocation of
workers regionally and industrially, technological change, and economies of scale. The evidence across individual industries confirms this
general pattern even amid industrial variation. In two industries (hats
and cordage), the increase in the number of workers accounts for only
a minor portion of the output growth. In six industries (cotton goods,
carriages and wagons, furniture, granite, cordage, and drugs), the
lower-bound estimate falls below 50 percent; in six others (boots and
shoes, machinery, sugar and candy, glass, hardware and cutlery, and
precious metals), employment gains actually exceeded output growth.
In the biggest industries for which data are available (cotton, boots
and shoes, machinery, and woolens), the proportion of output growth
accounted for simply by employers' addition of more workers was
huge.

These estimates are consistent with Robert Gallman's (1960, p. 34)
finding that the increased supply of workers between 1839 and 1899
accounted for at least two-thirds of the growth in commodity production. This estimate may be misleadingly low, if it is not kept in mind
that "commodity production" includes agriculture. Hence, in
Gallman's estimate the shift of workers between sectors (primarily the
migration from farming to capitalist industry), which accounts for
another 10 percent of the growth in output, is treated separately.

It might still be argued that the one-tenth to two-fifths of growth
derived from sources other than the simple reproduction of operations using existing techniques represented a substantial, even if
minor, share. But this pattern contrasts sharply with the following
period, that of the second social structure of accumulation based on
homogeneous labor (see Chapter 4). Woytinsky (1953, p. 29) found
that output per worker was stagnant in the 1860s, rose by 8 percent in
the 1870s, by 17 percent in the 1880s, 21 percent in the 1890s, and 44
percent from 1899 to 1909. Moses Abramovitz (1956) has calculated
that worker hours in per capita terms hardly changed from the decade of the 1870s to 1944–1953 and that the combined increase in
labor *and* capital inputs increased by just 14 percent; yet output rose
by 248 percent. And Robert Gallman (1960, p. 34) estimated that less
than one-fifth of the increase in commodity production between 1899
and 1949 derived from the increased supply of labor. In other words,

such factors as technological change and the reorganization of production rather than the increase in employment (and capital) accounted for most of the growth during this later period. By contrast, the period of initial proletarianization was dominated by the transfer of existing techniques into the capitalist sector.[20]

A very careful analysis of production performed by Bruce Laurie and Mark Schmitz (1981, tables 11, 12) tends to confirm this view. Estimating production functions for Philadelphia's manufacturing sector for 1850 and 1880, Laurie and Schmitz find a virtual absence of economies of scale. Analyzing seventeen industries in both 1850 and 1880, they find only seven of the thirty-four scale estimates to be greater than unity (indicating positive returns to scale), and none is statistically different from zero; on the other hand, twenty-three of the estimates are significantly less than unity, suggesting that in such industries as refined food, boots and shoes, machine tools, and even metal-working, smaller firms were more resource-efficient (though not necessarily more profitable) than big firms.

The persistence of traditional techniques within the capitalist sector, even within those large works employing a substantial labor force, could be seen in diverse industries. In boot and shoe manufacture, craft production had endowed the industry with a well-defined organization. As late as 1840, even the tools of the trade had hardly changed in centuries. New machinery, especially sewing machines and stitchers, would shortly thereafter be added to the shoemaker's kit, and such devices, because they made for both uniform quality and variety of style, would become mandatory parts of the business. But even so, the big change occurred in organization (Hazard, 1921, p. 98):

> The Factory Stage [up until 1875] did not come into existence in the boot and shoe industry because, as it is commonly supposed, the central shop was replaced by a larger building called a manufactory or factory, nor because of the installation in it of heavy expensive machinery, nor the use of power to run it, but because industrial organization, in order to secure uniformity of output, economy of time, labor, and stock, demanded foremen to superintend, and regular hours of steady work on the part of men and women employed in all of the processes of shoemaking.

In carpet-weaving, large establishments had appeared and flourished long before the introduction of the Bigelow or Jacquard looms. As Arthur Cole and Harold Williamson (1941, p. 20) put it: "No changes on either the technological or labor [productivity] side seem to have contributed" to the success of the early factories; instead, "one must, it seems, look elsewhere to find adequate explanation of the rapid expansion just mentioned."

In other industries, where craft production had not been so strongly organized and hence had left fainter marks on subsequent methods, production in big enterprises in many cases nonetheless consisted of the agglomerated operations of small shops rather than integrated production using subdivided tasks. In metallurgy and machine shops, for example, although power equipment permitted handling and fabricating bigger products, the basic shop organization remained largely unchanged. Alfred Jenks's machine works in Philadelphia, one of the largest in existence in the 1850s, was described as a vast complex of foundries, shops, sheds, and yards, where

> each department or room housed groups of skilled workers who plied their trades simultaneously with the assistance of apprentices, helpers, and unskilled laborers who used both hand tools and some of the most modern machines and equipment in the world. Lathes were found along with chisels and crude grinding wheels in the machine shops; steam-powered hammers and old anvils were within arm's reach of the blacksmiths; cranes began to compete with hand hoists in the assembly rooms (Laurie and Schmitz, 1981, p. 57).[21]

Even two decades later the huge Baldwin locomotive works had much the same character. Here and elsewhere the size of an enterprise, even the use of power-driven equipment, did not necessarily imply that production methods had departed much from traditional ways.

The main exception to this reliance on traditional technique was probably in textiles, where (except for weaving) there was no craft background and where employers from the start took a lead in reordering the labor process. The Waltham system entrepreneurs transformed the workplace as much as they invented the dormitory system, and from the first their factories relied upon new technology. Yet even here the case may be overstated. The central power sources provided motion for all the machinery, yet it did not truly integrate the process; basically, spinning rooms remained filled with independent machines operated separately from the carding and weaving functions. Moreover, much of the industry – that around Philadelphia and in Rhode Island, for example – retained the small shop organization throughout the middle part of the century. Still, textile mills had carried the transformation of production processes the furthest by the decade of the 1870s (see also Dublin, 1979, and Lazonick, 1980).

Much as the reliance on existing craft and artisan techniques of

86

production would later hinder capitalists, initially it was not only a necessity but in many cases a highly positive feature. Little choice existed, because employers were not usually in a position to preempt the workers' knowledge of production. Beyond that, using existing methods reduced costs: by lowering the capitalization that was required, because ordinary tools and machinery, often owned by the workers themselves, could be employed; by economizing on training and learning times; by freeing hard-pressed resources from experimental (and hence temperamental) machines; and by reducing the need for technical oversight and direction, since a large portion of those tasks remained in the workers' own hands. In all these ways the adoption of existing techniques reduced the capitalists' costs. The labor process was extensively reformulated only in an industry like textiles, where the earlier start in Britain meant that much of the tinkering and development costs had already been borne.

The adoption of existing techniques was modified where necessary to accommodate their siting in larger enterprises and the possibility of employing powered equipment. We have already seen described the use of powered trip hammers side by side with ancient blacksmithing tools in the foundries and machine shops. In the boot and shoe industry, steam power was frequently introduced to drive particular machines, especially machines for making heels and the McKay sewing machine, but leaving other operations to be carried out by hand. Moreover, employers increasingly encouraged skilled workers to use more helpers, apprentices, and assistants, shifting the composition of the labor force by breaking the old craft limits on apprentices and thereby cheapening the work force while retaining its organization (see Hazard, 1921; Dawley, 1976; and Weiss, 1976).

The employers' heavy reliance on existing techniques meant that most of the tremendous diversity in precapitalist workplaces was also transferred wholesale into capitalist places of business. In perhaps the most useful analysis, Bruce Laurie (1980; and with Mark Schmitz, 1981) has conceptualized, for mid- and late-nineteenth-century Philadelphia, the simultaneous existence of five alternative "work settings": factories, or large industrial plants equipped with power sources, such as were found in textile and metallurgical production; manufactories, or large plants without power-driven machinery, such as characterized shoemaking, printing, and furniture manufacture; sweat shops, or small plants, almost never with power-driven machines, such as prevailed in the needle trades, leather goods production, light metals, and tobacco; outwork, or household production that remained important for tailored goods, handloom products, hats and millinery goods, and other products; and artisan shops, or small

87

shops with three or five or eight workers, which included bakers, butchers, blacksmiths, cabinetmakers, and so on.

Each work setting tended to have distinct methods of organizing work, in each case (except for factories) in large part continuing traditional methods. While enterprise size increased substantially over the period 1850 to 1880, in Philadelphia, at least, all five of the work settings remained important at the end of the period. For example, in 1880 over half of all food workers and about one-third of those employed in glass and furniture production were still employed in places classified as artisan or sweat shops. In Philadelphia as a whole, only 57 percent of manufacturing employment in 1880 was concentrated in "factory" establishments. Moreover, even in manufactories and factories, traditional methods persisted alongside more modern operations.

Why did these other forms of production persist? Why were they not driven out by the new and larger factories? The answer follows from our previous discussion. The factories were larger, but they were not necessarily more efficient. Laurie and Schmitz (1981) provide other evidence that supports their findings on the absence of economies of scale and helps emphasize the competitiveness of traditional techniques of production. They classify establishments by type of production – into factories, manufactories, small factories, artisan establishments, and sweat shops – and are able to compare labor productivity within industries among these five types of firms. They find (table 13) that average labor productivity in the factory was often lower than in the more traditional kinds of establishment. "Small factory" productivity was higher than "factory" productivity in six of nine cases, for example, whereas "artisan" firms had higher productivity in four of nine cases, and even "sweat shops" outperformed their factory competitors in three of eight comparable cases.

The heterogeneous character of capitalist production contained a spatial dimension as well. In the period from the 1840s through the 1870s, industry developed most intensively in the smaller industrial towns rather than the biggest cities; towns like Reading and Lynn and Syracuse rather than New York and Philadelphia led the way. David Gordon (1978b, p. 39) has calculated that between 1860 and 1870, manufacturing employment in the three largest cities increased by only 53 percent, while it increased by 79.5 percent in the cities ranked twenty-first through fiftieth in population. In contrast, industrial growth during the exploration phase of the next long swing (that is, the years from the 1870s to 1900) was paced by heavy development in the big cities: Between 1870 and 1900 manufacturing employment grew by 245 percent in the three largest cities and by only 158 percent in the cities ranked twenty-first to fiftieth.

These differing spatial patterns were directly related to the differing forms of capital accumulation. Built upon proletarianized but untransformed labor, accumulation in the earlier long swing gave the preponderant advantages to the smaller towns, the first stop on the country-to-city migration route, where such labor was available. Capital accumulation in the period of homogenization, relying much more on the discipline of substitutable labor, swung the advantages back to the bigger cities, with their heavy infusions of (mainly unskilled) foreign immigrants and their potentially wider labor markets.

These various factors – the use of proletarianized but untransformed labor in highly diverse work settings mixing traditional and "modern" techniques and spread throughout small industrial towns – constituted in substantial measure a response to the available and growing supply of workers. The old lament of a chronic "labor shortage" was largely stilled. Native-born white males, departing hardscrabble farms or declining trades, sought out employment in the new centers of industry. Craftsmen, whether foreign-born or native, left their "ten-footers" and shops to join, however reluctantly, the factory recruits. Females, especially those young girls or unattached women who could make no claim on a family wage, swelled the pool of mill hands. Then, with increasing force after the Civil War, the succeeding waves of unskilled immigrants washed over every industry, providing a low-wage labor force that employers could assign to the unskilled or menial production tasks.

As long as the capitalist did not enter the sphere of production and truly revolutionize production techniques – that is, as long as the capitalist relied on traditional production methods – the effect of this growing labor supply was selective and fragmented. In such jobs as that of mill operative, where prior skill acquisition was minimal, the competition among job holders and job seekers was quickly felt. In many lines of work, however – and here the skilled jobs in railroading, printing, steel mills, and machine shops are illustrative – competition was more indirect. Unskilled labor could not directly displace skilled. Still, the presence of an expanding pool of potential workers put pressure even on the skilled workers. Just as ambitious masters had earlier sought to increase the use of assistants and apprentices, so now skilled workers came under pressure to reassign parts of tasks to (low-wage) helpers, to fragment their work, and to conform to standards covering hours and output. The growing supply of labor of all types thus operated to strengthen the bosses' hands, to discipline even skilled workers, and to add a growing element of coercion within the capitalist sector itself.

The success of the social structure during the years from the 1840s through the 1870s in creating conditions that contained and dampened class conflict also facilitated rapid capital accumulation. It was not simply that the workers' movement during these years failed; rather, what was important was that the movement failed largely because it had to struggle on such unfavorable terrain.

Workers were unable to achieve much through collective action during the boom years. As Norman Ware (1964, ch. 14) notes, the labor movement in the 1840s was largely "defensive," in the sense that most of its activities sought to protect or restore the deteriorating position of the artisans, craftsmen, and mechanics in society. Utopian and associationist philosophies attracted great interest, and industrial strikes often split workers, many of whom retained illusions of a "community of interest" between employer (master) and employee (jour). In the textile mills, where factory conditions made inescapable the acceptance of capitalist relations, operatives walked out on a number of occasions to demand the ten-hour day and other improvements. Despite occasional successes, this movement largely failed (Ware, 1964, ch. 8; Foner, 1972, vol. 1, ch. 11).

By the 1850s the workers had been forced to recognize the permanence of the new relations of production, and increasingly they sought to gain better conditions within this new system rather than attempt to restore prior conditions. Although utopianism would hang on as an important force throughout the century (Eugene Debs for a time in the 1890s would advocate a worker "resettlement" scheme), the movement, in Norman Ware's phrase, became "aggressive." Beginning with the Typographers in 1852, national craft unions were organized in several crafts, and, more importantly, local crafts organized for better hours, wages, and conditions of work. Yet for other workers, most notably mill operatives, little successful organization and virtually no progress occurred during the 1850s. The heavy influx of immigrant labor made organization difficult, and employers used the growing labor supply to their advantage. The short business depression in 1857–1858 provided a further setback, destroying much local organization in the crafts and eliminating all but two of the nascent national unions (Ulman, 1955, ch. 1.).

In the 1860s, especially after 1862, when labor shortages began to occur, the workers' movement achieved greater solidity. A widely supported Massachusetts shoemakers strike in 1860 obtained substantial wage concessions (although only limited recognition of their Mechanics Association). In 1863 and 1864 membership in craft unions grew rapidly, reaching two hundred thousand or so by the end of the war. Unions were organized in sixty or more trades, and attempts at national organization were revived (see Ulman, 1955, pt. 1; Montgomery, 1967, appendix C). This movement restricted itself almost entirely to craft organization, and by far the most effective efforts occurred at the local level. By the end of the 1860s consolidation or reorganization had built strong unions among molders, ironworkers, construction workers, and most of the other skilled trades.

The labor movement failed to achieve much during the boom years, then, until a national structure and a solid groundwork of local craft organization appeared, at the end of the sixties. Although workers and their leaders were still preoccupied with establishing themselves, what they were establishing was clearly capable of making bigger challenges.

Organization of the labor process. The system of control within the labor process, a crucial element in the social structure of accumulation, emerged from the traditional methods of production and incorporated their diversity. Diversity is noted here not simply because of the existence of disparate forms of organizing work but rather because these forms retained an economic importance throughout the period.

In the first instance there existed an entrepreneurial or shop method of organizing work, what elsewhere has been termed *simple control* (see Edwards, 1979, ch. 2). Simple control existed mainly in those industries or workplaces, such as textile mills and metallurgical shops, where prior craft traditions were relatively weak, or, alternately, in those small shops where the capitalist, having risen from the ranks, acted as head worker. Simple control was constituted on the personal power and authority of the employer. In Stephen Hymer's (1972, p. 152) words, the boss "saw everything, knew everything, and decided everything." The entire firm was the workshop of the capitalist, who interceded quickly to solve problems, reassign personnel, direct workers to their tasks, and discipline and reward on the spot.

Inside contracting represented a quite distinct method of organizing the labor process (see Clawson, 1980, ch. 3, for an excellent discussion). Inside contracting relied on labor contractors who worked solely for the company and often received a day wage, but who also hired their own employees and supervised the labor process in return for a premium or for profit on the contracted work. As Clawson stresses, inside contractors differed from independent subcontractors in that the former worked exclusively for one capitalist, operating inside the capitalist's premises and using the company's own tools and machinery; the inside contractors hired, organized, and supervised the firm's work force, or parts of it, within the general framework (length of the workday, etc.) established by the company.

Inside contracting was used most extensively in machine shops; in firms like Colt and Winchester, which made small arms; and in some manufacturing concerns, like the Singer Sewing Machine Company and Waltham Watch (Clawson, 1980, pp. 75–76). The giant Pullman works and the Pepperill textile mill used the system for at least some of their operations, and it appeared in scattered form elsewhere.

Yet a third method of organizing the labor process relied directly upon the skilled craft worker to oversee production. Although related to inside contracting, the *craft system* lodged control of production clearly in the hands of producers rather than, as with inside contractors, a group of labor drivers. In those instances where craft skills remained essential to production – the work of molders, for example, or shipwrights, or puddlers, rollers, and others in the iron industry, or blacksmiths, or certain fine-goods weavers – craft workers frequently retained the right to hire, fire, and supervise their assistants and helpers, and employers depended upon it. In some cases, the craft worker was paid a price instead of a wage, the "tonnage rate" in iron being a well-known example, and the proceeds were then divided up among the various workers and assistants according to a carefully established schedule (Brody, 1960; Stone, 1975). In the full craft system, capitalists and plant foremen had little opportunity to intervene in the labor process, since technical knowledge of production resided with the skilled workers.

Structure of labor markets. The highly heterogeneous populations attracted to wage labor and the great diversity in labor process organization produced a system of fragmented, localized, and unconnected labor markets. Splintered and separated by craft or calling, industry, locale, and custom, labor markets during this period can be understood only as myriad balkanized specific markets.

The diverse methods of organizing work both reflected and reinforced the diversity of labor supply. On the one hand, the four groups mentioned above – native-born (noncraft) white males, craft workers, females and children, and immigrants – were spread unevenly across the jobs in the capitalist sector, and different methods of organizing work grew out of, and in this sense reflected, the unevenness in the available labor supply. On the other hand, different methods of organizing work attracted different groups of workers and hence tended to reinforce the disparate labor availabilities. These forces combined to produce the system of highly fragmented and isolated labor markets.

92

To take immigrant and native-born labor first, we find that foreign-born workers tended to distribute themselves in highly skewed fashion across industries. In 1870 the foreign-born represented slightly over a fifth of the total U.S. wage-labor force.[22] However, in some industries they represented a relatively minor force: Less than 15 percent of the millers were foreign-born, for example; less than 14 percent of the lumber workers and about 10 percent of the printers were immigrants. By contrast, in other industries immigrant labor clearly was crucial: among iron and steel operatives (43 percent foreign-born), boot and shoe workers (37 percent), cotton mill operatives (36 percent), and woolen mill workers (43 percent). Among miners the foreign-born actually dominated, providing fully 63 percent of the hands.

Moreover, particular nationality groups provided heavy labor supplies to specific industries. Nearly a quarter of the huge railroad employment consisted of Irish-born workers. Miners from the British Isles accounted for a third of all miners in U.S. mines. German-born workers dominated baking (41 percent) and sugar making (56 percent).

As these figures suggest, immigrant labor tended to be hired into two types of industries. First, employment in iron and steel plants, cotton and woolen mills, on the railroads and elsewhere reflected primarily the attraction of unskilled workers to industries with few craft precedents or with extensive segments of production using unskilled labor that coexisted with the skilled operations. For these workers especially, the conclusion of the 1911 U.S. Immigration Commission rang true; with comparatively few exceptions, the commission (vol. 1, p, 185) wrote, the immigrant "is essentially a seller of labor seeking a more favorable market." Second, the minority of immigrants possessing skills that were in demand (the German bakers and candy makers and English potters, for example) tended to act much more like other craft workers, foreign-born or not, in seeking out employment where craft organization persisted.

Females also found employment restricted to certain spots in the industrial sector.[23] They were overwhelmingly located in the needle trades, textiles, and boot and shoe industries; indeed, these three industries accounted for over 70 percent of all females in manufacturing in 1870 (*Ninth Census*, vol. 3, table 20). By contrast, such industries as ironmaking, flour milling, and carriage and wagon construction employed virtually only males. In those industries that employed female labor, women represented a substantial fraction of the work force: in cotton goods, women over fifteen years of age provided nearly half the labor in 1870 (with children of both sexes contributing another 17 percent) and in clothing, well over half; in boot and shoes, women provided only 15 percent of the work force. Even within industries, moreover, jobs tended to be highly sex-typed; despite the presence of large numbers of women in cotton mills, for example, printing cotton goods was almost entirely a man's job.

Craft workers, where they could defend the viability of their skills, forced employers to deal with them in what amounted to separate labor markets. Local organizations were always more effective than national bodies, and locals frequently obtained substantial collective bargaining rights. These craft unions sought, with varying success, to achieve uniform conditions of employment, to raise wages and restrict wage competition, and to provide benefits for sick or disabled workers or their widows. The success of these efforts renewed the enthusiasm for national associations, with the most notable results being the founding of the International Typographical Union in 1850, followed within the next few years by the Stonecutters, Hat Finishers, Molders, Machinists, and Blacksmiths (Foner, 1947, vol. 1, chs. 12, 17; Daugherty, 1951). After the collapse of most of these organizations at the end of the 1850s, they and some twenty more were reconstituted toward the end of the next decade. The issue of limiting the number of apprentices and restricting the entry of immigrant labor was always a key to the success of craft workers in protecting their status.

For native-born males who entered the wage-labor force without craft privileges, the scanty available evidence suggests that most made short migrations from rural areas to the nearby urban centers rather than move substantial distances in response to wider labor market incentives. Of the slightly more than five hundred artisans, operatives, laborers, and assistants who were employed in Reading's (Pa.) Spruce Ward in 1850, for example, more than 70 percent had been born in Berks or the adjacent counties. Most of the rest were immigrants, only about 10 percent having been born elsewhere in the United States.[24] Of course, migration may well have occurred between birth and entry into the labor force, so evidence on migration during adulthood would necessarily show even less movement in response to labor market pressures than is suggested by the above figures.

Aggregate wage data are consistent with this view of splintered labor markets; see Chapter 4, pp. 119–20 and note 9.

The period of decay: 1870s to 1890s

In September 1873, the financial house of Jay Cooke and Company went bankrupt, throwing the entire financial and credit system into panic. Just as, a half-century later, a stock market crash would destroy business confidence and thereby emphatically punctuate the onset of a depression that was already being generated by other forces, so now the financial panic triggered the Long Depression of the 1870s and signaled the beginning of the long downswing that would persist until the end of the century. The seventies and the nineties would see terrible depressions, and the mid-eighties could only be characterized as hard times indeed. The long boom was clearly over.

The social structure of accumulation based on proletarianized but untransformed labor, which had provided the context for the long boom, became the focus of increasing attack and conflict after the mid-1870s. The inadequacy of this structure accounts for the long downturn, which in part reflected the growing tensions and in turn contributed to the crisis and collapse of this social structure.

The attacks came from two directions at once. On one side, capitalists responded to the growing competitiveness in the economy at large by attempting ever-deeper intrusions in the labor process to revolutionize it and transform labor itself. On the other side, and in substantial response to these employers' efforts, workers of all sorts, but especially craft workers, struggled to defend their status and advance their interests.

The result was a period of prolonged, intense, bitter, and spreading class conflict. The conflict culminated in the economic and social crisis of the 1890s, during which the labor challenge was decisively defeated. On the basis of its victory, the capitalist class was able to construct a new social structure of accumulation, one based on the homogenization of labor.

The very success of accumulation during the long boom generated the increasingly severe competition of the last three decades of the century. One significant effect of the rapid accumulation was to encourage and provide the resources for capitalists to attempt to extend their operations into new markets for their products (see Edwards, 1979, pp. 39–42). Everywhere local producers sought to expand into city-wide or regional markets, bringing them into competition with other producers. Simultaneously, the heavy investments in transportation and communications, especially railroads, battered down the cost advantages that protected local producers from wider competition (Chandler, 1977, part 2). Long-haul and (less so) short-haul freight rates dropped precipitously, and previously isolated local product markets came more and more to be connected into regional or even national markets. Individual capitalists experienced this phenomenon both as an expanding set of opportunities and as rapidly intensifying competition.

As intercapitalist competition and economic instability intensified

95

during the 1870s and 1880s, the effects were quickly transported to capital–labor relations. Prices began to fall rapidly from the mid-1870s, in particular, and capitalists felt mounting pressure to reduce costs in order to preserve their margins. Although they sought wherever possible to reduce wages, capitalists faced increasingly militant workers who frequently made it impossible to reduce workers' wages as rapidly as final product prices were falling. (Long's data series [1960, p. 154] show rising real wages for both "skilled occupations" and "laborers" from 1873 to 1890; and Lebergott's series [1964, table A-19] on annual earnings for nonfarm employees also show rising real annual earnings from the mid-1870s through the early 1890s.) This situation placed growing pressure on the production process itself, both toward cost reduction and greater intensification of labor.

The traditional systems of labor management did not readily provide opportunities for either cost reduction or labor intensification. Two critical weaknesses in these systems of control soon became apparent. First, craft workers continued to exercise vast influence over the pace and character of production. Because so many production processes still depended upon the special skills and knowledge of experienced craft workers, employers were perpetually vulnerable to their power to slow down production and to bargain effectively over their wages. Robert Ozanne's (1967) chronicle of labor-management relations at McCormick from the Civil War through the 1880s provides a typical example of this kind of craft domination (see Chapter 4, this volume, under "The period of exploration").

Second, even where craft workers had relatively little influence, there were problems with the intensity and reliability of labor control over production. The pace of production was often irregular. The authority of employers and foremen was problematic, depending heavily on the particularities of an industry's craft traditions, its technology, and its system of direct worker supervision. (See Nelson, 1975, pp. 35–42, for a discussion of these variations among industries and regions.) Management in general had relatively little control over the pace at which the labor power it had hired was transformed into directly productive labor activity. This kind of unpredictability prompted Frederick Taylor's first studies of new management techniques. As Taylor observed about his experiences as a foreman in the 1880s, "As was usual then . . . in most of the shops in this country, the shop was really run by the workmen and not by the bosses. The workmen together had carefully planned just how fast each job should be done" (Taylor, 1911, pp. 48–49). In those industries where a substantial degree of craft control had been eliminated, such as boot and shoe and agricultural implements, "internal management techniques, particularly those involving relations between the factory managers and workers, were not fundamentally different from what they had been in the craftman's shop" (Nelson, 1975, pp. 3–4). "In this respect," Nelson continues, "the factory . . . remained a congeries of craftmen's shops rather than an integrated plant."

The successful accumulation of the boom years had also generated a rapid expansion in plant size (see Chapter 4, under "The period of exploration"). This rapid increase in factory size had a corresponding effect on the social relations of the factory. Work that had been organized by relatively particularistic relations between supervisor and supervisee was transferred to the larger factories, where personal relationships were much more difficult to sustain and authority became more impersonal. Reliance on hired officials introduced an unstable and often dysfunctional element into the firm's management (Nelson, 1975; Edwards, 1979, ch. 2).

Finally, capitalists were stymied in their efforts to reduce costs by the growing ability of important elements of the emerging labor movement to limit further increases in the length of the working day. Millis and Montgomery (1938, p. 468) document this trend in a summary of surveys of twenty-one industries, which suggests that a gradual reduction in average hours of labor per day began after the Civil War.

Hemmed in by these constraints, yet driven by the intensifying intercapitalist competition, employers began attacking the basic foundations of the social structure of accumulation: the untransformed character of proletarianized labor, the diverse and intractable systems for controlling the labor process, and the splintered (and in that sense noncompetitive) structure of labor markets. We review the thrust of their attack in Chapter 4, under "The period of exploration."

Workers no less than capitalists arrayed themselves against the prevailing arrangements, as intensifying class conflict signaled the growing inadequacy of the system. Whereas earlier the social structure had created a terrain that limited the effectiveness of the workers' movement, the very success of the accumulation process, by intensifying competition among firms, eroded the conditions underlying that structure.

The workers' challenge did not lag much behind the onset of hard times. Although high unemployment and severe downward pressure on wages after 1873 destroyed many craft unions, they activated industrial workers. The miners' "Long Strike" in the summer of 1875 (and the associated "Molly Maguire" incidents) and a major walkout by textile operatives in the fall of that year marked the prelude to this new class warfare (Foner, 1947, vol. 1, ch. 23; Broehl, 1964). Then, in 1877, what Jeremy Brecher (1972, ch. 1) has aptly described as the

Table 3.5. *Index of strike frequency, 1882–1892*

Year of business-cycle peak[a]	Three years averaged	Three-year average index of strike frequency (1927–1929 = 100)[b]
1882	1881–1883	65
1887	1886–1888	180
1890	1889–1891	215
1892	1891–1893	203

[a]Business-cycle peaks from Burns and Mitchell (1946, p. 78).
[b]Index of strike activity calculated from Peterson (1938, p. 21).

"great upheaval" began: the first national railroad strike and, with it, strikes spreading to associated industries and general strikes in Pittsburgh, St. Louis, and elsewhere. This first American experience with the *mass* strike was defeated in the end only by the intervention of military and police force.

Through the 1880s and early 1890s, working-class unrest spread more and more widely among industrial wage earners. Historians have richly described the working-class upheavals of these years, and we will not recount that history here.[25] We should note, however, that the character of the struggles themselves changed. Haymarket, Homestead, and Pullman, like the great upheaval of 1877, were not simply isolated conflicts affecting one industry or region; rather, they essentially became class battles, seizing the nation's attention, integrally involving state and federal governments, and having crucial class-wide consequences.

Moreover, the available evidence documents the widening dimensions of this protest. According to reasonably comprehensive figures collected by the federal government, workers waged strikes with mounting frequency from the early 1880s. Table 3.5 summarizes data on the frequency of strikes, comparing three-year moving averages centered around the peaks of short-term business cycles (when strike activity reached its cyclical maximum during these years). Although the three-year average of the strike-frequency index dropped slightly as the 1893–1897 recession began, its values at the end of the 1880s had nonetheless climbed to roughly three times its levels at the beginning of the decade. Other series from these data suggest that this increase largely reflected a spread rather than a deepening of strike activity. The average number of workers per strike did not increase through these years, but the number of establishments affected each year increased sub-

98

stantially, with the average number of establishments affected in the peak years of 1887 and 1890 climbing to five times the number affected in 1882 (Peterson, 1938, p. 29). The spread of strikes was apparently also guided by more active union leadership; the percentage of strikes ordered by labor unions increased from 48.5 percent in the peak of 1882 to 71.3 percent in the peak of 1890 (p. 32).

Under the twin pressures of growing competitiveness (and hence declining profit margins) and rising class conflict, the old social structure of accumulation, like a horse-drawn dray in the railway age, could no longer carry the load. A new vehicle was needed, and its design was already faintly discernible amid the attempts to patch up the decrepit and obsolete structure.

4

The homogenization of labor: 1870s to World War II

The initial creation of a wage-labor force proved to be an inadequate foundation for capital accumulation in the late-nineteenth-century U.S. economy. While employers could count on a fairly continuous supply of labor power, as we have seen in the previous chapter, they could not necessarily count on a steady and adequate flow of labor activity in production. The rapid growth during the 1850s and 1860s had partially masked this problem. As the crisis of the 1870s and 1880s deepened, however, the insufficiency of the prevailing wage-labor system grew more evident. Employers began to search for more effective systems to extract labor from their workers.

These late-nineteenth-century explorations led eventually to the dominance of a new stage in the organization of the labor process and the structure of labor markets in the United States: the *homogenization* of labor, a spreading tendency toward the reduction of jobs in the economy to a common, semiskilled denominator. However, homogenization did not become a fully dominant process until the beginning of the new stage of capitalism at the turn of the century. The consolidation of new methods for organizing the labor process awaited a new period of rapid expansion in the economy and a new social structure of accumulation, including institutional innovations to defuse the worker conflict that early steps toward homogenization had at least partly provoked. Homogenization then remained the dominant tendency through the economic crisis and labor upheavals of the 1930s.

We argue, in short, that the period from the 1870s until World War II constituted a period of "homogenization of labor" in the U.S. economy. Because this period of homogenization overlapped with the periods of proletarianization and segmentation, it seems important to highlight in advance some of the principal distinctions among the three periods.

As the preceding chapter showed, initial proletarianization left the labor process largely untransformed. Proletarianization was compatible with a wide range of labor systems, and indeed, the capitalist

100

sector still contained a substantial variety of labor processes during the late nineteenth century. As homogenization subsequently came to dominate the labor process, the range of variation in modes of labor organization in the capitalist sector began to narrow. By the first two decades of the twentieth century, the organization of capitalist production had become much more uniform. In particular, more and more work tasks had been reduced to detailed, atomized, semiskilled operations. This new system enhanced employers' control over production and consequently enabled expanded extraction of labor from their workers. (See Edwards, 1979, chs. 4, 7, for related treatment.)

Task reduction has continued through the present, of course, affecting not only blue-collar factory jobs but many office jobs as well (see Braverman, 1974). However, the economic context in which this continuing degradation occurs has changed since World War II. During the period of segmentation, the economy has produced a *divergence* in systems of labor management and labor market structures. Whereas homogenization tended to create more uniform working conditions among American workers in the capitalist sector, segmentation reversed that tendency, creating increasingly distinctive working conditions among different groups of workers.

This chapter traces the emergence, dominance, and decline of the tendency toward the homogenization of labor. We begin with a summary of the rhythms of the capitalist economy from the 1870s through the 1930s, then turn to a detailed discussion of homogenization through an analysis of its respective phases of exploration, consolidation, and decay.

Growth and stagnation in the world economy

Chapter 3 traced some of the dimensions of the spreading economic stagnation at the end of the nineteenth century. By the late 1880s, the crisis had grown to mammoth proportions.[1]

Some economic variables help indicate the severity of the crisis. The rate of growth in real Gross National Product (in constant prices) had dropped from an annual average of 6.5 percent in the 1870s to 3.6 percent in the mid-1890s (Gallman, 1966, table 2). Firms began to disinvest and to reduce their inventories. Between 1889 and 1898, net capital formation in producers' durables fell to half the average levels of 1868–1888, whereas net inventory additions as a percentage of GNP dropped from 5 percent in 1869–1878 to less than 2 percent in 1889–1898 (Kuznets, 1961a, pp. 92, 97). The periodic business cycle itself changed shape, as we saw in the appendix to Chapter 2, with shorter expansions and longer contractions. The economic deterioration also manifested itself in spreading rates of bankruptcy. The rate of business failures per 10,000 listed enterprises exceeded 100 in thirteen of the sixteen years between 1883 and 1898; by way of comparison, the incidence of business failures exceeded 100 in only three of the ten Depression years between 1930 and 1939 (*Historical Statistics,* 1975, series V-23).

Contemporary observers frequently noted the severity of the continuing depression. The economist J. W. Jenks wrote in 1897 about the depression's "great waves covering a score or more of years and bearing the panic fluctuations on their surface like mere ripples" (quoted in Kirkland, 1967, p. 8). David Wells concluded in 1895 (p. 1) that the economy had witnessed "a most curious and, in many respects, unprecedented disturbance and depression of trade, commerce, and industry . . . Its most noteworthy peculiarity has been its universality."

With the recovery of the world economy from the long recession of 1893–1897, rapid capital accumulation resumed. Particularly in the United States and Germany, much larger units of capital drew on new sources of finance for burgeoning investment. Imperialist colonization triggered a rapid expansion of trade throughout the capitalist world economy. At least in the United States, regional decentralization and metropolitan suburbanization generated vast new infrastructural investments in sewage, electricity, and urban transit. As Hansen concludes about the United States (1941, p. 41), "an era of buoyant prosperity was generated by the growth of four great industries: street railways, telephone, electric power, and automobile industries." The dynamism that Henry Adams (1918, pp. 339 ff.) anticipated at the Chicago Exposition of 1893 seemed to carry the economy on a steadily cresting wave of expansion.

This restoration of rapid accumulation both depended upon and facilitated a new social structure of accumulation, involving a multidimensional transformation of the U.S. and world capitalist economies. The world market was rapidly transformed as interimperialist rivalries intensified and advanced capitalist countries captured colonies around the globe (Mandel, 1975, ch. 2). Particularly in Germany and the United States, huge new consolidated companies achieved dramatically increased market power (see discussion later in this section). New systems of transportation facilitated alternative sources of natural and intermediate supply. As Mandel (1975, ch. 2) argues in detail, systems for the production of raw materials changed around the turn of the century, moving quickly toward a more capitalist organization of the extractive industries. As Hansen notes

(1941, pp. 45–46), the new stage of accumulation "had less to do with mere extensive growth and expansion into new territory, and involved a much more radical transformation in consumption habits and ways of living." The pace of technological development also intensified, at least partly through corporations' systematically harnessing research and development (see Noble, 1977). Dramatic changes affected the relationship between the private sector and the government (Kolko, 1963), and major changes also occurred in the financial structure and the structure of administrative management (see, for example, Chandler, 1962, 1977; and Kotz, 1978).

Once the new stage of capitalism had begun to take shape, rapid capital accumulation occurred in the world capitalist economy through World War I. Most analysts agree that worldwide recovery began from the trough of the 1893–1897 recession. Dupriez (1947, vol. 2, p. 567) provides a proximate series of physical output for the leading advanced countries; his data indicate that the average annual change in physical output per capita between 1895 and 1913 was 1.75 percent, almost exactly twice the rate of increase for the years from 1880 to 1894. As the data reported in our appendix to Chapter 2 show, world trade increased at an average annual rate of 5.42 percent between 1891–1895 and 1913, roughly 50 percent more rapidly than during the previous period of contraction. Few would disagree with the general conclusions reached by Hobsbawm (1976, pp. 85, 87): "In a purely economic sense, capitalism seemed set for a long and untroubled future around 1900 . . . [The] international capitalist economy . . . had, by and large, . . . an astonishing run for its money . . . until 1914."

Although some economists have doubted the extent of continuous expansion in the U.S. economy during these years (see, for example, Baran and Sweezy, 1966, pp. 240 ff.), aggregate data indicate that the U.S. economy shared in world prosperity throughout these expansive twenty years. Average rates of increase in real output in the United States between 1894 and 1914 substantially exceeded those in the United Kingdom, Germany, and France (see Chapter 2, Table 2.1). According to Fabricant's data (1942, p. 183), manufacturing employment grew rapidly and fairly steadily throughout the period, increasing by 131.1 percent between 1899 and 1919. Rates of gross capital formation also remained high, with the ratio of gross capital formation to GNP dropping only slightly during the 1910s (Kuznets, 1961a, p. 92). As in the earlier long expansion from the 1840s to 1873, the average business cycle expansion was longer than the average period of contraction (see Chapter 2, Table 2.2). The rate of business failures also dipped, rising above 100 (per 10,000 listed enterprises) in only five of the twenty years between 1899 and 1918 (*Historical Statistics,* 1975, series V-23).

The relatively higher unemployment rates in the United States from 1908 to 1915 (see *Historical Statistics,* 1975, series D-86) reflected rapid increases in labor supply much more than stagnation in aggregate output.[2] During periods of business cycle expansion, average annual growth rates remained as high toward the end of this period as during the onset of prosperity. From the trough of 1896 to the peak of 1903, for example, real GNP grew at an annual average rate of 6.9 percent per year, while the comparable figure for the trough-to-peak expansion from 1908 to 1913 was 6.2 percent per year. Similarly, peak-to-peak annual growth rates of real GNP stood at 3.3 percent in 1907–1910 and 3.1 percent in 1910–1913, respectable by historical standards and hardly indicative of stagnation (*Historical Statistics,* 1975, series F-3, F-4; per capita figures moved similarly).

After 1920, the world economy slid gradually into the instability that produced the Great Depression. The political instability that both triggered and remained unresolved by World War I underlay a continuing and intensifying instability in world trade. This instability helped undermine the foundations for growth in almost all the advanced countries. England felt the instability in spreading stagnation, while the German economy soared through wild inflationary spirals.

By contrast, the U.S. economy grew rapidly, although unevenly, in the 1920s. Many scholars would argue that the U.S. economy remained buoyant until 1929, although virtually all recognize that increasing problems appeared after 1925. Real GNP grew by 3.5 percent annually between 1919 and 1929, and capital per worker, virtually constant between 1909 and 1919, now jumped by about 3.2 percent annually. With these impressive statistics, Alvin Hansen concluded (1941, p. 31):

> On balance, we believe it is a defensible thesis, though certainly not proven, that the basic underlying economic conditions from 1920 were relatively unfavorable, but that special factors growing out of the first World War, along with certain technological developments especially favorable to the United States, differentiate the experience of [the United States] from that of western Europe . . . It is possible that the most reasonable classification is to make 1920 the turning point for the European countries and 1929 the turning point for the United States.

We follow this dating scheme in our periodization for the United States, tracing the period of consolidation through the 1920s, although we view the long-swing contraction in the *world* economy as beginning after World War I.

Even in the apparently prosperous twenties in the United States, however, the economy performed unevenly. In particular, capitalists did well but farmers and workers fared poorly. After the rapid expansion of commercial farming during World War I, agriculture entered a period of relative depression during the 1920s (Soule, 1947, pp. 229-234). Although industrial output rose rapidly, employment in manufacturing stagnated, declining slightly (in absolute numbers) from 1918 through 1929 (Fabricant, 1942, p. 183). As R. A. Gordon notes (1974, ch. 2), both real investment in structures and equipment and the rate of increase in productivity began to slacken after 1925. This slackening real investment appears to have dampened economic growth as the 1920s progressed. In the three short-term business cycles in the United States between 1920 and 1929, average annual (peak-to-peak) growth in real output declined successively from 6.2 percent per year in 1920-1923 to 4.8 percent in 1923-1926 to 2.4 percent in 1926-1929; per capita figures showed similar patterns (*Historical Statistics*, 1975, series F-3, F-4). As the decade advanced, commercial speculation increasingly fed upon industrial profits, and the foundation for continuing prosperity began to weaken. Compared to the period from 1898 to 1918, the incidence of business failures increased dramatically, exceeding 100 in eight of the nine years from 1921 through 1929 (*Historical Statistics*, 1975, series V-23). (In general, see the parallel discussion in Lee and Passell, 1979, pp. 363-368.)

These diverse movements had a predictable effect upon income distribution. Inequality increased substantially, with the income share received by the richest 5 percent of the population expanding from about a quarter to a third of total income. The richest 1 percent of the population did spectacularly well: Its share ballooned from 12.2 percent to 18.9 percent of all income (*Historical Statistics*, 1975, Series G-339-342).

As Kindleberger (1974) argues at length, these elements of instability contributed to the collapse in 1929-1930. The rest of the story requires little documentation. The U.S. economy joined the rest of the capitalist world in sustained depression until World War II. From World War I through 1939, prices, physical output, and world trade all stagnated in the world economy as a whole. Hobsbawm (1976, p. 87) provides one dramatic index to capture the cumulative impact of the contraction: "In 1938 world trade was little more than two-thirds of what it had been in 1913 . . . There had been no setback of this kind since the beginning of the industrial revolution."

"Monopoly capital" and the challenge to big business

Many analysts, particularly those within the Marxist tradition, treat the period after 1900 as a new stage of "monopoly capitalism" (see, for example, Lenin, 1917, and Baran and Sweezy, 1966). The emergence of much larger, consolidated units of capital plays an important role in our own analysis of the process of labor homogenization, as it helped establish the foundations for the new system of labor management in production. But there has been much confusion over the significance of the merger movement. It therefore seems important to examine this structural change in greater detail, to trace what did (and did not) change in the U.S. economy as a result of the merger movement at the turn of the century, and to see what course business had to follow in order to overcome the obstacles in its path.

Historical background. As economic instability spread during the 1870s and 1880s, firms began to seek some means of insulating themselves against competition and the threat of bankruptcy. Andrew Carnegie noted the pervasiveness of this concern in 1889 (quoted in Clark, 1929, vol. 2, p. 175):

> The condition of cheap manufacture is running full . . . Manufacturers have balanced their books year after year only to find their capital reduced at each successive balance. While continuing to produce may be costly, the manufacturer knows too well that stoppage would be ruin . . . It is in soil thus prepared that anything promising relief is gladly welcomed. The manufacturers are in the position of patients that have tried in vain every doctor of the regular school for years, and are now liable to become the victim of any quack that appears. Combinations, syndicates, trusts – they are willing to try anything.

We know from hindsight that the holding company merger provided the eventual basis for an institutional solution to this entrepreneurial problem. But the solution did not come overnight. It appears that three main developments provided a permissive basis for the merger movement of 1898–1902. First, the completion of the national rail network and the standardization in the early 1880s of rail gauge and equipment, rate schedules, and timetables permitted a scale of market that both invited and was compatible with large-scale concentration of capital. Freight rates fell rapidly from the early 1880s to the end of the century (*Historical Statistics,* 1975, series Q-281, Q-345), making more extensive sales possible, dissolving the geographic barriers protecting local and regional monopolies, and eventually requiring strong measures to protect the strongest firms from intensive competition (see Kirkland, 1967, chs. 3-6). Second, investors' experience with outside capital investment in the railroads gradually supplied the model for a more general stock market for industrial securities and eventually provided easy and reliable access for financiers and promoters to much larger sources of capital. As Navin and Sears note (1955), the market for industrial securities emerged and grew rapidly during the 1880s and 1890s. Third, the New Jersey holding company legislation of 1889 finally provided the legal model facilitating corporate consolidation (Kirkland, 1967, pp. 204-205). Despite the apparently aggressive antitrust language of the Sherman Antitrust Act, the act would become a significant force only somewhat later, and then for only a decade. As Kirkland concludes (1967, p. 205), "the holding company signalized the final triumph of the corporation, for now corporations could be made to combine corporations."

Once the economy had recovered from the recession of 1893-1897, prosperity unleashed the consolidation movement. There were 3,653 recorded mergers between 1898 and 1902, twenty-five times the total number in the preceding three years and six times the number in the succeeding five years (*Historical Statistics,* 1975, series V-39). According to Nelson's data, between one-quarter and one-third of the *entire* U.S. manufacturing capital stock experienced consolidation between 1898 and 1902 (Nelson, 1959, p. 37; Edwards, 1979, pp. 216-217). And as Moody (1904) reported, 236 of the 318 important "trusts" (or consolidations) active in 1904 had been incorporated *after* January 1, 1898. The corporate landscape would never again be the same.

Despite the magnitude of those changes, however, the importance of the consolidation movement by itself should not be exaggerated. It must be understood as the culmination of drives toward consolidation which developed over a period of at least twenty years. The merger movement was not something that happened to the economy as a result of unique events during those five years. Much more fundamentally, the earlier contradictions of the economy produced the merger movement. Firms and bankers sought industrial consolidation as part of a potential solution to urgent economic problems that had plagued them with increasing severity at least since the early 1880s.

Impact of the mergers. The effects of that prospective solution were mixed. While the merger movement produced a qualitative transformation of firm size and internal behavior, it was only a necessary (and far from a sufficient) condition for the solution to firms' problems of competition and economic insecurity.

The effects on firm size are clear. During the 1880s, according to Navin and Sears (1955), firms were "very large" if their net assets (invested capital plus reinvested profits) exceeded $10 million. By these standards, only a handful of manufacturing firms were "very large"; six "processing trusts" and a few other industrial firms controlled more than $10 million in assets. (Fifteen or so of the highly capitalized railroads also exceeded this level of capital assets.) By 1903, at least a hundred industrial firms had assets exceeding $15 million, and about ten corporations controlled assets exceeding $100 million (Edwards, 1975a). For at least a few notable corporate examples, this greater size facilitated immediate quantum leaps in (at least potential) market power. By 1904, the newly consolidated International Harvester Company controlled 85 percent of harvesting machine output. By 1900 only the General Electric and Westinghouse corporations survived to control the new electrical industry. By 1902, the United States Steel Corporation, representing the agglomeration of about 165 separate companies, controlled approximately 60 percent of the entire steel market (Edwards, 1979, p. 42).

The effects of consolidation on the shape of firms were just as dramatic (see Chandler, 1962, 1977; and Edwards, 1979, ch. 3). Through the 1880s, firm ownership and management were almost always concentrated within the families or partnerships of their founding entrepreneurs. Only the railroads, textile companies, and a few other firms were more widely owned. Many of the larger manufacturing firms – like Best and Company, the McCormick Company, and all the large iron companies – were family-held firms or partnerships. Since there were no effective outside capital markets, net investment almost always flowed from internally generated retained earnings, and since little outside borrowing or stock sale occurred, net profits almost always remained inside the family or partnership. Because firms were small and outside sources of managerial capacity had not yet emerged, internal administrative structures were simple and internally staffed.

The mergers effectively transformed these characteristics of the entrepreneurial firm. Few of the largest firms were still controlled exclusively within the founding families or original partnerships; outside stock ownerships and, in particular, bank financing came to be decisive. With borrowing and stock equity sales outside the firm, the ratio of internal financing to external financing became a critical variable for corporate attention. As the size of firms grew and administrative problems became increasingly complex, firms turned quickly to recruitment of managerial personnel and development of administrative systems.

Despite the importance of these changes, however, the new consolidations still faced intense and unstable product market competition.

The evidence on the continuing intensity of competition seems reasonably strong. The centralization process did not immediately produce firms that securely dominated their respective industries. Through World War I, large firms continued to suffer sudden declines in market position or relative size. Some even faced bankruptcy. Data developed by Edwards (1975a; 1979, ch. 3) demonstrate this persistent instability. Of the 100 firms with the greatest assets in 1903, only 45 remained large enough to be listed among the top 100 in 1919. Moreover, 9 of the top 100 in 1903 had experienced bankruptcy and liquidation by 1917; 7 had been acquired by other firms; and 57 others, while still in business in 1917, had assets worth less in real terms than they had had in 1903.

Contemporary corporate leaders were painfully aware of this continuing instability. As Edwards argues (1979, ch. 3), most of the corporations involved in consolidation had already achieved technical economies of scale in plant and equipment *before* the mergers. They were not faced with a problem of finding the magic investment that would enable more efficient production or lower prices. Rather, most firms were seeking to translate their new market power into higher profits and greater corporate security. Unless they could achieve positions of perfect product market monopoly, large corporations required intraindustry oligopolistic cooperation before they could take advantage of their larger size. But this quest for security was not immediately fulfilled.

The large corporations (and the finance capitalists who controlled them) faced a series of obstacles to their plans. Most fundamentally, their rapid consolidation and predatory intent divided the capitalist class and permitted the mobilization of a loose, sometimes self-contradictory multiclass alliance in opposition to the corporations (see Edwards, 1979, pp. 65–71).

Small business constituted one element in this anticorporate opposition. In many historical contexts, small manufacturers, small-town bankers, store owners, and other small businessmen form the junior or subordinate element within the general "business community." With its superior resources, power, and prestige, large capital – big bankers and corporate owners – usually provide the leading element. Small businessmen dream of joining the ranks of big business, with its status (and success), and usually defer to its representatives.

But the rapidity of the consolidations and the obvious intent to trustify industry completely opened a split within this capitalist class coalition. Small business feared that its own interests were becoming imperiled by the growing monopoly power of the new giants. Although it never explicitly joined in concerted political activity with the other oppositional elements, small business composed the constituency that made Republican antitrust policy and reformism possible.

The split within the capitalist ranks opened the way for other oppositional elements to be effective. Middle-class reformers and Socialists (the two groups often overlapped, as in the cases of Upton Sinclair and Walter Lippmann) mounted a compaign to curb the activities of the large corporate and financial interests. Their activitites produced movement toward the "Progressive Era" reforms, including establishment of the Federal Reserve System, the Federal Trade Commission, and other regulatory agencies.[3]

Most notably, reformers forced the launching of an unprecedented (and unrepeated) enforcement of antitrust legislation, an effort aimed at rolling back the results of consolidation. In the ten years following the 1904 Northern Securities decision, major antitrust suits were filed against Standard Oil, American Tobacco, International Harvester, U.S. Steel, and other giants – seven of the largest ten corporations and others (like General Electric and Du Pont) that had emerged in control of particular industries.

The Socialists presented another locus of opposition. The great fear of socialism among propertied classes made the arguments of middle-class reformers more compelling. Beyond that, however, the Socialist and labor opposition made it impossible for big capital to achieve the political consensus necessary to carry through its program.

Big capitalists initiated one effort to build consensus by organizing the National Civic Federation (NCF). Drawing together elements from big business, labor (mainly American Federation of Labor [AFL] leaders), and the "public," the NCF attempted to forge a national agenda for reform of industrial relations and governmental policy (Weinstein, 1968). Still, the real opposition to the corporate program prevented substantial action until the war.

Although divisions among capitalists and a rising opposition prevented the installation of the full corporate program, big and small capitalists were united on one major issue: Both opposed unions and sought to limit or destroy them. Throughout the period during which

Morgan representative George Perkins sat in NCF conferences with Samuel Gompers and other labor leaders to discuss a new system of industrial relations, the Morgan-dominated U.S. Steel Corporation suppressed and eliminated the remnants of the old Amalgamated Association in its mills. As late as the 1919–1920 steel strike, U.S. Steel countered attempts to organize with maximum force.

If possible, small capitalists were even more hostile to labor. The "employers' offensive" during the opening four or five years of the century (like that at the beginning of the 1920s) obtained most of its support from small employers, who insisted on smashing unions and maintaining the "open shop." On this issue they had no differences with big capital (Commons et al., 1935, vol. 4).

Thus, on the one hand, the prewar multiclass opposition prevented big capital from installing the overall regime that it wanted. On the other hand, big and small capital was unified with respect to that particular part of the new social structure of accumulation that we analyze in the remainder of this chapter, namely, the labor process and labor markets. Here, the results of the new regime did not await big capital's triumph; instead, the changes date to the very beginning of the century.

The coming of the war completely altered the constellation of class forces that had forestalled the corporate program. Beginning in 1915 or so, small business as well as big capital began to feel the effects of the war-induced growth in demand. Big profits loomed, and small business readily fell in step with big capital, resuming its customary junior role in the increasingly unified "business community." Middle-class reformers turned their attention to winning the war to save democracy, and the reform impulse collapsed. Socialists and militant labor groups like the Industrial Workers of the World were harassed, imprisoned, and utterly defeated.

After 1915 and even more so after 1920, big capital had eliminated its opposition. Antitrust was relegated to occasional regulation for the general business interest of exceptionally rapacious corporations and the labor movement was gutted and impotent. The profit boom of the 1920s reflected these auspicious circumstances.

Their new dominance permitted corporations to use their increased size, greater preoccupation with the medium and long run, and expanded leverage over their environments to move toward systematic, rational planning for the future of both their internal and external environments. More and more, firms could now devote (and were compelled to apply) resources to the development of policies and practices which served the long-run interests of the corporation but which, in earlier and more immediately competitive times, might have threatened short-term survival. Entrepreneurial firms before the merger movement more closely resembled the traditional neoclassical model of the representative competitive firm, taking prices and other variables as given parameters of their environments in the short run. After 1919 corporations began actively seeking changes in their economic environments beyond the short run (see also Galbraith, 1967, and Averitt, 1968).

As important as these changes in corporate structure became, it is also important to reemphasize our more general argument that the economy experienced many other dimensions of structural transformation as well. (See the brief summary earlier in this section.) We think that many writers in the Marxist tradition have overemphasized the singular importance of the shift from "competitive capitalism" to "monopoly capitalism." While changes in firm size and market power were critical and obviously helped trigger the new stage of accumulation, changes in firm structure alone cannot explain all of the changes that took place between the end of the nineteenth and the beginning of the twentieth centuries. Perhaps even more important, an exclusive focus on the emergence of "monopoly capitalist" firm structure and behavior provides virtually no explanation for some of the qualitative changes in the logic and dynamics of the world capitalist economy between the periods before and after World War II.

While changes in the structure of firms at the turn of the century constituted a necessary condition for the new stage of capitalism, they did not, in short, provide a sufficient basis for that stage of accumulation, and they fail to provide a sufficient explanation of the course of twentieth-century capitalist development. As we argued in Chapter 2, a more complex and multidimensional analysis of stages of capitalism – building upon the interdependence of long swings and social structures of accumulation – provides a more fruitful guide to the dynamics of capitalist development and, more specifically, to the transformation of the labor process and labor markets. Within this expanded analytic framework, it becomes possible both to appreciate and to avoid exaggerating the historical importance of the consolidation of corporate size and power around 1900.[4]

The homogenization of labor

We argue that a tendency toward the homogenization of labor emerged gradually after the early 1870s and came to dominate the development of the labor process and labor markets during the early-twentieth-century stage of capitalism. We develop this argument in three main sections, examining in turn each of the respective phases through which the process of labor homogenization passed.

The period of exploration: 1870s to 1890s

In the 1860s, as we saw in Chapter 3, the organization of capitalist production in the United States remained primitive. Craft workers still controlled many spheres of production. Even outside these spheres of artisanal influence, the pace of production was irregular and the returns to productive capital investment still fairly unpredictable. As the crisis of the 1870s and 1880s deepened, the problems created for capitalists by this relative lack of control began to seem more and more acute. Pressured by falling prices, capitalists were forced to seek new and more effective means of reducing production costs. Traditional systems of labor management, as we also saw in Chapter 3, did not readily permit either cost reduction or labor intensification. Employers had virtually no other option but to begin exploring new methods of gaining increasing control over the labor process. Relying primarily on new methods of mechanization, industrial capitalists began in the early 1880s to explore and increasingly to implement new production techniques that typically eliminated skilled workers, reduced required skills to the barest minimum, provided more and more regulation over the pace of production, and generated a spreading homogeneity in the work tasks and working conditions of industrial employees.

The first steps toward this kind of mechanization occurred during the Civil War, when interchangeable parts were introduced into the watch and clock, sewing machine, and munitions industries (see Clark, 1929, vol. 2, chs. 2, 30). In industries that adopted these innovations, Rosenberg concludes (1972, pp. 254-255), employers achieved a virtual "elimination of dependence upon handicraft skills, and the abolition of extensive fitting operations." During and after the Civil War, the McKay machine and the Goodyear welt machine provided boot and shoe employers with comparable increases in control over the pace of production, undercutting the advantages of craft work by enabling unskilled operatives to reproduce fine shoes (Hazard, 1921, pp. 123-126). During the 1870s and early 1880s, meat processors began to develop a primitive precursor of the assembly line: Moving hooks passed along the butchers' work benches. One butcher no longer carved an entire animal; instead, semiskilled workers remained at individual positions on the moving line making single or several slices at their designated targets (Clark, 1929, vol. 2; Giedion, 1948; Brody, 1964). Cyrus McCormick's technical innovations in 1886 eliminated the skilled molders with new machines which "common labor was [now] used to operate" (Ozanne, 1967, p. 20).

Similar changes had begun to take place in the steel industry during the 1880s, as employers sought to introduce technology that would reduce their dependence on the skilled puddlers, mechanics, and rollers. Indeed, their principal complaint against the union concerned the restrictions against the introduction of the new machines that had become both feasible and necessary by the late 1880s. Frick wrote to Carnegie in 1892: "The mills have never been able to turn out the product they should owing to being held back by the Amalgamated men" (quoted in Stone, 1975, p. 34. On steel, see also Clark, 1929, vol. 2; and Brody, 1960, ch. 2).

Mechanization spread more and more widely through the 1890s. Data on installed horsepower per wage earner in manufacturing, for example, indicate an increase of 8 percent from 1869 to 1879, an increase of 13 percent from 1879 to 1889, and an increase of 36 percent from 1889 to 1899 (National Industrial Conference Board, 1923, p. 139). Since these data calculate horsepower per worker, they reflect an *intensification* of mechanization and cannot simply be attributed to the more *extensive* spread of the factory system itself.[5]

At the same time, it is important to emphasize that this process of mechanization did not represent only a technical process, governed solely by the rate of technological innovation and diffusion. Two additional dimensions of this initial stage of mechanization were crucial.

First, mechanization involved as much, or more, a social as a technical dynamic. As Marglin (1974) argues about the earlier Industrial Revolution in England, the principal barrier to mechanization arose from organizational, not technical, factors. Employers had to discover and apply systems for organizing production that would accommodate and regulate the labor of semiskilled workers and new kinds of machines. Where they had previously relied on the coordinative as well as technical skills of craft workers, employers now had to provide new systems effecting coordination in order to reduce their dependence on craft workers' technical skills. Among economic historians, at least, this point does not seem controversial. For example, Lebergott notes (1972, p. 210) that "the transition from hand to machine labor took considerably longer than the availability of a new technology would indicate." Giedion also concludes (1948, p. 96) that "the attention of industrialists was being claimed not so much by new inventions as by new organization." An industrial engineer reviewed the early experience with mechanization in 1899 (quoted in Clawson, 1980, p. 200): "It is not merely sufficient that the technical portion of [industrial] operations be modernised. Automatic and stop-machines . . . must be themselves made part of a system arranged to suit the changed conditions of work."

The second point is more controversial. In many instances, it appears that employers sought mechanization largely in order to enhance their general control over production and not exclusively (or even partially) in order to effect quantitative reductions in unit factor costs in the short run.[6] Three examples illustrate this dynamic.

In the iron industry, Dank's puddling machine was a way station in the series of technological developments that led to the Bessemer process. Victor Clark concludes that the craft workers' militance was the principal stimulus for the machine's adoption (1929, vol. 2, p. 79):

> This furnace consisted of a horizontal revolving cylinder in which the iron was treated much as in an ordinary furnace, but with a great saving of hand labor. Puddlers were among the highest paid and most intractable of workers in the iron trade, and their frequent strikes caused constant interruption in the business. That was the principal motive for devising a mechanical method to perform the service they rendered.

A similar substitution occurred in the textile industry. In the southern New England area, textile manufacturers had stayed with the putting-out system longer than the Boston manufacturers. After the Civil War, in transforming their production, employers adopted English mule-spinning equipment. They needed the English craft workers to operate the equipment, and the English workers brought trouble (Clark, 1929, vol. 2, p. 106):

> Following the English mules came English spinners, bringing with them the trade unions and labor traditions of the mother country, with the result that labor conflicts were much more frequent during this period in Southern New England than along the Merrimac. These difficulties accounted in part for the later restoration of ring spindles for spinning warp.

Indeed they did. As one employer summarized their actions (quoted in Gutman, 1973, p. 560):

> On Saturday afternoon after they had gone home, we started right in and smashed a room full of mules with sledge hammers. On Monday morning [the spinners] were astonished to find that there was no work for them. That room is now full of ring frames run by girls.

Ozanne's study (1967) of the history of McCormick/International

Harvester provides the third example. By 1884–1885, McCormick had had enough with his craft workers. After the successful skilled workers' strike in 1885, McCormick immediately invested $500,000 in new machinery "to displace all of the company's skilled molders." The molders tried to organize other workers to protect their position, and they struck again in 1886. The strike was broken and the union lost its influence.

> As the days [of the strike] wore on, more and more workmen, mostly unskilled, were successfully recruited. Unskilled workmen were available in abundance . . . The union's prime weapon, the ability to withhold the worker's labor at peak spring production rushes, had declined because the introduction of machinery made the molders' skill obsolete (pp. 22, 25).

There can be little doubt, Ozanne concludes (p. 26), that "in the case of the molding machines for the McCormick foundry, the main purpose was clearly to destroy the union."[7]

It is, of course, impossible to estimate the relative quantitative importance of these kinds of examples. At least some contemporary observers nonetheless considered this "social control" imperative to have been critical. David Wells, reviewing the mechanization experience in 1895, concluded (pp. 67–68):

> One influence which has been more potent in recent years than ever before in stimulating the invention and use of labor-saving machinery, and which should not be overlooked in reasoning upon this subject, has been undoubtedly the increasing frequency of strikes and industrial revolts . . . As [an English engineering review] has already pointed out, the remedy that at once suggests itself to every employer of labor on the occasion of such trouble with his employes [sic] is, 'to use a tool wherever it is possible instead of a man.'

This early process of mechanization generated a corresponding increase in plant size. The new machines required larger establishments, and those larger establishments in turn required a larger volume of production to support the capital investment. Throughout U.S. manufacturing, the number of workers per establishment increased dramatically after the 1860s. Although aggregate data for the late nineteenth century are biased downward because they include "hand and neighborhood industries" in which little mechanization took place, the decennial census series nonetheless indicates a 48 percent increase in the average number of wage earners per establish-

The homogenization of labor

Table 4.1. *Increase in average establishment size, by industry,*
1860–1900

Industry category	(1) Average establishment size, 1860	(2) Average establishment size, 1900	Column 2/ column 1
Agricultural implements	8	65	8.14
Carpets and rugs	31	214	6.91
Cotton goods	112	287	2.56
Glass	81	149	1.84
Hosiery and knit goods	46	91	1.98
Iron and steel	65	333	5.13
Leather	5	40	8.00
Malt liquors	5	26	5.20
Paper and wood pulp	15	65	4.33
Shipbuilding	15	42	2.80
Silk and silk goods	39	135	3.46
Slaughtering and meat packing	20	61	3.05
Tobacco	30	67	2.24
Woolen goods	33	67	2.03

Source: U.S. Bureau of the Census (1903, table 17, p. lxxii).

ment between 1869 and 1889 (National Industrial Conference Board, 1923, p. 97). More revealing are the data for individual industries in which the spread of mechanization was most dramatic. Table 4.1, drawn from the 1900 *Census of Manufactures,* provides data on the increase in average establishment size for fourteen leading manufacturing industries. Establishment size more than doubled in all but two of those fourteen industrial categories.

In Philadelphia, to take a more local example, the increases were equally noticeable (Laurie and Schmitz, 1981, tables 4, 5). In 1850, only 43.1 percent of all employees worked in establishments with fifty-one or more employees; by 1880, that percentage had grown to 65.9 percent. In the paper, fuel, shipbuilding, textile, and clothing industries, more than three-quarters of all workers were employed in establishments with more than fifty workers.

This rapid increase in factory size undoubtedly had a significant impact on the social relations of the factory. Up through the 1860s plant size remained small enough to sustain relatively personal relations between supervisor and supervisee (see Edwards, 1979, ch. 2, for a summary). As factories rapidly expanded, however, intimate and particularistic relationships were much more difficult to sustain.

117

Authority became less personal, and each worker became increasingly liable to the threat of dismissal and more vulnerable to the fear of replacement by a member of the reserve army. Ozanne emphasizes this effect in his study of the McCormick factory during this period. By the 1870s the Chicago Works had employed several hundred workers, and, he concludes (1967, p. 10), the larger factory size "destroyed the personal contact which had formerly characterized the Works. The size of the plant now made it inevitable that the workmen would henceforth deal only with hired managers."

Viewed in combination, the skill reduction effected by early mechanization and the increasing impersonality of larger factories jointly generated the final strand of this early movement toward homogenization. As the quantitative and qualitative importance of skilled work was reduced and as the impersonality of supervisory relations eroded more intimate relations between employers and workers, more and more wage earners in manufacturing shared the experience of working in similar kinds of jobs. Almost anyone could work in the large factories because jobs in those factories increasingly required only nominal skills. Under the craft system there had been apprentices, journeymen, helpers, assistants, and master craftsmen, all with widely disparate job tasks and skill levels. Now, more and more, there was a single class of semiskilled factory operatives who required virtually no skills in order to perform their jobs. As David Wells concluded (1895, p. 93):

> The individual no longer works as independently as formerly, but as a private in the ranks, obeying orders, keeping step, as it were, to the tap of the drum, and having nothing to say as to the plan of his work, of its final completion, or of its ultimate use and distribution. In short, the people who work in the modern factory are, as a rule, taught to do one thing – to perform one and generally a simple operation . . . The result has been that the individualism or independence of the producer in manufacturing has been in a great degree destroyed.

These initial decades of emergent homogenization are partially reflected in several aggregate indicators of job structure and labor market outcomes.

Although census data on the occupational distribution of the work force before 1900 do not provide sufficient detail to trace the effects of homogenization with full rigor, the aggregated data do permit some rough approximations. The compilations by Sogge (1933, pp. 199–203) estimate that "industrial wage earners" increased their share of the total economically active population from 26.6 percent in 1870 to 35.3 percent in 1900. The more detailed compilations by Alba Edwards (U.S. Bureau of the Census, 1943, pp. 104 ff.) indicate that male operatives and laborers increased their share of male manufacturing employment from 38.6 percent in 1870 to 42.0 percent in 1900. More detailed data that accounted for the changing working conditions in which specific occupational groups labored might more accurately reflect this first movement toward homogenization.[8]

Aggregate wage data for these decades are also consistent with our argument about the early stages of homogenization. In the three decades from 1870 to 1900 a large and continuing number of immigrants entered the country. Most scholars agree that the immigrants were less skilled on the average than native-born workers (see Hutchinson, 1956). Regardless of their skills, many immigrants entered unskilled jobs that did not make use of the skills they had (Medoff, 1971).

If supply factors alone had influenced occupational wage differentials, it seems likely that the rapidly increasing supply of unskilled workers would have depressed the wages of unskilled workers relative to those of skilled workers. In fact, available wage data compiled by Lindert and Williamson (1977, pp. 78, 121) indicate that the ratio of unskilled workers' wages to skilled workers' wages *increased* by roughly 5 percent (from cycle peak to peak) from 1873 to 1896. This narrowing seems to indicate that the relative demand for unskilled workers increased even more rapidly than the supply.[9]

Although quantitative evidence on labor market mobility is scarce, it appears that the emergent process of homogenization also helped foster the growth of a national labor market.[10] Thernstrom and Knights (1970) summarize their quantitative studies of urban mobility with the conclusion that highly mobile unskilled urban residents increasingly "formed a class of permanent transients who continued to be buffeted about by the vicissitudes of the casual labor market." Most studies of immigration during this period suggest that surplus immigrant workers both searched for available jobs on their own and were frequently recruited for factory work by labor recruiters (see, for example, Erickson, 1957). In his study of immigrant labor in Milwaukee, Gerd Korman emphasizes both effects. On the one hand, he writes (1967, p. 27), new arrivals were drawn to Milwaukee because "agents in New York and Chicago recruited and distributed immigrants"; on the other hand, once they arrived (p. 28), "most men made the rounds of the factory gates."

If this labor market homogenization had cumulative and significant effects, one would expect to find evidence of a tendency toward increasingly homogenous wages for semiskilled and unskilled workers across regions and industries. Scattered evidence suggests precisely this effect. Lebergott (1972, pp. 211–218) summarizes a variety of evidence indicating that regional wage differentials diminished substantially between the Civil War and the turn of the century; this narrowing suggests a more mobile labor supply.[11] Relying on scattered evidence, Clark concludes (1929, vol. 2, p. 143) that "wages varied more widely" at the end of the Civil War than at the turn of the century. Ulman (1955, pp. 64–67) suggests that the geographic mobility of labor increased during the second half of the nineteenth century, peaking before World War I. Finally, Montgomery argues (1979) that a kind of "class wage" had begun to emerge by the end of the nineteenth century, created by the fluidity of an increasingly homogeneous labor market. "Common labor earnings turned out to be not only homogeneous as among occupations," he concludes, "but remarkably stable over the years" (p. 36).

One important exception to this tendency toward increasingly homogenous labor markets involved female workers. Having constituted the first wave of the wage-labor force in the textile industry through the 1840s, women did not share in the rapid growth of industrial employment after those initial decades. They remained relatively concentrated in just a few jobs and industries and did not experience the impact of early tendencies toward homogenization as much as their male counterparts.

Even this exception should not be overstated, however. Although these general impressions are certainly accurate as an overview of the difference between the experiences of male and female workers between 1870 and 1900, female workers did begin to move out of their traditional jobs, at least to some degree. While the magnitudes of movement were not momentous, the early tendency toward homogenization nonetheless seems to have significantly affected the occupational composition and labor market outcomes of female as well as male workers.

A number of indicators support this conclusion.[12] Female nonagricultural employment increased rapidly, growing from 1.5 million in 1870 to 4.3 million in 1900. This growth reflected a notable increase in female labor force participation rates – from 13.1 percent in 1870 to 18.8 percent in 1900 (*Historical Statistics,* 1975, series D-13). The employment of women in manufacturing grew more rapidly than industrial employment itself; female manufacturing workers increased as a percentage of total manufacturing employment from 13.8 percent in 1870 to 19.2 percent in 1900. This increase in female industrial employment was not confined exclusively to traditional strongholds in clothing and textiles; the share of female manufacturing workers employed in the clothing and textile industries declined from 83.8 percent in 1870 to 71.9 percent in 1900. This moderation of the relative concentration of female industrial workers in the apparel sectors was accompanied by a correspondingly moderate spread of female workers into several other manufacturing industries. Between 1870 and 1900 in particular, women increased their proportion of total employment in printing and publishing from 15.2 percent to 24.0 percent; in leather goods from 4.1 percent to 14.5 percent; and in food processing from 2.8 percent to 9.8 percent. These developments help account for the simultaneous reduction in the historic concentration of women in just two kinds of employment – the apparel industries and domestic and personal service. The percentage of female nonagricultural employment accounted for by the apparel industries and by domestic and personal service declined from 87.4 percent in 1870 to 80.4 percent in 1880, 74.9 percent in 1890, and 66.8 percent in 1900 – a cumulative decrease over those three decades of nearly one-quarter.

One final observation about the employment patterns of women is important in order to follow through on earlier developments. We noted under "The period of exploration" in Chapter 3 that the early employment of women was often linked to the employment of children. It was not until the 1880s that the emergence of child labor legislation began to cut into the employment of children under fifteen. (Between 1870 and 1880, female employment and child employment increased at roughly the same rate, but the employment of children then declined absolutely from 1880 to 1890, dropping by 34 percent [Wright, 1895, p. 206].) As children left industry, it appears that women replaced them. Wright concludes (p. 211): "So the facts certainly indicate that women, instead of crowding upon the men to as great an extent as is generally supposed, are rapidly taking the places of boys and girls and doing the work which they formerly did in our factories."

Homogenization and spreading class conflict. Our analysis of this period of exploration leads us to one final argument as background to the consolidation of homogenization after the turn of the century. Throughout the 1880s and early 1890s, as we saw in Chapter 3, working-class unrest intensified. Workers struck more frequently (see Table 3.5). And between 1880 and 1900 the number of union members in the work force increased fourfold (Commons et al., vol. 2, 1918, p. 47; Wolman, 1936, p. 16). We attribute part of this growing unrest to the intrinsic contradictions of homogenization itself. The more that workers shared common working circumstances, the more likely that they would share protests over their jobs.

A first level of evidence on spreading workers' unrest comes from data on unionization and strike activity. By both these measures, workers' militance and unrest appears to have continued its growth and extension beyond the 1880s to the turn of the century, acquiring new momentum during the depths of crisis in the 1890s and mushrooming until at least 1903–1904.

During the sustained stagnation of the 1870s and 1880s, recessions nearly wiped out union membership and strength. But in the recession of 1893–1897, for the first time in U.S. history, the trade unions successfully maintained their organizational integrity in the face of spreading unemployment. Although union membership dropped quantitatively during the recession of the early nineties, unions were not demolished. Membership dropped from its peak of nearly one million in 1886–1887 to roughly half that level in the depression of 1893–1897 (Millis and Montgomery, 1945, p. 82). Between 1897 and 1904, according to Wolman's internally consistent data series on average annual trade union membership (Wolman, 1936; tabulated in *Historical Statistics*, 1975, series D-952), union membership rose from 447,000 to 2,072,700, an increase of more than 300 percent. As Samual Gompers, head of the American Federation of Labor, noted with prescience and pride in 1899 (quoted in Millis and Montgomery, 1945, pp. 81–82),

> while in every previous industrial crisis the trade unions were literally mowed down and swept out of existence, the unions ... have manifested not only the power of resistance, but of stability and permanency ... the organization remains intact during dull periods of industry, and is prepared to take advantage of the first sign of an industrial revival.

Led by their own unions, workers also struck with increasing regularity during the initial years of transition. Table 4.2 continues the data series presented in Table 3.5, comparing three-year moving averages of strike frequency around peak years of the business cycle. After the "dull-periods-of-industry" dip during the sustained recession of 1893–1897, strikes recovered quickly and climbed by 1902–1904 to an average frequency almost twice the highest level reached during the crisis of the 1880s and early 1890s (see Table 3.5 for comparison).

Peterson's data tabulations (1938) also provide evidence that, by the early 1900s, strikes were involving larger segments of workers, affecting broadening numbers of establishments, focusing increasingly on "noneconomic" demands, and benefiting more from labor union leadership. Table 4.3 summarizes data on these dimensions of strike

Table 4.2. *Index of strike frequency, 1892–1903* [a]

Year of business-cycle peak[b]	Three years averaged	Three-year average index of strike frequency (1927–1929 = 100)[c]
1892	1891–1893	203
1895	1894–1896	162
1899	1898–1900	214
1903	1902–1904	417

[a]Since federal data collection was interrupted between 1906 and 1916, it is difficult to extend this consistent series further beyond the turn of the century.
[b]Business-cycle peaks from Burns and Mitchell (1946, p. 78).
[c]Index of strike activity calculated from Peterson (1938, p. 21).

activity for three-year moving averages around business cycles peaks from the early 1880s through 1902–1904.[13] The data in the table suggest two tentative conclusions.

First, although a growing percentage of workers was involved in strikes (see col. 1), the increase in this percentage was not as rapid as the increase either in the incidence of strike activity (see Table 4.2) or in the percentage of establishments involved (Table 4.3, col. 2). This disparity suggests that *broader* segments of the working class were participating in strikes, rather than that larger numbers of workers were participating, on average, in each strike. Indeed, the rate of increase in establishments affected (col. 2) roughly matches the rates of increase in strike frequency (see Table 4.2); and other data in Peterson (1938, p. 29) indicate that the *average* number of workers per strike declined from peak levels in the 1880s and early 1890s to nearly half those levels in 1902–1904.

Second, trends in workers' focus on noneconomic demands (col. 3) and trends in the growth of labor union sponsorship (col. 4) appear to have moved together. Both figures were low in the early 1880s, climbed somewhat as unions grew more active in the late 1880s and fought more vigorously for union recognition, fell with union membership itself during the mid-1890s stagnation, and then rose quickly to new heights in 1902–1904.

Some labor historians, particularly Montgomery (1976), are inclined to attribute spreading strike activity after the mid-1870s to the growing militance of craft workers and their trade unions. Skilled workers were indeed restive in this period. If the protest was largely

Table 4.3. *Characteristics of strike activity, 1882–1903* [a]

Year of business-cycle peak[b]	Three years averaged	(1) Percentage of workers involved	(2) Percentage of establishments involved	(3) Percentage of workers in "non-economic" strikes[c]	(4) Percentage ordered by labor unions[a]
1882	1881–1883	n.a.	n.a.	9.0	50.8
1887	1886–1888	n.a.	n.a.	20.3	62.6
1890	1889–1891	4.5	2.0	26.8	71.1
1892	1891–1893	n.a.	n.a.	27.3	71.6
1895	1894–1896	n.a.	n.a.	26.0	60.5
1899	1898–1900	5.1	2.8	24.5	62.6
1903	1902–1904	6.8	5.5	37.2	79.7

[a] Because federal data collection was interrupted between 1906 and 1916, it is difficult to extend this consistent series further beyond the turn of the century.
[b] Business-cycle peaks from Burns and Mitchell (1946, p. 78).
[c] For method of calculation, see note 14.
[a] Series tabulated from Peterson (1938, p. 32).

limited to skilled workers, however, which we do not believe, it would not support our hypothesis that the homogenization of working conditions was beginning to generate increasingly widespread working-class protest and beginning to knit together workers in different kinds of occupations.

Since there are no available survey data on the occupational backgrounds of participants in strikes and protests during this period, it is apparently impossible to test these alternative interpretations with anything approaching full historical rigor. We advance three fragmentary kinds of evidence in support of the plausibility of our hypothesis about the contradictions of homogenization.

First, some accounts of strike activity during the 1880s and 1890s suggest that many strike protests, whether initiated by craft unions or through more informal and spontaneous auspices, quickly spread to virtually the full labor force in large factories. Ozanne notes (1967, pp. 22 ff.) the ease with which the skilled molders at McCormick mobilized the entire work force in 1885–1886. Brecher (1972), Grob (1964), and Ware (1959) all emphasize the degree to which local chapters of the Knights of Labor were able to attract widespread support in manufacturing cities, particularly around the May Day upheavals of 1886. It appears that the full work force mobilized in support of the skilled workers' battles against Carnegie at Homestead in 1892 (see Brecher, 1972). Although reporting on a slightly later labor battle, Nelson (1974, pp. 169 ff) reports that the skilled molders at National Cash Register were able to win strike support from the entire unskilled work force at National Cash Register in 1900–1901. Since the American Federation of Labor had already begun to disavow cooperation with operatives and laborers by 1886 (Millis and Montgomery, 1945, pp. 69 ff.), one can hardly attribute these examples to the *official* policies of the craft unions themselves. We suspect that these instances of solidarity on a plant-wide and community-wide basis reflect the increasing bonds among factory workers which the early tendencies toward homogenization helped forge. As Selig Perlman concluded (1922, p. 80), the great upheavals of the mid-1880s "signalled the appearance on the scene of a new class which had not hitherto found a place in the labor movement, namely the unskilled."

A second piece of fragmentary evidence comes from instances of early efforts at industrial unionism. Throughout the period after the Civil War, the labor movement was dominated by organizations of skilled workers seeking to protect their wages and working privileges against "degradation." Except for the much more evanescent organizing efforts of the Knights of Labor, most labor historians cite Eugene Debs's American Railway Union and the mineworkers' union as the single examples of industrial union organizing before 1900. If one focuses only at the national level, this conclusion seems justified. But there appear to be *local* examples of industrial union organizing on a primitive basis which seem to indicate that many other workers had begun to appreciate, even before 1900, the importance of multioccupational solidarity. Reich (1981, ch. 6) cites several examples of multiracial union organizing in the South just before the turn of the century (see also Worthman, 1969), for example, and both Wright (1905) and Tuttle (1969) indicate that multiracial plant-wide organizing had begun in the Chicago stockyards before the turn of the century, providing the foundation for the unified industrial strikes of 1904–1905. Given the extent of AFL domination of the trade union movement in the 1890s, it would be difficult to explain these instances except as the product of progressive homogenization of working conditions.[14]

We note, finally, that working-class protest in the 1880s and 1890s often had a kind of contagious character. Many protests took place in downtown factory districts. Given the concentration of factories and working-class housing in the largest industrial cities (Gordon, 1978b; Hershberg et al., 1981), protests launched in one plant or neighborhood quickly spread. Contemporary observers frequently used the epidemiological metaphor in describing the diffusion of protest. Graham Taylor (1915, p. 23) describes one employer's perceptions of the late-nineteenth-century atmosphere: "Every time the strikers paraded past his plant a veritable fever seemed to spread among the employees in all his workrooms." Korman provides a parallel account of labor unrest during the 1880s (1967, pp. 85–86): "Men marched from factory to factory, gaining strength with each rally, and, by leaving their work benches *en masse,* temporarily halted the entire machinery of the industrial community." This density and intensity of "communicable" protest, we suggest, both took root in the increasingly homogeneous working conditions of masses of wage workers and helped contribute to these workers' spreading consciousness of common problems and conditions.

Based on this partial evidence, we suggest a tentative hypothesis about the last decades of the nineteenth century: The first tendencies toward homogenization in production and in labor markets began to generate an increasingly widespread and unified protest among industrial workers. Our general argument states that this period was one of exploration and that the period of consolidation followed later. Hence, this hypothesis about the early phase of homogenization requires little more than a perceptible trend toward more unified industrial protest – evidence of which we have already reviewed – and at least some evidence that employers and public observers perceived this trend. However subjective, these perceptions of spreading unrest seemed common. As one Wisconsin labor official reported in 1886, for example, workers' "agitation permeated our entire social atmosphere" (quoted in Brecher, 1972, p. 40). The commissioner of the Connecticut Bureau of Labor Statistics echoed this perception, conducting a small informal sample of employers and "representative public figures" in 1887 and finding, according to Garraty's summary (1968, p. 136), that "all agreed that the workers' discontent was both deep and pervasive." Something had to be done. As Korman concludes about the 1890s (1967, p. 76), "a major change in the relations between management and worker was in the offing." Management appeared to be itching for revenge. "I do not believe," one manufacturer avowed in 1901, "that a manufacturer can afford to be dictated to by his labor as to what he shall do, and I shall never give in. I would rather go out of business" (U.S. Industrial Commission, 1901, vol. 7, p. 352).[15]

The period of consolidation: 1890s to 1920s

The economic crisis of the 1880s and 1890s required institutional resolution. In particular, it had become more and more apparent that early employer explorations of labor homogenization had been sufficient *neither* to restore profitability *nor* to curb workers' unrest. The new stage of capitalism that took shape in the United States after the mid-1890s both depended upon and helped foster the consolidation of labor homogenization. Whereas continuing class conflict slowed the implementation of many other institutional features of the new social structure of accumulation, the transformation of the labor process and of labor markets proceeded almost immediately.

We argue in this section that the consolidation of homogenization, taking deeper and deeper root from the 1890s through the 1920s, helped restore stability to the production process and foster renewed control by the employer over production workers. We develop this argument in three parts. First, we provide evidence of continuing and accelerated homogenization from the turn of the century through the 1920s. Second, we review the wide variety of new and innovative corporate policies implemented after the turn of the century which helped facilitate the consolidation of homogenization and the greater control over workers upon which that consolidation rested. Third, we summarize evidence on the general impact of the processes of homogenization during this period.

The principal dimensions of homogenization. Given the new scale of corporate operations and finance after 1898–1902, many large corporations were able to pursue homogenization with growing vigor. During the first three decades of the twentieth century, the corporate push toward homogenization compressed more and more production jobs into relatively homogeneous, more or less semiskilled operative work. Many contemporary observers called the new system that this homogenization produced the *drive system* (see, for example, Slichter, 1919). The drive system involved three principal dimensions: (1) a reorganization of work, facilitated by both mechanization and job restructuring, which produced increasingly homogeneous employment for production workers; (2) a rapid increase in plant size, particularly among the larger corporations, which reinforced the spreading impersonality of wage labor; and (3) a continuing expansion of the foreman's role, which added an insistent supervisory impetus to the new system of employer control. A wide variety of evidence supports our hypothesis that all three of these principal dimensions of homogenization dominated the labor process and labor markets from 1900 to 1930 (see also Edwards, 1979, ch. 4). We review each of these three dimensions in turn.

1. Mechanization and task-compression proceeded as interdependent dynamics. Technical innovation supported new systems of labor management by helping embody machine control in production and by reducing employers' reliance on craft workers. Job compression helped facilitate the diffusion of new machines. Taken together, mechanization and job compression jointly reinforced the disciplinary effectiveness of the reserve army of labor, making it more and more possible to replace employees who refused to submit to the growing power of capital.

Specific industry studies provide ample evidence of this continuing trend toward homogenization in the production process. In steel (Brody, 1960; Stone, 1975), the electrical industry (Passer, 1952), food processing (Giedion, 1948), printing, glass, and stonecutting (Barnett, 1926), and automobiles (Reitel, 1964; Maltese, 1975; Russell, 1978) homogenizing mechanization took place from 1900 to 1930 with clear skill-reducing effects. Clark's discursive summary (1929, vol. 3) provides numerous concrete examples of this kind of mechanization. Jerome's classic study (1934) provides the most detailed and comprehensive review of the process of mechanization from the turn of the century, summarizing aggregate tendencies and reviewing specific details for nineteen separate leading manufacutring industries (pp. 55–119). Based on his careful analysis of the combined effects of these tendencies toward mechanization, Jerome concludes (p. 401) that the "aggregate effect may be accurately described as a leveling process producing fewer highly skilled jobs but also few really unskilled jobs."

Quantitative evidence on technical change in manufacturing further supports our hypothesis that mechanization from 1900 to 1929 followed the trajectory of change first charted after the Civil War. Table 4.4 summarizes the relevant quantitative indices for manufacturing from 1879 through 1929, providing estimates of trends in value added, capital stock, total production employment, horsepower per production worker, value added per worker, capital per worker, and the capital/output ratio. The data in the table indicate that the growth of manufacturing and the spread of mechanization continued fairly steadily throughout the period represented in the table. While the rate of decennial increase of several of the indices slows through the successive decades represented in the table, undoubtedly reflecting the low base of mechanization in the 1870s and 1880s, only one of the series (production employment in the 1920s) shows a decisive shift or point of inflection during the decades from 1899 to 1929.[16] The tremendous leap in mechanization during the 1920s reflects the culmination of this process. Capital per worker jumped by 36 percent over the period 1919 to 1929, while real value added per worker soared by nearly 75 percent.

Did mechanization proceed more rapidly in the newly consolidated corporate giants than in smaller firms with a more traditional entrepreneurial structure? Relevant data are not available for individual firms, but one can easily compare industries. For the purpose of this and later comparisons, we have defined a category of "consolidated" industries – industries in which the largest firms controlled 25 percent or more of total assets. Firm data provided by Edwards (1975a) permit the classification of two-digit industries in both 1903 and 1919 as either "consolidated" or "nonconsolidated."[17]

One would expect mechanization to have proceeded more rapidly in consolidated industries, other things being equal, because the new consolidations created by the merger movement had access to much larger pools of liquid capital for the purposes of investment. (Further, if rates of return were higher in consolidated industries, for reasons we shall discuss throughout this section, these initial advantages would be multiplied.) Available data on horsepower per worker confirm these expectations. The growth in horsepower per worker between 1899 and 1919 was 56 percent more rapid in consolidated industries than in nonconsolidated industries (calculations based on data reported in National Industrial Conference Board, 1923, p. 145).

Table 4.4. Indices of growth in manufacturing, 1879-1929

	(1)	(2)	(3)	(4)	(5)	(6)	(7)
Year	Value added ($)[a]	Capital stock($)[a]	Production workers[b]	Horsepower per production worker	Value added per production worker ($)	Capital per production worker ($)	Capital/output ratio
1879	3,201	4,821	2,733	1.25	1,170	1,760	0.547
1889	6,756	11,157	4,129	1.40	1,640	2,700	0.730
1899	9,916	18,626	5,098	2.07	1,940	3,650	0.803
(1899)[c]	(9,275)	(17,452)	(4,502)	(2.18)	(1,790)	(3,880)	(0.794)
1904	11,132	23,295	5,182	2.52	2,150	4,500	0.891
1909	13,674	31,563	6,262	2.88	2,070	5,040	0.967
1914	14,931	36,737	6,602	3.26	2,260	5,560	1.008
1919	18,042	46,094	8,465	3.33	2,130	5,540	1.022
1925	25,668	n.a.	7,871	4.37	3,261	n.a.	n.a.
1929	31,196	63,022	8,370	4.91	3,701	7,530	0.885

[a]Millions of dollars, 1929 prices.
[b]Thousands.
[c]The second series for 1899 (in parentheses) differs from the first as a result of the exclusion of "hand and neighborhood" factories from the universe of manufacturing establishments.
Sources: Col. 1: Creamer et al. (1960, table A-10, addendum, p. 258). Col. 2: Historical Statistics (1975, series P-123; drawn from Creamer et al., 1960, table A-8). Col. 3: Historical Statistics (1975, series P-5). Col. 4: Historical Statistics (1975, series P-73). Col. 5: Col. 1/col. 3. Col. 6: Col. 2/col. 3. Col. 7: Creamer et al. (1960, table A-13; this series is for total output, not for value added.)

Since the development of the automobile assembly line represents such an important example of mechanization during this period, it is especially useful to consider its relationship to our general argument. Many tend to view the assembly line as a new departure in American industry, considering what some call Fordism as a decisive turning point in the development of modern technology (for example, Aglietta, 1979). Without depreciating the importance of Ford's innovations, we would suggest nonetheless that the purely technical dimensions of the assembly line did not represent major advances over earlier systems. On the contrary, the assembly line seems to represent a culmination of the successive movements toward homogenizing mechanization that had spread since the Civil War. The major difference between the assembly line completed in 1913 and the earlier systems used by Ford himself involved the extension of material handling methods from moveable gravity slides to continuous line operations. As such, the assembly line simply completed a logical development in the organization of technology that had begun with interchangeable parts and continued through the primitive moving hooks of the slaughterhouses in the 1870s and 1880s.

It seems equally important to emphasize that the automobile assembly line, like the earlier efforts toward mechanization, arose at least partly as a result of corporate efforts to gain greater control over production. Ford himself acknowledged that growing employer concern over labor unrest helped spark the sequence of innovation that led to "mass production" (Ford, 1929, pp. 38–39; italics in original):

> The early factory system was uneconomical... Mere massing of men and tools was not enough; the profit motive, which dominated enterprise, was not enough. There remained the scientific motive which grew eventually into what is called mass production.
>
> The advent and progress of financial control of industry were marked by two developments, the corporation and the labour revolt. Artificial combination of industrial plants into vast corporations for financial purposes was the first movement toward *mass* in industry. It proceeded on the theory that complete financial control would automatically bring complete profit advantage. The theory ignored many vital principles of business and its fallacy became apparent, but not before serious social hostility had been incurred... it was out of the social strife thus engendered that the idea began to emerge that possibly the difficulty lay in the neglect of scientific manufacturing principles.

Ford knew his own history. Evidence suggests that the urgency of Ford's experimentation leading to the assembly line can be at least partly attributed to growing labor unrest in Detroit from 1909 to 1912, which prompted more intensive efforts to reduce skilled workers' control over production and to eliminate social contact among semiskilled operatives (see Maltese, 1975, Meyer, 1979, pp. 107–116; and Russell, 1978, for a summary of some of this evidence).

In this respect, Ford's innovations in mass production are particularly representative of the more general tendency toward homogenization. Mechanization was always most effective if it proceeded within the context of fundamental changes in the more "social" aspects of production – changes, for example, in labor-management practice (see Edwards, 1979). This was evident at the Ford Motor Company, where both the owner and his planners were consistently disappointed with the productivity dividends reaped from purely physical and technical changes in the production process. John R. Lee, Ford's first personnel manager, expressed this disappointment in 1916: "We confess that up to this time [of the final completion of the assembly line at Highland Park in 1913] we believed that mechanism and material were of larger importance [than the human element] and that somehow or other . . . our men were taken care of automatically and needed little or no consideration" (quoted in Meyer, 1977, p. 89). Company data on productivity help confirm the need for a change of view: The increases in average worker productivity resulting from the first major personnel policy innovations in 1914 were nearly five times greater than the average annual increase in worker productivity resulting from the previous four years of primarily technical innovation between 1909 and 1913 (based on data reported in Meyer 1977, pp. 88, 306).

If we take Ford's mass production techniques as exemplary of the broader movement toward homogenization, do we find evidence at Ford of the touchstone of the homogenization process, of the reduction of jobs to a common, semiskilled denominator? Meyer (1977) has carefully tabulated available data on the occupational composition of production workers at Ford and in the Detroit metal industries from which bicycle and then auto manufacturing initially evolved. Table 4.5 summarizes these data on a comparable basis for the Detroit metal industries in 1891, long before homogenization had eroded the craft structure in the metal trades; and then for samples of Ford workers in 1910, near the beginning of the rapid movement toward mass production; in August 1913, reflecting the final installation of the assembly line; and in 1917, after mass production had been in effect long enough to have acquired its characteristic shape. However approxi-

132

Table 4.5. *Job homogenization at Ford Motor Company, 1910–1917*

	Total production worker employment (%)			
	Detroit metal industries, 1891	Ford Motor Co., 1910	Ford Motor Co., 1913	Ford Motor Co., 1917
Skilled workers	39.8	31.8	28	21.6
Semiskilled operatives[a]	30.6	29.5	51	62.0
Unskilled laborers	29.6	38.6	21	16.4

[a]The jobs represented in this category had various names during this period. Meyer has inspected production operations with sufficient care to feel comfortable designating this band of jobs with the general "semiskilled" label.
Source: Meyer, 1977, tables 1–4.

mate, the figures in the table provide dramatic confirmation of the occupational impact of homogenization in this relatively prototypical case: In 1910, the job structure at Ford still closely resembled the earlier structure of craft production in the metal industries. In particular, in 1910 the semiskilled job category had the lowest representation among the three skill levels, being considerably outnumbered by both skilled and unskilled occupations. By 1913, this pattern had been dramatically reversed. By 1917, semiskilled operatives had grown to more than three-fifths of total production worker employment. Within just seven years, the occupational structure had been compressed and effectively transformed. A new class of homogeneous, semiskilled jobs now dominated employment in this classic case of mass production. (Elbaum, 1982, provides parallel results for steel.)

2. The continuing trend toward mechanization also produced continuing increases in plant size. In addition, the rapid growth of the largest firms after the 1898–1902 merger wave permitted a dramatic increase in the size of the largest factories during the first two decades of the twentieth century. This widening of the tail of the distribution of plant size had a moderate and significant effect on the rate of increase in plant size over the full period from 1870 to 1920.

The evidence concerning the size of the largest factories seems clear. Nelson (1975, pp. 6–9) shows that these factories increased from roughly 1,500 workers per establishment in 1880 to a range of 20,000 to 60,000 during the 1920s. This expansion took place disproportionately among the largest firms in recently consolidated industries, reflecting the increasing capacity of those firms to finance and

Table 4.6. *Establishment size in manufacturing, 1880–1920*

Year	(1) Workers per establishment	(2) Average annual percentage change in (1)	(3) Workers per establishment, 7 industries	(4) Average annual percentage change in (3)
1880	10.8		67.7	
		−0.2[b]		+2.8
1900	10.4[c]		105.6	
	(22.7)[c]		(119.3)[a]	
		+1.8		+5.1
				(+4.0)[a]
1920	31.4		213.7	

[a]The data for 1900 are not precisely comparable between the two sources for three of the seven industries; the figures in parentheses represent the alternative series using 1900 data from the *Historical Statistics* time series.

[b]The actual *decline* in average establishment size between 1880 and 1900 appears to be a product of the depression of the early 1890s. There was a positive rate of increase in establishment size during the 1880s. In any case, since these numbers include "hand and neighborhood industries," the data in col. 3 are more meaningful for the purposes of comparison.

[c]The first figure is the average for factory and hand and neighborhood production, comparable to the 1880 figure. The number in parentheses is the average for factory industries only, comparable to the 1920 figure and to the base for which the figures in col. 3 were calculated.

Sources: Col. 1: National Industrial Conference Board (1923, p. 97). Col. 3: Average (unweighted) establishment size data for seven industries with comparable definitions and complete series, from U.S. Bureau of the Census (1903, table 27); and *Historical Statistics* (1975, series P-58, P-60). Several textile industries were omitted from this comparison because they did not experience substantial consolidation after 1900.

manage large factories. Nelson tabulates (pp. 7–8) the seventy factories with 2,000 or more workers in 1900. Of those seventy factories, 81.4 percent were owned by firms in consolidated industries; consolidated industries accounted for only 48.4 percent of total manufacturing capital in 1899. Perhaps more revealing, our own calculations show that the average number of workers per establishment in consolidated industries averaged more than twice that in nonconsolidated industries in 1900; and average plant size in consolidated industries grew by nearly 100 percent from 1899 to 1919, whereas average plant size in nonconsolidated industries remained virtually constant.[18]

Although it is difficult to compare data on plant size in the aggregate before and after 1900, this rapid increase in the size of the largest factories after 1900 appears to have had an accelerating impact on the aggregate rate of increase in plant size. Census data on manufacturing establishments do not separate "hand and neighborhood" establishments from factories before 1899, so that perfectly consistent comparisons of the rate of growth in factory size from 1870 to 1920 are not possible. Consistent time series for seven important (roughly two-digit) manufacturing industries are available, however. Table 4.6 compares the aggregate indices for factory wage earners per establishment with the weighted average indices for these seven disaggregated industries. Both series dramatize the continuing increase in factory size throughout the period. As column 4 shows, the annual increase in wage earners per establishment rose significantly from its rate of increase in the pre-1900 years to the two decades after 1900.

3. In order to achieve greater control over the labor process, corporations made heavier and heavier use of foremen and superintendents. As skills were reduced and craft workers were replaced in many industries, foremen substituted their own authority for the coordinative and managerial activities that craft workers had formerly provided. The first three decades after 1900 culminated in what Nelson calls (1975, ch. 3) the "foreman's empire" (see also Edwards, 1979, ch. 2; Jacoby, 1981, ch. 2). The growth in the supervisors' power lent a further commonality to the working conditions of semiskilled operatives, for all workers were equally vulnerable to the power and caprice of the bosses' representatives.

This increasing reliance on foremen and supervisors is clearly revealed in the data. The number of foremen in manufacturing increased from 90,000 in 1900 to 296,000 in 1920, an increase of more than 300 percent, whereas total manufacturing employment increased by only 96 percent over the same years (*Historical Statistics*, 1975, series D-393, D-130). This growth contributed to the rapid expansion of the salaried occupations in the manufacturing sector. According to the Fabricant-Kuznets data compiled by Delehanty (1968, table A-1), the ratio of salaried employees to wage earners rose steadily, from 8.76 per 100 wage earners in 1899 to 16.32 in 1919, nearly doubling in twenty years.[19] And this relative growth in the salariat is not solely attributable to increases in nonsupervisory white-collar occupations. According to disaggregated census data for the decade from 1909 to 1919, the increase in the relative share of "superintendents and managers" (not including "salaried officers of corporations") was double the growth in the relative share of "subordinate salaried employees" (National Industrial Conference Board, 1923, table 13).

Corporate policies to reinforce homogenization. We noted in our discussion
of the exploration of homogenization that all three principal dimensions of homogenization had already begun to emerge in U.S. industry by the 1880s. We also hypothesized that this early exploration of
homogenization contributed to spreading worker unrest through the
turn of the century. We have now traced the trends toward mechanization and job compression, larger plants, and the "foreman's empire" through the 1920s. If these trends had continued unaccom-
panied, our analysis of the exploration period would lead us to expect
further intensification of worker militance and rebellion after 1900.
And yet, in our general discussion of this stage of capitalism, we have
argued that corporations consolidated a new system of control over
the labor process and restored their power to forestall worker unrest.
How did this happen?

We argue in this section that the final consolidation of homogenization was accompanied by, and partly depended upon, a variety of
direct and increasingly self-conscious corporate policies to reinforce
the homogenization of labor. Employers began pursuing these
strategies almost exactly around 1900. "They became aware of the
deeply-seated nature of labor's discontent," Slichter concluded (1919,
p. 414), and they sought ways of reducing the disruptiveness of that
discontent. Their efforts were not coordinated, and they did not
apply a master boardroom strategy. The kinds of strategies they pursued, as a result, were varied and scattered.

Despite the disparate character of these policy innovations, however, almost all of them shared a common thread dictated by the
corporate effort to consolidate the homogenization of labor. Corporations had learned that they could potentially increase both their profits and their control over workers by restructuring the labor process.
This restructuring established more and more common working conditions among many production workers. In order to curtail the
spreading worker unrest that these commonalities were apparently
helping to foster, corporations recognized that they needed both to
increase the disciplinary effectiveness of the reserve pool of labor and
to dissolve the emergent unity that homogenization seemed to forge.
All of the most important corporate policy innovations after 1900
were conceived and implemented, at least partly, we argue, either to
improve the effective credibility of the reserve army as a threat to
currently employed production workers or to divide and fragment
working-class solidarity on the job. We trace the several most important examples of these new policy directions in the following
paragraphs.

Many corporations began almost immediately after the merger movement to install centralized personnel offices. As one consequence, they gained greater flexibility in the containment of labor problems. Through the end of the nineteenth century, the foreman in each shop had held virtually unlimited discretionary authority to hire, fire, and promote workers. While this authority often helped foremen maintain discipline in the shops, it sometimes also led to a kind of clannishness from department to department, with foremen hiring workers of their own ethnic background and maintaining cozy relationships on that basis. These "old-fashioned hiring methods," as Slichter called them (1919, p. 247), frequently undermined efficiency. Foremen were likely, according to Jones (1925, p. 392), "to hire the friends of the employees of his department on the basis of friendship rather than fitness" and to "sell jobs" or "hold his favorites in soft assignments."

Many large firms sought to remedy these problems by establishing central "employment managers" (see summary and conclusions in Slichter, 1919, pp. 282 ff.). Nelson reports (1974, p. 176) that National Cash Register established the "first modern personnel department" in 1901 after a crippling strike. Slichter concludes that many large firms quickly followed. The primary function of these new offices, according to Jones's summary (1926, p. 390), was to supervise hiring and transfer. From the National Cash Register model through the 1920s, one of the major priorities in hiring and transfer decisions was to break down worker solidarity and weed out troublemakers. At National Cash Register, for example, the Labor Department kept a list of workers "whose records were at all objectionable and . . . tried to weed them out, including socialists." The office involved a "new, less formidable role for foremen and no role at all for independent labor organizations" (Nelson, 1974, p. 177). In general, Slichter reports (1919, p. 298), personnel departments applied a clear principle: As soon as workers "began to show a clannish spirit, it was necessary to separate them . . . Many firms prefer to put the source of difficulty in another department." Although this new effort undercut the foreman's authority over hiring and firing, it was not intended to and apparently did not undermine the foreman's discipline in the shop itself. As Cyrus McCormick, Jr., concluded about this period: "Several years ago the average employer in big factories took away from the individual foremen the right of hiring and firing, and gave it to the employment manager. At that time it was said that that would ruin the foreman's ability to discipline his men. It didn't" (quoted in Jones, 1926, p. 421).

Although recent historical research on these developments has not yet adequately followed up the clear suggestions in contemporary accounts such as those by Slichter and Jones – see the notable exception of Jacoby (1981) – there is sufficient evidence available to point toward two main hypotheses. First, centralized personnel departments emerged immediately after 1900 and became a crucial method for bringing the disciplining effect of the reserve pool of labor to bear upon an increasingly homogenized and substitutable work force. Second, only firms with sufficiently large operations to warrant such departments could afford to install them. By 1928, according to a study by the National Industrial Conference Board (1929), only 12 percent of all firms had personnel departments, but 34 percent of firms with more than 250 employees had organized central personnel offices (see also Slichter, 1919, pp. 282 ff.; Riegel, 1942, pp. 28 ff.; and Jacoby, 1981, ch. 6). In his influential critique of this system in the 1920s, Feldman (1925, p. 341) referred to this method "as a system of labor clearances based on the possibilities of moving workers about like armies."[20]

Many employers also began to reduce workers' unity by creating artificial divisions and distinctions among jobs. While the homogenization of the labor process was itself reducing labor tasks to increasingly similar kinds of work activity, employers were seeking to create differentiation among employees through the definition of varied job titles and the creation of new job ladders. Stone (1975, pp. 45–59) traces the development of these kinds of job ladders in the steel industry, dating them from the period between 1900 and 1920. Both Slichter (1919, pp. 290 ff.) and Bloomfield (1921, pp. 295 ff.) confirm that such artificial job ladders became increasingly common through World War I. Slichter (1919, p. 290; italics added) emphasizes, indeed, that the "positions are divided into several grades and promotions made *regardless of the specific operation*" which those workers performed. Looking back at these new methods, Smith (1939, p. 31) confirmed that "such uneven assignments ... prevented the formation of worker teams whose members would have common problems and a sense of group morale. But above all they aggravated the dependence of the workers upon management by making any common action impossible."

Large corporations also appear to have filtered planning decisions about plant location through a kind of divide-and-conquer calculus (see Gordon, 1978b, pp. 47–51, for further details). After several decades of concentrating factories in central-city factory districts, employers began, during the later 1890s, to move their factories out to what were then called "industrial satellite suburbs" (see Taylor, 1915).

Gary, Indiana, is the best known of such examples. This decentralization of manufacturing employment continued at a rapid pace
through World War I and paved the way for the accelerated development of motor transportation after the war.

Location theorists have traditionally explained the decentralization
of factories by citing the development of the truck and the rapid
diffusion of land-intensive automated processing technologies. It is
difficult, however, to explain the inauguration of factory decentralization by either factor (Gordon, 1978b). Trucks did not develop as an
adequate substitute for rail freight transport until the 1920s. And, as
we have already argued in our discussion of the consolidation of
homogenization, there were few significant qualitative changes in
the character of processing technology between the last half of the
nineteenth century and the first two decades of the twentieth.

The concern of employers with labor discipline seems a more plausible explanation of the first stages of decentralization. Factory owners,
who had become increasingly aware of the strikes and demonstrations
that surrounded and infected their downtown factory workers,
thought that moving to the suburbs would isolate their respective
factory workers from "dangerous" influences and help forestall the
threat of unionization. Only the larger (and mostly consolidated)
firms could afford such a move, with its heavy infrastructural investment costs. Once installed at a sufficient distance from the center of
labor agitation, these firms achieved a measure of insulation from the
epidemics of central-city strike activity to which they had previously
been vulnerable. In moving to the suburbs, corporations sought to
isolate their work forces from central-city unrest; insofar as the evidence can provide such indications, they at least partially succeeded.[21]

More or less simultaneously, large corporations also changed plant
design significantly. As plants grew larger, firms gradually abandoned the classic nineteenth-century model of the single open shed. A
number of important technical innovations, such as reinforced concrete for construction and electrical power for traveling cranes, railroads, and other handling equipment permitted more flexible plant
design. After 1895–1900, as Nelson concludes (1975, p. 23), most
modern factories "consisted of a series of interrelated buildings rather
than a single large structure." For example, foundries were located in
separate structures, isolated from the main assembly areas. Even
within the general flow of assembly production, plant activities were
fragmented among disparate shops and structures.

This increasing fragmentation of plant design might simply have
involved a technical accommodation to the difficulties of larger factory size and an adaptation of some technical innovations. It becomes

important for our story, however, because departmental separation began to require more centralized personnel administration within the firm and because the physical fragmentation of factory design was consistent with the new centralized personnel policies of "labor clearances." Although we have no evidence that architects were "ordered" by their employers to fragment plant design for explicit purposes of labor control, it would not be implausible, given the timing and context of these design innovations, to propose such a speculative hypothesis as a guide to further research.[22] In any case, the departmentalization of factory design, itself an outgrowth of larger factory size and technical improvements in plant construction, helped facilitate the general transfer of employees among departments.

Large employers also began to experiment with wage incentive schemes that created differential rewards among employees and helped create competition among them. Before the 1890s, most employers relied on simple day rates in paying their wage earners. Nelson (1975, p. 53) and Clawson (1980, pp. 168 ff.) date the introduction of simple piecework and more sophisticated incentive plans from the mid-1890s. When companies installed piece-rate systems, they would almost always "adjust piece prices to a level that allowed workers to earn somewhat more than their day wage – so they would continue to have a material interest in high output – but only about one-third more, no matter how great the increase in output" (Clawson, 1980, pp. 169–170). Workers increasingly resented these adjustments. As an industrial engineer noted as early as 1899 (quoted in Clawson, 1980, p. 170), "the result is frequently not peace, but soreness." This reaction led many personnel experts to propose more complicated incentive schemes. Ford Motor Company introduced one of the most systematic wage systems, dividing production workers into six pay groups with three pay grades within each group (Slichter, 1919, p. 360). Stone reports (1975, pp. 44–45) that "between 1900 and World War I, piecework and premium plans became more and more prevalent in the steel industry." Many other industries also experimented with similar plans (see Jones, 1925, ch. 21).

Two characteristics of these incentive schemes seem particularly noteworthy for our analysis. First, the systems could not be implemented in isolation; they depended on the establishment of personnel offices, on greater supervisory authority, and on the standardization of labor activities which homogenization provided. As Jenks concluded (1960, p. 436), "Nearly all [wage systems] called for changes in shop organization; standardization of shop practice, equipment, and routine procedures; a realignment of tasks; and some augmentation of supervision and clerical personnel" (see also Korman, 1967, pp. 65 ff., and Clawson, 1980, pp. 182 ff.). Second, the wage systems were not designed solely to influence individual workers' output through graduated piece-rate incentives. Equally or more important, the systems were aimed at dividing workers and minimizing collective worker action. "Piecework was not merely 'payment by results,'" Mark Perlman concludes (1961, p. 28); "it was predominantly a new concept of the job." As one manufacturer explained his introduction of the schemes (in National Industrial Conference Board, 1929, p. 25), "When each worker is paid according to his record there is not the same community of interest . . . There are not likely to be union strikes where there is no union of interest."[23]

Employers in this period also experimented with "welfare" plans, seeking to increase worker motivation by tying them to pension and benefit schemes (see, for example, Korman, 1967, ch. 4; Brody, 1968; and Nelson, 1975, ch. 6). These plans also frequently supported the divide-and-conquer strategies. Some employers explicitly sought to limit the applicability of the welfare benefits to a small group of workers so that workers would compete among themselves for access to the plans and would be divided into those who shared their benefits and those who did not. (See Maltese, 1975, and Meyer, 1977, for a summary of the intentions and impact of welfare schemes at Ford.)

Another dimension of corporate policies toward labor during this period involved employers' manipulation of racial and ethnic differences among their workers (see, for example, Brody, 1960; Brecher, 1972; and Gutman, 1976). Several features of this general approach deserve special emphasis.

First, corporate manipulation of ethnic and racial differences was not limited solely to initial hiring practices. Employers did prefer to rotate hiring among different ethnic groups in order to create competition among workers of different nationalities.[24] But insufficient emphasis has been placed on the allocation of workers within the plant once they were hired. It appears that many corporations began during this period to maintain explicit occupational segregation by ethnicity among departments and job categories; such ethnic differentiation was intended to reinforce the division that artificial job differentiation was also intended to create. Summarizing their detailed studies of immigration, the U.S. Immigration Commission concluded (1911a, p. 531) that "in many cases the conscious policy of the employers [is] mixing the races in certain departments and divisions . . . preventing concert of action on the part of the employees." Immigrants were not only separated from native workers, they added (p. 538), but also "subdivided into smaller groups . . . in order to insure more ease in handling." The commission concluded (p. 540) that

141

there had been "a sharp segregation . . . into distinct occupations" within a very short space of time.

Second, differentiable groups of workers were subject to these policies on a relatively common basis; employers do not appear to have made distinctions, for example, between racial and ethnic differences. When blacks were first introduced into Northern factories, their assignments among jobs paralleled the allocation of Southern and Eastern European immigrants. Indeed, some evidence for this period suggests that within certain manufacturing industries blacks were located not at the bottom of the occupational ladder but above several Eastern European ethnic groups (see Hessen, 1974; Bodnar, 1976; and Klaczynska, 1976).

Third, this explicit divide-and-conquer strategy was linked to employers' more general efforts to forestall and weaken workers' resistance and unionization. The Immigration Commission concluded (1911, p. 538) that most large corporations "realized that by placing recent immigrants in these positions they would break the strength of unionism for at least a generation . . . [Their policies] made it possible for the employers to carry out their policy of undermining the unions' elements of strength and control in the industry."

Fourth, this explicit divide-and-conquer strategy for manipulating ethnic and racial divisions represented a new strategic innovation, an approach that employers had not systematically applied earlier. The substantial immigration from the 1840s through the 1890s had obviously created a more ethnically differentiated labor force. But the early exploratory phase of homogenization appears to have promoted more rapid occupational assimilation among different immigrant groups, and employers did not actively promote explicit competition among different ethnic and racial groups for the purposes of forestalling worker unrest.

The evidence on occupational assimilation is obviously fragmentary, since few systematic studies of occupational distributions by ethnicity have been conducted for the late nineteenth century. But some evidence supports this conclusion. For the early 1870s, Montgomery concludes (1967, pp. 35–36) that "there was no simple promotional ladder in industry bearing different ethnic groups on successive rungs . . . Most immigrants . . . blended into the scenery with amazing rapidity." Hershberg et al. (1981) conclude from their detailed analyses of census records for Philadelphia in 1880 that immigrants were segregated residentially by blocks but that there was a much less systematic pattern of ethnic segregation by plant or by occupation within a plant. Laurie et al. (1977) conclude that Irish and

German immigrants remained in much the same occupations between 1850 and 1880 – during the earlier consolidation of initial proletarianization – but that their native-born son had already begun during those years to move into a distribution of jobs much more closely resembling that of native white males. Ehrlich (1974, pp. 529–530) concludes about the 1870s and 1880s in general that "most immigrants were quickly absorbed into the general labor market, and were therefore subject to the vicissitudes common to all its members."

The evidence on strikebreaking and explicit manipulation of ethnic groups is equally fragmentary. Ehrlich's (1974) detailed survey of the labor press for 1878–1885 indicates that those employers who used immigrant labor to help break strikes, particularly in the mines and along the railroads, were "most often directed at enlarging the labor supply and thus driving wages down and encouraging docility on the part of employees." This contrasts with the increasingly widespread policy after 1900 of using strikebreakers and different ethnic groups explicitly to create divisions among already employed workers and to exacerbate whatever divisions already existed. The earlier policy, in other words, sought to tap the general reserve army of labor, many of whom were immigrants, for the general purpose of reducing workers' bargaining power. After 1900, by contrast, employers increasingly sought to take advantage of the differentiated character of the reserve army so as to have a much more explicitly divisive effect upon their employees.[25]

Militant antiunionism provided the final and most sweeping element in the employers' new approach to labor. Particularly after 1902, corporations waged an aggressive "employers' offensive" against trade unions and Socialists, seeking to combat the spreading radicalism of the working-class movement. As Commons et al. notes (1935, vol. 4, p. 129), the employers' "mass offensive" against unions between 1903 and 1908 was motivated more by the general threat to managerial prerogatives than by the nuisance of specific labor demands. The National Civic Federation (NCF) began to emphasize, in particular, the necessity of a general corporate effort to combat militant unionism and the socialist movement (see Green, 1956, and Weinstein, 1968). As the executive secretary of the NCF wrote in 1912 (NCF Archives, Box 49B):

> Every man who has a dollar's worth of property in this country is interested from a selfish standpoint alone in the fight against socialism. When a body of men who openly preach confiscation of property and the overturning of all American

institutions can quadruple their vote in twelve years – now having over a million – it is time for every man of property to wake up.

In order to further this general effort, many corporations cooperated with the conservative elements of the trade union movement, largely represented by the American Federation of Labor, thereby separating them from industrial unionists and Socialists and weakening the general effectiveness of the working-class movement. In this respect, moderate corporate cooperation with the AFL reflected yet another effort to moderate and limit spreading working-class unrest.[26]

As should be evident from the preceding pages, large corporations played the pivotal role in forging and applying these strategies. Until the merger movement of 1898–1902, few corporations had either the margin to develop such strategies or the resources with which to implement costly innovations such as centralized personnel departments. After the consolidations, large firms could begin to tackle their labor problems and the contradictions of homogenization with far greater resources and leverage than their smaller counterparts. Although the process of homogenization dominated virtually all U.S. manufacturing, only the larger corporations were able to pursue and apply many of the divisive strategies that reinforced the corporate institution of new systems of labor management. This advantage of the large corporations undoubtedly played an instrumental role in the continuing centralization of capital that has occurred in the twentieth century.

Yet, large corporations were not solely responsible for these new directions in labor-management strategies; they received very active support and cooperation from important elements of the organized labor movement. As Weinstein (1968) notes, several important AFL leaders, Samuel Gompers and John Mitchell in particular, joined with large corporations in the National Civic Federation, consolidated their opposition to more militant and radical expressions of the working-class movement, and contributed to the nativist hostility toward more recent immigrants from southern and Eastern Europe. As Green (1980, ch. 2) argues in greater detail, union leaders oriented toward "business unionism" gained greater power in, or control over, a number of the most important unions around the turn of the century, notably the United Brotherhood of Carpenters and Joiners, from which the more militant Peter J. McGuire was ousted in 1900; the United Mine Workers, in which Mitchell consolidated his power after 1897; and the Boot and Shoe Workers Union, in which the transition toward business unionism appears to have been completed by 1903. The developments in the building trades were apparently typical of this increasingly common orientation. Green concludes (p. 33):

> The building trades sacrificed much of their nineteenth-century militancy, abandoning the sympathy strike – one of their strongest weapons – in order to obtain trade agreements. The new centralized organizations created by the business agents contributed to bureaucratic efficiency, but their growth reduced local autonomy and rank-and-file democracy.

We conclude this discussion of corporate policies with two final comments that will help distinguish our analysis of homogenization from our later analysis of segmentation.

The first involves a clarification of the role of large consolidated companies, or "monopolies," in establishing the foundations for homogenization. We have argued that initial proletarianization involved untransformed labor and that the subsequent consolidation of homogenization eventually transformed the labor process through the institutionalization of a drive system. It is our hypothesis that this drive system was applied more and more universally in the capitalist sector during the period from 1900 to 1930 – in durables and nondurables, across regions, among both small and large firms. In emphasizing the innovations pursued primarily by larger corporations, we do not mean to suggest that large corporations developed a qualitatively different set of labor-management practices from those pursued by small firms. Rather, we would argue that, in the larger firms, the more effective consolidation of homogenization led to what Edwards (1979, ch. 7) has termed "technical control" – the conscious embedding of the drive system in the technological structure of production. This technical control helped large firms reap profit advantages from the drive system by extending and supplementing it. In contrast, as we argue in the following chapter, segmentation occurred in large part as a result of growing qualitative differences between core and peripheral firms.

The second comment follows from the first. Our analysis of homogenization and the drive system leads to a corollary hypothesis about corporate labor-management policies. Recent attention to "scientific management" and "Fordism" has led many observers to conclude that major qualitative changes in corporate policies occurred from roughly 1900 to 1920. Our own analysis leads us to conclude that these arguments are historically misleading and that neither scientific management nor Fordism became important as qualitative modifications of the drive system until explorations with new systems of internal control during the late 1920s and early 1930s.[27]

This conclusion seems at odds with much of the recent attention that has been paid to scientific management. Especially since the revival of interest in Frederic Taylor, generated by Braverman (1974) and others, many observers have traced the development of new ideas about scientific management during these two decades, attributing great importance to the implementation of those ideas.

We share Palmer's skepticism (1975) about the importance of actual experiments in scientific management during this period (see also Edwards, 1979, pp. 97–104). While Taylor, Gantt, the Gilbreths, and others tinkered with new ideas, almost all employers practiced the simpler systems facilitated by homogenization. The evidence supporting this general observation seems persuasive. Thompson (1915, pp. 264–265) reports on his careful contemporary survey of "scientific management" plans in operation by 1914. There were only 140 documented applications of those schemes in operation, involving 120 factories. (There were 268,436 manufacturing establishments in 1914 [*Historical Statistics,* 1975, series P-1].) Those 120 factories represented slightly less than 1 percent of the employees in factories with more than 100 employees in the previous census of manufactures.

Nelson and Campbell (1972) provide details on one interesting case study of efforts by experts to install scientific management techniques in a large factory. After some initial experimentation, the proponents of the scientific management techniques lost out to advocates of a simple reliance on mechanization and wage incentive systems because those simpler techniques still seemed to work. Palmer (1975, pp. 35 ff.) reviews other evidence which also suggests that the impact of operating scientific management plans before World War I was extremely limited. Scientific management, as we shall see in the next subsection, was an idea whose time had not yet arrived.[28]

We draw similar conclusions about the spread of Fordism or other policies that lead eventually to the growth of structured internal labor markets. We develop this argument in detail in later sections, on the decay of homogenization and the exploration of segmentation. It is sufficient for our purposes to emphasize here that the drive system constituted the dominant system of labor management in the United States during the first three decades of the twentieth century and that the continuing effectiveness of that system through the 1920s continually pushed back the clock on major reforms of its internal logic.

Impact of the consolidation of homogenization. We have argued that homogenization continued through the first three decades of the twentieth century and that innovative corporate policies helped secure its consolidation after 1900. A wide variety of indicators suggest the significant and far-reaching impact of the process of homogenization upon both the labor process and labor markets. In the following pages we review the aggregate impact of homogenization upon corporate profitability, accidents, labor turnover, occupational composition, wages, the composition of the labor force, and the dynamics of working-class struggle.

A first measure of the impact of homogenization is in many respects the most general. We argued at the end of Chapter 3 that the stagnation of the 1880s and 1890s had produced a crisis of profitability for capitalist firms. If homogenization provided a partial resolution of these problems, we should be able to trace its impact through measures of profitability itself.

There are no reliable aggregate data on profit rates during this period, but we can rely on an indirect measure instead. We have calculated *gross surplus* in manufacturing from 1870 through 1930, defining gross surplus as the share of revenue from value added that manufacturers were able to retain after covering their production workers' wages. (This is equivalent to 1.00 minus the production workers' wage share.) If gross surplus rises, it means that corporations have a greater margin from which to retain higher relative profits. If gross surplus falls, in contrast, it augurs a potential squeeze on manufacturing profits.

According to our calculations, gross surplus had fallen during the previous period of decay from 62.7 percent of value added in 1869 to 55.6 percent in 1889. Between 1889 and 1929, after the period of consolidation, gross surplus increased to 64.4 percent.[29] There are many other potential sources of this earlier fall and subsequent recovery of gross surplus, of course – most notably, the effects of aggregate demand upon capacity utilization – and we have not been able to disentangle them for the purposes of this analysis. At a purely nominal level, in any case, the trends in gross surplus are at least consistent with our hypotheses about the consolidation of homogenization. The fact that the peak in 1930 exceeded the earlier peak in 1870 – despite all the working-class unrest and unionization during the intervening sixty years – provides one approximate measure, from the capitalists' perspective, of their ability to restore and even to improve upon the conditions necessary for successful accumulation.

Another apparent impact of homogenization involved an upsurge in industrial accidents. Homogenization permitted an intensification of the pace of labor, as the notion of a drive system obviously conveys. As workers were forced to work harder and as the machines drove them faster, accident rates appear to have soared. Comprehensive time series on accident rates do not extend back before the 1920s, so we must rely on more impressionistic qualitative accounts for the earlier years. Commons et al. (1935, vol 3, p. 366) conclude tentatively that death rates from industrial accidents reached a historic peak, compared to earlier periods, between 1903 and 1907 (see also Eastman, 1910). A detailed study of accidents in New York State for 1911 to 1914 further concluded that "of the various causes of non-fatal accidents by far the most significant was power machinery" (cited in Lauck and Sydenstricker, 1917, p. 198; for a more general summary, see pp. 192–212). Aggregate data are available from 1926. Although they are not fully comparable with the figures for the period after World War II, the average from 1926 to 1929, at the end of the period of consolidation of homogenization, was nonetheless almost twice the average during the period from 1950 to 1970, when the drive system had finally been superseded (*Historical Statistics*, 1975, Series D-1029).

The effects of the process of homogenization also appear in studies of labor turnover. Because the first systematic studies of turnover appeared only in the 1910s and 1920s (Slichter, 1919; Brissenden, 1923), we cannot accurately follow trends in turnover rates from the nineteenth to the twentieth centuries. A number of contemporary observers seem to agree that turnover did accelerate after the turn of the century (see Jacoby, 1981, ch. 4). The problem arose, according to those analyses, because the declining skill requirements of most operative jobs and the easy substitutability of factory workers for one another removed any inducements for workers to remain on the job. Slichter emphasizes (1919, pp. 150 ff.) that turnover occurred because of the large pool of unattractive jobs, not because the workers were "habitual floaters."

Slichter (1919, p. 21) provides the most comprehensive data on turnover rates. Of 105 plants surveyed in 1913–1915 (with average annual employment of 226,038), two-fifths of the factories (with two-fifths of the average annual employment) had turnover rates exceeding 100 percent per year; more employees terminated their employment during the year than the average total employment in those factories. Both Slichter (1919, pp. 33 ff., 57 ff.) and Brissenden (1923, pp. 987 ff.) confirm that turnover rates were far higher among semiskilled and unskilled workers than among skilled workers. Slichter (1919, pp. 169–200) also reports that turnover rates were highest in the largest factories and that independent measures of worker dissatisfaction were highest in the largest plants. These studies seem to indicate, in short, that the process of homogenization was generating rapid labor turnover, with substantial labor market movement and labor market "friction." The rising turnover reflected the contradiction, Slichter concluded (p. 411), between policies which simply "economize labor or which tend to improve relations between the company and its help."

The process of homogenization continued to increase the relative role of factory workers and, among them, semiskilled operatives and laborers. According to census data compiled by Alba Edwards (1943), the share of male operatives and laborers in total male manufacturing employment increased from 38.6 percent in 1870 and 42.0 percent in 1900 to 55.0 percent in 1930.[30] This somewhat imperfectly reliable data source is supported by the later standardization of the decennial tally of occupations from 1900. According to those data, unclassified general operatives and laborers in manufacturing increased as a percentage of total manufacturing employment from 36.7 percent in 1900 to 52.1 percent in 1930 (*Historical Statistics*, 1975, series D-174, D-498, D-614). Both series underscore the occupational impact of homogenization after 1900.

Data on wage differentials are also relevant to our hypotheses about homogenization and the effects of employers' divisive strategies. We saw in the previous section that the rapidly increasing demand for relatively unskilled labor between 1873 and 1896 narrowed wage differentials despite huge increases in the labor supply of unskilled workers. Between 1900 and 1920, the demand for labor increased at least as rapidly, as Table 4.2 shows. Other things being equal, we would have expected a continued narrowing of the wage differential, with the wages of unskilled workers relatively rising.

Wages are determined by more complex factors, however, and other things were *not* equal. First, average annual rates of gross immigration more than doubled after 1900 (until World War I interrupted the flows).[31] Second, large corporations acquired relatively more monopsonistic power in many industries, and they sought, as we have already seen, to weaken workers' bargaining power by manipulating ethnic differences and by buying craft workers' cooperation through moderate policies toward the American Federation of Labor. Both factors were likely to have complementary countervailing effects, serving to reduce unskilled workers' bargaining power (compared to the earlier decades), to increase skilled workers' relative wages, and therefore, *ceteris paribus*, to widen the wage differential.

These countervailing factors appear to have reversed the earlier wage dynamic. Whereas unskilled workers' real hourly wages had increased at an average annual rate of 1.3 percent between 1882 and 1896, the same index remained roughly constant after the turn of the century, rising by only 0.2 percent a year between 1896 and 1913. Skilled workers fared much better, and the ratio of unskilled to skilled wages fell consistently (from business-cycle peak to peak) after 1896, declining by 12.3 percent from 1896 to 1913. Only with the end of mass immigration and the mass strikes of the war years, when millions of industrial workers were able to take advantage of the "battle for war-time production," did the wage differential begin to narrow once again, barely returning, by 1919, to its 1896 level.[32]

A similar dynamic appears to have shaped wage movements during the 1920s. Despite the sudden interruption in immigration after 1924 and the consequent slowdown in the inflow of unskilled workers from abroad, unskilled workers were unable to maintain their wages against the combined force of homogenization and continually agressive corporate policies. The nominal hourly wages of unskilled workers fell, according to the data compiled by Lindert and Williamson (1977, table A.1), from fifty-three cents per hour in the business-cycle peak of 1920 to forty-nine cents in the peak of 1929; given falling prices during the 1920s, real hourly unskilled wages remained roughly constant. In contrast, skilled workers were able to increase their real earnings. After the brief narrowing of the gap during the war years, the unskilled/skilled wage differential resumed its earlier decline. By the business cycle peak of 1926, it had already fallen to its 1913 level and, despite a slight narrowing by 1929, closed the decade nearly 10 percent below its (business-cycle-peak) levels of the early 1920s.[33]

Our analysis of the process of homogenization and the new corporate strategies can also be related to trends in the relation of women and minorities to the labor force during the new stage of capitalism.

More and more women joined the wage-labor force. Female labor force participation rates rose from 17.4 percent in 1890 to 22.0 percent in 1930. Growing numbers of married women, in particular, began to work; the percentage of married women in the labor force more than doubled between 1890 and 1930 (*Historical Statistics*, 1975, series D-13, D-60). However, the increasing segregation of jobs among different groups of workers affected the paths along which women entered the labor force.

Women did not share proportionately in the expansion of manufacturing employment. Despite the rapid increases in female employment overall, for instance, the female share of the operative and labor occupations dropped from 19.1 percent in 1900 to 15.6 percent in 1930 (*Historical Statistics,* 1975, series D-191–192, D-225–226). Women also continued to be confined to just a few manufacturing industries. By 1930, a little more than half of all women in manufacturing still worked in the apparel industries (Edwards, 1943, table 10), and women were still unable to enter many other key manufacturing sectors. The failure of women to increase their share of manufacturing employment was caused in part by many pieces of protective legislation during this era. Craft unions had grown more sensitive to competition for employment (at least partly in response, obviously, to employers' divide-and-conquer strategies), and they participated in exclusionary paractices (Hartmann, 1976).

Instead, women dramatically expanded their share of white-collar employment. As late as 1900, women accounted for less than one-quarter of all clerical and kindred workers; by 1930, their proportion of clerical employment had increased to over half (*Historical Statistics,* 1975, series D-186, D-220). Better-educated women were able to work as professionals, mostly as teachers; the number of women in the professions in 1930 was 3.4 times the number in 1900 (*Historical Statistics,* 1975, series D-218).

These patterns of occupational segregation continued to mean that a few kinds of jobs accounted for very high proportions of female employment. Of the 9.8 million nonagricultural female employees in 1930, 79 percent worked as teachers, clerical workers, retail sales-workers, operatives in the apparel industries, or domestic and personal service workers.[34] This occupational segregation meant that most employed women had not yet been affected by the job differentiation among different ethnic and racial groups that was beginning to develop throughout the corporate capitalist sector. Women were employed in female occupations, whereas male workers felt the principal impact of the process of homogenization and the new corporate strategies.

We do not mean to imply that female workers were in any way better off than male workers, for women experienced a special kind of discrimination and exploitation on the job. We intend a much more specific point: Teachers, clerical workers, and service workers did not experience the real pressures of homogenization that we are analyzing more generally. Even women working in the clothing industries did not experience divide-and-conquer strategies with the same force as workers in most other manufacturing industries because textile firms, faced by continuing competitive conditions, were unable to adopt many of the innovations pursued by larger consolidations. Indeed, we would tentatively suggest a further hypothesis. It was precisely the relatively weak bargaining power of women, and their neglect by the male unions, that helped contribute to the ability of corporations to isolate women and continue to manage female labor with relatively traditional techniques.[35]

One can similarly relate our analysis to the situation of black workers in the capitalist sector during this period. Blacks remained outside the capitalist sector, by and large, until the end of European immigration during World War I and in the early 1920s. In 1910, 70.2 percent of all blacks in the United States still lived in the rural South; even after World War I, 63.7 percent still lived there. In 1910, fewer than 190,000 blacks worked in Northern manufacturing; blacks accounted for only 2.2 percent of all nonagricultural employment in the Northern and western regions (Reich, 1981a, ch. 6). Meanwhile, as Baron notes (1971, p. 18), "the Irish largely displaced blacks in streetpaving, the Slavs displaced them in brickyards, and all groups moved in on the once-black stronghold of dining-room waiting."

Those few blacks who did work in capitalist manufacturing were channeled into specific corners. Employers' use of blacks as strikebreakers in the North began in the 1890s in the coal mines. The first black strikebreakers were brought to the Chicago stockyards in 1894 and again on a more substantial scale in 1904 (Tuttle, 1969). The most dramatic example occurred during the steel strike of 1919, when between 30,000 and 40,000 blacks were brought north by employers to help break the strike (Brody, 1960). Much of the early employment pattern of blacks in manufacturing is explained by these selective uses of blacks as strikebreakers. Of the twenty-one major industries for which the U.S. Immigration Commission secured information in 1908 to 1910, blacks composed more than 5.0 percent of employment – their cumulative average among all industries in the survey – in only five of the twenty-one industries. One industry, cigars and tobacco, had offered employment to blacks in the South after the Civil War. A second, construction, had been a traditional locus for black employment in the South after the Civil War and, to a very slight degree, in the North. The other three provide the three main instances of the use of blacks as strikebreakers between 1890 and 1910: coal mining, iron-ore mining, and meatpacking (see U.S. Immigration Commission, 1911a; and analysis in Lauck and Sydenstricker, 1917).

This selective use of blacks as strikebreakers began to have some important effects on black incomes and social status. In the North, free blacks had traditionally worked as craft workers and had enjoyed relatively free income and occupational opportunities. After 1900, as blacks selectively entered the competitive labor market along with the steady streams of European immigrants, it appears that relative black income and occupational standing began to fall. Bodnar (1976) provides one detailed study that charts these effects in Steelton, Pennsylvania, from 1880 to 1920. In 1905, lower proportions of blacks than foreign-born immigrants worked in unskilled occupations, and blacks stood higher on the wage scale. By 1920, blacks had the highest percentage of unskilled workers among any racial or ethnic group and began to experience much lower rates of occupational mobility.

The movement of blacks to the North during World War I accelerated during the 1920s. The figures on net decennial black outmigration from the South tell the story: 221,000 in 1900–1910, 408,000 in 1910–1920 and 689,000 in 1920–1930 (*Historical Statistics*, 1975, series C-46-62). In this period blacks moved increasingly into slotted positions in the occupational structure, and they were exposed to systematic race-conscious divide-and-conquer policies for the first time (Korman, 1967, pp. 66 ff.; and Reich, 1981a, ch. 6).

Perhaps the most important evidence of the impact of the consolidation of homogenization derives from the history of working-class movements during this period. Many labor historians have tended to treat the entire period from 1898 through World War I as a nearly undifferentiated period of spreading labor unrest and growing working-class militance, followed by a collapse after wartime and postwar repression and corporate offensives. This view overlooks some important variations in the rhythms of the labor movement during this period. It is clear, as we noted at the end of the section "The period of exploration," that labor unrest spread from the 1890s through 1902–1904. After 1903, however, employers intensified their offensive against labor. Both the effects of an augmented reserve army of labor – continually replenished through immigration and rising labor turnover – and the success of corporate innovations in labor management began to dampen the effectiveness and curb the spread of homogeneous working-class protest. We would argue that both the contours and the composition of working-class struggle between 1903 and 1929 provide considerable support for our general hypotheses about the consolidation of homogenization and help construct a more complete outline of class struggle during this period than has been available in the traditional literature.

Trends in union membership provide one straightforward index of the relative success of workers' protest. Union membership had increased by 300 percent between 1897 and 1904. After the employers' offensive, the growth in membership stopped abruptly. From 1904 through 1910, union membership remained almost constant, fluctuating in a narrow range, between 1.907 million members in 1906 and 2.140 million in 1910. More strikingly, membership did not increase during periods of business upturn and actually declined from the trough of 1904 until just before the peak of early 1907. After 1910, membership began to grow again, but only slightly. From 1910 through 1916, it increased to 2.773 million. This increase amounted to a growth rate of 30 percent over six years, a tepid gain compared to the 300 percent growth from 1897 to 1904 (figures based on data compiled by Wolman, 1936, tabulated in *Historical Statistics*, 1975, series D-952).

Union membership soared again during World War I as craft workers were able to take advantage of tight wartime markets and of considerable government pressure on employers for reasonable concessions over hours and union recognition. Union membership itself rose from 2.8 million in 1916 to a peak of 5.0 million in 1920.

Employers appear to have believed that, despite wartime losses, they could quickly restore the balance of power over labor unions through continuing pursuit of homogenization. The companies' self-confidence and aggressiveness is perhaps best illustrated by their performance at a critical labor-management conference called by Woodrow Wilson in 1919 (see Hurvitz, 1977). Wilson had hoped to promote labor-management compromise and, through such moderation, reduce the level and intensity of class struggle which had spilled over from the war itself. The business delegates represented the largest corporations in the country. While labor leaders pledged their support for compromise, the business representatives, in Hurvitz's words (1977, p. 519), "advocated a campaign to extirpate unionism, root and branch, from the United States." Given the power that companies had constructed within the plants of their corporate empires, they were particularly opposed to any kind of *national* bargaining and compromise. They wanted plant-based labor management because their power was greatest there. The business representatives concluded that "each shop should work out its own machinery for resolving conflicts; industry-wide standards, rules, and policies were rejected as unnecessary and counter-productive" (p. 522). The employers' intransigence made the conference futile; it was disbanded after two scant weeks.

The large corporations had judged correctly. Although workers' strength had indeed grown during the war, employers counterattacked (with considerable help from the government) as soon as the war had ended (see the summaries in Millis and Montgomery, 1945; Perlman, 1968; and Brody, 1980). Radical leaders were harassed and often deported while a variety of company union plans undercut the basis for union organizing (see also Brody, 1980, ch. 1). Union membership fell quickly from its 1920 peak of 5 million to 3.5 million in

Table 4.7. *Trends in strike activity, 1903–1929*

Business-cycle peak	(1) Percentage of gainful workers involved in strikes	(2) Percentage of gainful workers involved in strikes on "non-economic" issues	(3) Percentage of gainful workers involved in successful strikes
1903	2.1	1.2	0.8
1907	1.0	0.4	0.3
1910	1.5	0.6	0.5
1913	2.2	0.9	0.8
1918	5.0	1.9	1.6
1920	5.4	1.9	1.4
1923	2.3	1.1	1.0
1926	0.8	0.4	0.3
1929	0.6	0.3	0.2

[a]Business-cycle peaks from Burns and Mitchell (1946, p. 79).
Sources: Col. 1: Griffin, 1939, table 7. Col. 2: Griffin, 1939, table 9 times col. 1. Col. 3: Griffin, 1939, table 11 times col. 1.

1924 and stayed at approximately that level for the rest of the decade (*Historical Statistics*, 1975, series D-952). (See also Wakstein, 1969.)

Further evidence on the dynamics of working-class protest builds upon indicators of strike activity. This evidence remains somewhat fragmentary, since the federal government did not collect comprehensive data on workers involved in strikes – despite the earlier series collected through the turn of the century – for the years 1906 through 1916 (Peterson, 1938). Seven states did continue to collect their own strike data during these years, however, and these states included the heavily industrial areas in which, as we show in note 21 of this chapter, a large proportion of strike activity was concentrated. Griffin (1939) has performed the interpolations necessary to link these state data with the aggregate series reported by Peterson (1938). Although the series on absolute strike frequency is somewhat unreliable because of the uncertainty of data weights, Griffin's compilations for strike incidence and characteristics suggest an interesting story of the ebb and flow of working-class protest and power during this period.

Table 4.7 summarizes strike data for 1903 through 1929 – presenting, as with earlier tables, three-year moving averages around business-cycle peaks; the table combines aggregate data in 1903 and 1918–1929 with interpolated data for 1907–1913. The table summarizes figures for the percentage of gainful workers involved in strikes; the percentage of gainful workers involved in strikes focused on "noneconomic" demands; and the percentage of gainful workers involved in successful strikes.

The data in Table 4.7 indicate the success of the consolidation of homogenization, revealed by the overall change from 1903 to 1929. Despite some substantial variation during those years (about which we comment shortly), all three series indicate a moderation of working-class protest by the end of the 1920s. The proportion of gainful workers involved in strikes fell by 1929 to less than one-third of its level in 1903. The percentage of workers participating in strikes over "noneconomic" demands, primarily involving protests over working conditions and hiring and promotion policies, declined to one-quarter of its extent at the beginning of this period of consolidation. The percentage of gainful workers involved in victorious strikes, finally, fell by 75 percent.

The variations in these indicators of working-class protest also reveal some important dynamics of workers' struggles after the turn of the century. All three indicators suggest a substantial moderation of working-class struggle immediately after the employers' offensive of 1903–1905. Through the two succeeding business cycles, according to these data, the breadth and effectiveness of strike activity subsided (cols. 1 and 3) while the percentage of strikes focused on "noneconomic" (or what Montgomery, 1974, calls "control") issues fell from 55 percent in 1903 to 40 percent in 1907 and 1910 (based on the underlying data). Other data reported by Griffin (1939, table 10) indicate that the average duration of strikes declined by more than half between 1903 and 1910; in view of the simultaneous decline in the percentage of successful strikes, this suggests that even those workers who did strike against their employers after 1907 were relatively more on the defensive than before the employers' offensive had begun.

The data in Table 4.7 indicate a resurgence of working-class protest after 1910, reflected in the numbers reported for 1913 through 1923. Given the more general decline in protest activity through the late 1920s, it is important to interpret these data on resurgence carefully. We turn to this problem in detail in succeeding paragraphs, but one conclusion seems evident from the series in Table 4.7 alone. It is not adequate to treat the resurgence of working-class protest simply as a political phenomenon, fueled by the opportunities of World War I and extinguished by the sharp political attacks on radicals during and immediately after the war. Strike activity had resumed its earlier intensity by 1913, even before the onset of the war in Europe, and workers continued to wage a relatively more militant struggle through

1923 (when the percentage of gainful workers involved in strikes was higher than in 1903), two full business cycles after the end of the war. This pattern suggests the need for a more detailed, at least partly economic, examination of working-class protest during this period in order to clarify the sources of its ebb and flow and to investigate further its consistency with our more general hypotheses about homogenization.

Such investigation prompts us to offer further hypotheses about the factors affecting both the character and relative effectiveness of workers' protest in the first three decades after 1900. Each of these hypotheses serves further to amplify our analysis of the impact of homogenization and to link the dynamics of class struggle with the broader structure and contradictions of the new social structure of accumulation. These additional hypotheses focus, in turn, on the factors influencing the relative effectiveness of unified workers' struggles aimed at *industrial* unionism; the evolving character of *craft* unions' strike activity; and the character and impact of more explicitly *Socialist* and *syndicalist* struggle during these years.

Industrial unionism. We have already emphasized that many corporate policies after the turn of the century were aimed explicitly at fragmenting the workers' opposition that early explorations of homogenization appear to have stimulated. This would lead one to expect that the relative success of workers' efforts at industrial unionism would hinge substantially on the relative power of large corporations within the industries in which workers sought industrial unions and, correspondingly, on the degree to which large corporations had adopted policy innovations aimed at increasing leverage over their employees. The most intensive industrial union drives during the first three decades of the 1900s occurred in the mining, men's and women's clothing, and steel industries. Workers succeeded in the first two industries and failed in the third. We propose that these different outcomes resulted in large part from the different industry structures and corporate policies in effect in these three industrial situations. Workers in all three industries had experienced substantial homogenization of the labor process by the time the industrial union drives began – the unified struggles undoubtedly reflected, in large part, the contradictions of this homogenization. Only in the steel industry, however, were employers able to pursue the kinds of corporate policies that reduced the effectiveness of workers' opposition to this homogenization.

Mine workers were impelled toward more broadly organized struggle and the creation of the United Mine Workers of America

157

(UMWA) by their employers' successful push toward homogenization of the production process near the end of the nineteenth century. As craft workers' control over production ebbed, both former artisans and others with fewer skills turned to industrial unionism for protection from more and more intensive exploitation. The homogenization of labor, according to one contemporary observer in 1904, "created in time a somewhat vindictive reaction [among the mine operatives] which, encouraged by the remaining influence of those they superseded, is now expressing itself in persistent organized demands for better conditions" (quoted in Thompson, 1979, p. 84). As Thompson concludes, "the central contradiction of the success of the capitalists to achieve control of the work processes through this homogenization of labor was that in eliminating the hold of the craftworker, they created the broader opposition of the first major industrial union in the U.S., the U.M.W.A." (p. 91).

Why were the miners more successful than other industrial workers experiencing similar contradictions? We suspect that mine workers succeeded, particularly in the East and despite militant opposition by employers, because the companies could not "run away" from the pits (as many large corporations had been able to flee to "industrial satellite" suburbs) and also because the mining companies were still small and highly competitive; the only antiunion tools available to these smaller firms were the labor recruiting agencies and the goon squads that mine companies had begun marshaling against workers since their attacks on the Molly Maguires in the 1870s. As most larger consolidated companies in other industries had already discovered, those primitive weapons were hardly adequate to the task. As a result, the spread of the UMWA followed closely behind the spread of homogenization. Formed in the 1890s, the union was able by 1905 to sign up close to 80 percent of miners in the Midwest and rapidly rising proportions in Pennsylvania (data reported in Thompson, 1979, fig. B-22).

Similar arguments help explain the sudden and substantial success of the International Ladies' Garment Workers Union and the Amalgamated Clothing Workers of America between 1909 and 1916. Homogenization had spread rapidly in the apparel industries toward the end of the nineteenth century, with unusually rapid increases in the average number of workers per establishment between 1870 and 1900.[36] And yet, the women's and men's clothing industry remained competitive and firms remained relatively small: Among fourteen (roughly two-digit) industries for which the 1900 Census provides detailed data on the effects of "combinations," apparel and textiles ranked thirteenth in combinations' control of the total value of products.[37] Because of this competitive industry structure, clothing firms were unable to adopt some of the principal innovations implemented by larger firms in more consolidated industries. In addition, the clothing workers were densely concentrated in a few large factory districts (especially in New York and Philadelphia). When speedup intensified after 1908–1909, and especially after the disastrous Triangle Shirtwaist fire in New York in 1911, employers were unable to quell the contagious and widely supported strikes that followed. Homogenization and central-city concentration united and strengthened the workers, while persistent intraindustry competition kept divide-and-conquer innovations beyond the employers' grasp (see Green, 1980, ch. 3).

The contrasting case of steel has been amply documented (see Brody, 1960, and Stone, 1975). After the craft workers' union had been smashed in the period between Homestead in 1892 and the last significant Amalgamated strikes immediately after 1900, the large steel companies aggressively pursued a wide variety of policies aimed both at homogenization and at fragmenting their increasingly homogeneous employees. When workers finally organized the massive industrial union strike of 1919, employers were able to crush the strike by playing on ethnic and racial divisions and by importing thousands of black strikebreakers from the South. Despite the scale and intensity of the workers' struggle during that strike, the workers were unable to muster themselves for another major assault on the industry until the later years of the Great Depression.

Craft unionism. Our analysis of homogenization can also illuminate some of the central strands of craft union history from 1900 to 1930.

We suggested in the previous section that large corporations sought an accommodation with craft unions after 1900 and that many craft union leaders, increasingly oriented toward business unionism, reciprocated. This historic compromise led the craft unions to concentrate on consolidating and protecting member gains in the industries in which they had already established influence. Between 1906 and 1916, virtually the only absolute gains in union membership came from the successful formation of the industrial unions in the men's and women's clothing industries. Almost all the dramatic increase in union membership between 1916 and 1920 reflected the ease with which craft unions were able to extend their strength in the construction, machinist, and transportation trades during wartime; they did not seek significant extensions of their representation beyond these traditional domains.[38]

This perspective leads us to suspect that Montgomery (1974) has somewhat exaggerated the tendency within the craft union movement toward quasi-syndicalism and efforts at workers' control during the period between the formation of the National Civic Federation and the years following World War I. It is clear, as Montgomery demonstrates in detail, that syndicalist thought penetrated deeply into certain sectors and regions during these years. It is less clear, however, that this penetration deflected the more general tendency, which we have already noted, toward business/union and corporate/union cooperation. Montgomery postulates a shift toward workers' concern with "control" issues, for example, between 1909 and 1922. The aggregate data do not support this argument. The series augmented by Griffin's interpolations (upon which Montgomery did not rely) indicate that strikes involving wages-and-hours demands increased substantially after the compromises inaugurated from 1900 to 1905 had taken root. The percentage of strikes focused on wage-and-hour issues averaged 44.8 percent per year between 1901 and 1905, rose to 59.8 percent in 1906 to 1910, fell slightly to 58.8 percent during the clothing drives between 1911 and 1915, and then increased again to 63.5 percent during the intensive strike years between 1916 and 1920 (Griffin, 1939, table 9). These data indicate movement in an opposite direction from that which Montgomery suggests.[39]

This compromise was weakened by significant tensions after the beginning of the 1920s. However, the new corporate offensive, not a union deflection from their predominantly business orientation of the previous fifteen years, was primarily responsible. Faced with increasingly aggressive corporate attacks and with a sudden attrition in their membership between 1920 and 1924, unions were forced to resort to defensive strikes on issues of union rights and hiring and firing policies. The percentage of strikes prompted by wage-and-hour issues fell steadily after 1920 and averaged only 41.1 percent in the five years between 1925 and 1929, a drop of more than one-third from the proportionately greater focus on wage-and-hour issues during the war years.

Socialist and syndicalist movements. Many labor historians point to the growth of the Socialist Party and the emergence of the Industrial Workers of the World (IWW) from 1905 to 1913 as evidence of a continuous spread of working-class militance. Without denying the importance of those movements, we would nonetheless suggest that their growth does not contradict our general hypothesis concerning the impact of homogenization. First, the base of the Socialist movement was not exclusively or even predominantly in manufacturing or in the industries dominated by large employers. Much Socialist

Party strength came from small towns and rural areas, in some senses more of a successor to the agrarian Populist movement than a reflection of spreading working-class militance during those particular years (see Kipnis, 1952; Weinstein, 1967; and Green, 1980, ch. 3). Second, the problems that the IWW faced indicate the strength of the employers' movement as much as or more than the strength of working-class resistance. The Western Federation of Miners was itself weak when it helped launch the IWW, having suffered crippling defeats in their battles with western mining interests from 1902 to 1904 (Foner, 1972, vol. 4). The IWW had little luck with its strikes and organizing in manufacturing areas from its founding until the McKees Rock rebellion of 1909–1910 (Foner, 1972, vol. 4; Green, 1980, ch. 3). Even the notable successes in 1912 in Lawrence, Massachusetts, and Paterson, New Jersey, depended on the IWW's ability to overcome the ethnic divisions that employers had been able to manipulate with such success.

We have argued that corporations were able to consolidate a new structure of labor management after the turn of the century. Their growing ability to moderate, isolate, and overwhelm the various strands of working-class struggle was obviously critical for this consolidation. Our analysis suggests the factors that played the most important roles in supporting this attenuation of working-class protest: the growing disciplinary effectiveness of the reserve army of labor (a result of the increasing substitutability of semiskilled workers) and new corporate labor-management policies aimed at internal diffusion and fragmentation of workers' strengths.

Many economic historians, particularly Marxists, have placed virtually singular emphasis on the disciplinary force of the reserve army of labor. This factor clearly had important effects, particularly from 1900 to 1914, when the acceleration of immigration dramatically increased the rate of replenishment of the reserve army. But the simple reserve army analysis, although necessary, is not sufficient to explain all the major events of this period. We would conclude in general that the effectiveness of the reserve army was greatly strengthened by new corporate policies designed explicitly to increase the internal leverage of corporations over workers. It is difficult to explain the differential outcomes of the three principal industrial union drives of the first two decades, for example, with a simple reserve army analysis. All three groups of industrial workers were exposed to the continuing pressure of the reserve army and all three industries included large proportions of unskilled, semiskilled, and foreign workers. We have suggested above that these differential outcomes are attributable at least in part to the differences in industrial structure and corporate policies between mining and apparel, on the one hand, and iron and steel, on the other.

We are joined in this kind of general conclusion, as we have also noted above, by many contemporary observers: The U.S. Immigration Commission (1911a) concluded that self-conscious corporate manipulations of ethnic differences had clearly helped weaken the industrial union movement; Graham Taylor (1915) argued that plant movement to the suburbs had helped isolate workers and diffuse some of the spreading protest before the turn of the century; whereas Atkins and Lasswell (1924), Feldman (1925), Jones (1925), and Slichter (1919) all emphasized the impact of new corporate personnel policies designed to move workers around within the factory and to create artificial job and wage incentives for the purposes of dissolving potential worker unity.

At the same time, we would emphasize that it is not necessary to attempt to disentangle the separate effects of the reserve army and the new, explicit corporate policies designed to reinforce homogenization in order to compare their respective significance, since the effects of the reserve army and corporate innovations in labor management were interdependent and mutually reinforcing. The success of large corporations at consolidating their strength and profits between 1900 and 1930 derived from their ability to harness the force of the reserve army of labor with a new set of personnel policies capable of intensifying the reserve army's effects. The profound impact of the homogenization of labor resulted from this historically powerful conjuncture.

The period of decay: 1920s to World War II

The decay of homogenization, which began in the late 1920s, became full-fledged in the Great Depression. Most observers correctly note that employers were never stronger in their battles with workers than in the years immediately following World War I. Employers did benefit from their continuing homogenization of the work force and their successful assaults on the union movement. Upon closer inspection, however, it appears that some decay had already begun to develop in the systems of labor management. With the onset of the Depression, these weaknesses multiplied rapidly, and the need for new systems of labor management became all the more apparent.

The power and flexibility that the companies had created for themselves permitted an additional burst of mechanization and speedup in the first years of the 1920s. Labor productivity increased rapidly between 1921 and 1923 (Mills, 1932, pp. 197, 297). Value added per worker increased much more rapidly than it had during the previous two decades; this increase can not be explained by a correspondingly rapid increase in investment or in the value of the capital stock.[40] As Slichter noted (1928, p. 635, italics in the original) about the early 1920s, "physical output per worker is extremely flexible and *under favorable conditions,* can be quickly and substantially increased." Thus, the available data are consistent with the hypothesis that employers engaged in rapid speedup during the early and mid-1920s, taking advantage of labor's weakness; this speedup explains as much or more of the continuing increase in labor productivity during the 1920s as is explained by continuing mechanization.

In these respects, as we have already noted in the previous section, the early 1920s represented the final triumph of the consolidation of the drive system. Its successes had not masked its contradictions, however, and some problems in the system of labor management had already become apparent.

The first problem to appear was high labor turnover. Even during the triumphs of the early 1920s, labor turnover rates remained extremely high (see the discussion in Feldman, 1925, pp. 5 ff.). Observers such as Slichter and Feldman regarded high turnover as a sign that the drive system was not working well. It was becoming increasingly apparent, according to Feldman (1925, p. 62), that "behind the confusion of fluctuating labor requirements there is a greater chaos of inefficient management of sales, finance, production, and personnel." It was equally clear, as Slichter noted (1920, pp. 337, 343), that turnover rates had begun to serve for many employers as proxies for "the degree of discontent within the plant... [and] revolt against the ... drudgery of modern repetitive factory work."

The second problem apparently arose in response to the success of the earlier systems of homogenization and the employers' campaign against unions. In the earlier craft system, workers forged important bonds with one another through their social relationships in production. Where workers had unions, unions helped protect those social relations or helped create new ones. As a result of the process of homogenization and the weakness of unions in many sectors, worker resistance was effectively driven underground, particularly after World War I. Employers began to discover that workers had highly developed "informal work groups," which conducted a kind of subterranean restriction of output (Leiserson, 1931; Mathewson, 1931). On the surface, it appeared that the drive system had intensified production. Underneath the surface, it appeared that workers had developed informal methods for reducing their vulnerability to that system. The employers' success created a surprising contradiction: Greater employer power produced increasingly hidden worker resistance, which prompted ever-greater employer vigilance, thereby only heightening the spiral. Mathewson clearly noted this contradiction (1931, p. 68): "Time study . . . owes its origin largely to the feeling of working people . . . that they must hide from their employers their real capacity for work . . . [But further time study further] stimulates deliberate efforts on the part of employees to hold back production." The results seemed clearer and clearer by the end of the 1920s. As Mathewson's classic study concluded (p. 146), "restriction is a widespread institution, deeply entrenched in the working habits of American laboring people."

The so-called drive system thus created a situation in which employers were pulled in contradictory directions. By the mid-1920s it was already clear to observers like Feldman (1925, p. 239) that employers had to abandon "the old-time haphazard methods of hiring labor." The general dynamic of accumulation proved to be more powerful than the specific criticisms and proposals of people like Slichter and Feldman, however. The growth and high profits of the 1920s convinced many employers that the drive system was still in fine shape. The high rate of mechanization in the early part of the decade appears to have fostered high rates of "permanent separations" among industrial workers by the mid-1920s (Mills, 1932; Jacoby, 1981, ch. 6), reflecting workers' intimidation and inclinations to quit their jobs.[41] The system was still working well.

With hindsight, indeed, we can see that the drive system was working *too* well; the disproportions between stagnant workers' wages, rising labor productivity, and soaring profits soon brought the entire economy to a crash. And the Great Depression provided the context in which the formation of the great industrial unions delivered the fatal blow to the drive system. Companies had been unable to "extirpate unionism, root and branch" from U.S. industry. With the new industrial unions came shop stewards, contractual rights, grievance procedures – all representing an apparatus of organized worker power that circumscribed the tyranny of the foreman. The drive system could not survive these changes. The origins of labor segmentation began amid the decay of homogenization.

5

The segmentation of labor: 1920s to the present

The system of labor management institutionalized after the turn of the century in the United States displayed deepening problems during the 1920s and 1930s. But by the late 1950s, many of those problems had been solved. Labor struggle had moderated, productivity in both manufacturing and the services was rising rapidly, and large U.S. corporations were prospering in the world market.

The solutions to the earlier labor problems were developed through a historical process that operated at two different levels. At an aggregate level, the U.S. and world economies experienced a severe depression, a world war, a growth in governmental management of economic activity, and a reconstitution of the world capitalist economy in the late 1940s and early 1950s. At a microeconomic level in the United States, corporations sought new methods of solving their labor-management problems, workers finally succeeded in forming large and powerful industrial labor unions, and corporations and unions battled during the 1940s over the structure of their interdependent relationship. The aggregate developments occurred interactively with the microeconomic changes. Out of that process, new systems of control in the labor process and structures in labor markets became consolidated in the United States.

In this chapter we argue that these new structures shaping the labor process and labor markets produced a segmentation of labor. Jobs (and labor markets) became qualitatively differentiated in their logic and dynamics. More specifically, we argue that two processes of divergence produced labor segmentation. First, structured labor processes in a "primary" sector diverged from labor processes in "secondary" sectors. Second, within the primary sector, jobs involving relatively more "independent" work became increasingly differentiated from jobs involving relatively more "subordinate" work. These two processes generated three divergent labor segments – three qualitatively distinct groupings of jobs and labor market mechanisms. These three segments include the *secondary* segment and, within the group of primary jobs, the *subordinate primary* segment and the *independent primary* segment.

Before beginning our historical elaboration of these processes, it is important to warn against two possible misinterpretations of our argument. First, at several points in this chapter we appear to attribute a singularly determinate importance to the self-conscious and purposeful strategic planning of large corporations and to the responses of labor unions to those efforts. Such strategic efforts were indeed undertaken by both sides. But we also argue that broader systemic forces generated the dynamics of capitalist development in the United States and limited the range of possible solutions that corporations and unions could pursue. The effects of corporate planning and labor counterplanning, in other words, were constrained by the trajectory of the economy.

Second, it seems important to emphasize in advance that our argument traces historical tendencies and not final outcomes. Our argument could be interpreted as suggesting the static conclusion that all workers in the United States by the late 1960s could be categorized exhaustively into three different labor segments. This interpretation misstates our intention. We advance the hypothesis that the evolving structure of labor processes and labor markets was creating increasingly differentiated labor segments. But that argument does not lead us to conclude that all jobs could already be categorized into one of our three segments by the 1960s. Many jobs had not yet been affected by the tendencies toward segmentation, many jobs undoubtedly occupied intermediate positions, and many jobs (although a declining portion) lay essentially outside and remained mostly unaffected by the dynamics of the capitalist sector itself.

We develop our argument about the segmentation of labor first by reviewing the dynamics of the world and U.S. economies during the period from the 1920s until the present and then by tracing the tendency toward segmentation through its successive periods of exploration, consolidation, and, in the present period, decay.

Growth and stagnation in the world economy

Spreading economic instability during the 1920s led to the Great Depression of the 1930s. It scarcely seems necessary to review the magnitude of the crisis of the 1930s or to justify our calling it a crisis. However, four clearly recognized features of the Great Depression are important for the argument we make about its resolution. First, the stagnation and instability it generated required unusual collective political intervention, based partly on class interests, in the ordinary

166

process of capitalist economic activity. Second, the Depression lasted so long largely because it took several years for corporations, workers, and the state to work out a means of achieving this kind of collective intervention. Third, recovery from the Depression was stimulated largely by the preparation for and conduct of World War II; in this sense, the wartime years constitute as important a part of the period of the resolution of crisis as the years immediately before or after the war. Fourth, the character and intensity of class struggle in the United States from the mid-1930s through the late 1940s dramatize the importance of our general argument that the content of the new institutional structure is shaped by the character of the class struggle during the preceding period of crisis.

By the early 1950s, the world capitalist system had been substantially reconstituted. Few institutions necessary for capital accumulation looked anything like their counterparts immediately before or after World War I. The world economy had been stabilized, grounded in the strength and mediating role of the U.S. economy. The Bretton Woods monetary system set up under American leadership in 1944 created the conditions for the resurgence of international trade. Many large U.S. corporations expanded their international role, opening new markets and sites of production in both the industrialized and the underdeveloped worlds. The augmented power and stability of large U.S. corporations permitted much greater financial independence from banks and greater reliance on internal sources of investment funds. Throughout the industrialized nations, a collective bargaining structure accommodated labor unions and moderated working-class militancy. The state played a much more active role in guiding the economy and legitimating the institutions of advanced capitalist society. New sources of energy and intermediate products, building heavily upon the expanded petrochemical industries, helped facilitate both rapid expansion and new lines of products. Particularly in the United States, final demand was increasingly reconstituted around the automobile and single-unit suburban housing. In this context, the institutions structuring labor management and labor markets also experienced qualitative transformation.

The decisiveness of these institutional transformations is reflected in the aggregate economic data for the post–World War II period. Between 1947 and 1966, industrial output in the United States grew at an annual compound percentage rate of 5.0 percent; in the original six countries of the Common Market, 8.9 percent; and in Japan, 9.6 percent (Mandel, 1975, p. 142). Between 1938 and 1967, the volume of world trade grew at an annual cumulative rate of 4.8 percent per year, twelve times the rate of increase for the years from 1913 through 1937 (p. 142). In the United States, the real net value of structures and equipment in manufacturing (in 1958 prices) increased by 107 percent between 1947 and 1968 (*Historical Statistics,* 1975, series P-119). Output per worker in the private economy in the United States more than doubled over the same period, and real personal income per capita (in 1958 prices) increased by 70 percent during those twenty-two years (*Historical Statistics,* 1975, series W-22, F-25). To many economists who observed the U.S. and world economies in the mid-1960s, it appeared that stable and prosperous growth was here to stay.

In the early 1970s, however, the structure of the world economy began to disintegrate rapidly, ending an era of international economic prosperity. After 1973, growth rates suffered and productivity dramatically slackened in all of the industrialized countries. Inflation began to soar, and stagflation emerged as a new ghost haunting advanced capitalist economies. Beginning about 1967, increasingly intensive and frequent strikes by organized labor began to unsettle the labor peace that had dominated the 1950s and 1960s. Political instability soon followed, characterized by sharp debates about the levels of taxation and social services that were feasible in advanced economies.

Aggregate economic data indicate the end of the period of prosperity. Rates of growth in industrial output have slowed throughout the advanced capitalist world since the late 1960s (Organization for Economic Cooperation and Deveopment, various years). In 1975 the volume of world trade contracted for the first time since the 1930s (Mandel, 1977, p. 19). The median worker's real spendable earnings in the United States has stagnated since 1973, falling by 1981 to the levels of 1961–1962 (*Monthly Labor Review,* July 1981, table 20).

The crisis has also been reflected in the spreading instability of the world economy itself. Protectionist pressure has mounted throughout the advanced world. Third World debt to the advanced countries has continued to increase. Higher oil prices have wrought havoc in conventional trading and consumption patterns throughout the advanced world. Most business analysts project rates of growth through the 1980s at levels far below those of the 1950s and 1960s.

This pattern of economic growth and stagnation provides the backdrop to our analysis of labor segmentation in the United States. It would be misleading, however, to characterize this backdrop primarily in quantitative terms. The most important dimensions of this context of long swings in economic activity involved the qualitative institutional transformations effected by the emergence of a new social structure of accumulation.

The postwar social structure of accumulation

A new social structure of accumulation emerged from the class conflict and political realignment of the dozen or so years following 1935. The outcome was a set of institutions governing accumulation quite unlike what had existed before. Although the transformations occurred on a world scale, it is sufficient here to focus on their domestic dimensions.

Within the United States, the period during which these new institutions emerged can be divided into two distinct parts. The first half-dozen years, roughly 1935 to 1941, witnessed historic working-class victories. The most notable achievement involved the building of the Congress of Industrial Organizations and the unionization of the mass production industries, a goal pursued by the labor movement for at least half a century. But other victories might be counted as well: the entrenchment of labor in a central position in Democratic Party politics; the passage of the Social Security Act, the Wagner Act, and other legislation; and the first enduring and relatively comprehensive alliance of black and white workers. These advances ensured that any successful new social structure of accumulation would have to accommodate this new working-class power. At the end of the nineteenth century capitalists had largely defeated labor and had consolidated the new set of institutions that reflected their disproportionate class power. But in the post-CIO era, working-class groups maintained sufficient power to block any set of arrangements that excluded labor and did not express class compromise.

The phase of aggressive working-class gains came to a conclusion with the ambiguous results of the 1946 strike wave. The balance began to swing the other way, as antilabor forces pushed the persecution of the Communists, the curtailing of union powers contained in the Taft-Hartley Act, and the redirection of the social agenda from social reform to fighting the Cold War.

The new social structure of accumulation that emerged from this period thus necessarily reflected class compromise and explicitly incorporated a new level of working-class power. It was rooted in five central pieces of legislation or treaty: the Social Security Act, which provided the main underpinning to the welfare state; the Wagner Act, which legalized the rights of workers to independent unions; the Taft-Hartley Act, which restricted union weapons such as secondary boycotts, purged union leaders who were Communists, and in general limited the effectiveness of the union's industrial (strike) powers to bargaining within individual industries; the Employment Act of 1946, which committed the federal government to antidepression policies;

169

and, finally, the Bretton Woods monetary system, which promoted world trade and placed the dollar in the advantageous position of a privileged international reserve currency.

Beyond these legal foundations, the new social structure of accumulation incorporated a number of crucial arrangements. In what amounted to an effective quid pro quo, organized workers were deprived of their power to use industrial action (general strikes, sitdowns, secondary boycotts, etc.) in pursuit of class-wide gains; union resources and militance were directed instead to contestation over state policy and electoral politics. Thus, class conflict over minimum wage legislation, safety and health issues, provision of medical care, antidiscrimination policy, and so forth was deflected from the industrial to the state policy arena.

Other elements in the new "accord" included acceptance by major industries of the permanence of the unions (where already established); "pattern-bargaining" in wages, by which real wage gains tied to productivity increases regularly increased workers' incomes while maintaining an overall wage structure; and support by all groups, including the top AFL–CIO leadership, of the large military budgets that simultaneously created jobs at home and protected corporate investments abroad.

This new social structure of accumulation reflected the success of the New Deal coalition – the Democratic majority that emerged after the elections of 1934 and 1936 – in institutionalizing the new relations of power in ways that stabilized class relations and permitted rapid growth. Forty years earlier, Woodrow Wilson's election had marked the only interruption in Republican rule between 1896 and 1932; yet Wilson's years had confirmed rather than challenged the dominance of the Republican program by indicating how far the opposition Democrats had traveled to accept the outlines of the Republican solution. So too, in 1952, the election of the Eisenhower administration, explicitly committed to efficient administration (rather than repeal) of the New Deal programs, sealed the latter's permanence.

The segmentation of labor

The origins of segmentation date back to the explorations of the 1920s and 1930s; a new system of control in the labor process and corresponding labor market structures became consolidated after World War II; and these systems began to decay during the 1970s. We develop these arguments by tracing the process of segmentation through the three characteristic periods of its development.

The period of exploration: 1920s to World War II
In the early 1920s the large corporations appeared stronger than ever
before. By this date, as Edwards shows (1979, ch. 5), the leading firms
had finally achieved the stability of moderated product market competition for which the merger movement had been a necessary but not
sufficient condition. This external stability helped permit an intensive
internal reorganization of corporate structure (Chandler, 1962,
1977). The repression of radicals immediately after World War I and
the largely successful campaign against unions in the early 1920s provided corporations with a further margin for the intensive exploitation of labor. The drive policy and the homogenization of the labor
process and labor markets appeared to be working with great success.
success.

Once many large corporations and their management experts had
examined their production operations, however, they discovered that
the drive policy of labor management contained contradictions. Slichter anticipated many of these perceptions in his careful analysis of
labor turnover in 1919. "The pursuit of a 'drive'... policy engenders
animosity and antagonism among the workers," he concluded (1919,
p. 427), "which enormously complicated the problem of working out
a satisfactory program." Many large employers were becoming increasingly aware, he observed (p. 414), "of the fundamentally defective
character of their methods of handling men and of the superficial and
inadequate character of their devices for improving their relations
with their men." Even in the larger companies, Wilcock later observed
(1961, p. 282), the prevalent system of management "was rarely sufficient to the needs of the business, both because of internal problems
of control and because of outside pressures."

We noted at the end of Chapter 4 that many companies became
particularly concerned about problems of labor turnover and informal work group resistance. Perhaps even more important for the
argument that follows, many companies began to recognize that those
problems were produced by the prevalent systems of labor management, originating in the contradictions of the drive system itself.

Both Slichter (1919, pp. 200 ff.) and Feldman (1925, pp. 27 ff.)
emphasize that high rates of labor turnover were weighted heavily
with voluntary quits. The growing phenomenon of worker dissatisfaction represented one form of worker response to irregular employment, transfers, and arbitrary supervisory authority. Feldman (1925,
pp. 278 ff.) also presents evidence suggesting that the intensity of
informal work group resistance derived from resistance to the prevalent system of management, and, in particular, from "a general sentiment of disapproval among the workers against the use of the power

of transfer." Some personnel experts observed that the short-run effectiveness of the explicit strategies of divide-and-conquer became counterproductive in the longer run. Such policies only pushed workers faster toward industrial unionism to overcome those divisions. Slichter also anticipated this reaction (1919, p. 438), arguing that "coercive methods impede the [labor] movement only temporarily. In the long run they stimulate and strengthen it ... The temporary victory of the employers is achieved at the cost of increasing the strength of labor's forces."

Wishing to address these problems and prodded by the new "liberal" school of personnel management, many major corporations began to experiment during World War I and the 1920s with new methods of organizing production. To begin with, many large employers observed that effective systems of labor management depended upon successful systems of demand management. Given labor's resistance to irregular employment, personnel experts began to view regular employment as a necessary condition for more stable labor relations. But regular employment in turn depended on a stable volume of production; that depended, in large part, on relatively steady product demand. In his catalog of the wide variety of experiments at regularizing employment in the early 1920s, Feldman emphasized (1925, pp. 62, 74) that the experiments began with new methods for product distribution because regular employment "depends chiefly on the degree of control achieved over demand ... Back of these [experiments] is the fundamental policy of continuous operation." Increasingly, many large corporations came to see what Feldman called (p. 82) "sales engineering" as a necessary complement to more systematic policies of labor management.

Many large corporations also began to rationalize the operations of their labor production systems, to gain more control over design and knowledge of production, and to plan the individual labor activities of their workers in ever greater detail. These efforts were clearly related to Taylor's ideas of "scientific management." Riegel confirms (1942, p. 118) that "in the early years of the present century, the scientific management movement slowly took root, but in the twenties and thirties, it spread with remarkable speed."

Many large employers placed greater emphasis on developing personnel and labor-management departments that would plan and redesign the operation of production (see Atkins and Lasswell, 1924; Feldman, 1925; Jones, 1925; and Eilbert, 1959). In the 1920s, at least, this growth of personnel administration occurred by transferring supervisory functions from the foremen to the personnel administrators. Consequently, nonproduction workers did not grow in relative numbers. Delehanty (1968, table A-1) shows that the ratio of nonproduction workers to production workers remained essentially constant between 1920 and 1929, after an apparently rapid growth between 1899 and 1919. It is also notable, in further support of this point, that the number of foremen in manufacturing actually declined in absolute terms, from 296,000 to 293,000, between 1920 and 1930 (*Historical Statistics,* 1975, series D-393).[1]

Corporate managers began to organize job tasks more systematically in order to permit more control, greater differentiation among workers' tasks, and greater fragmentation of informal work groups. Slichter had argued in 1919 (p. 436) that "employers so far have not fully appreciated as a means of combatting unionism the tremendous possibilities of the plan of organizing the work in their plants into minutely subdivided jobs ... [with] systematic lines of promotion." Particularly when companies were introducing new technologies, as Smith emphasized (1939, pp. 18 ff.), they found it essential to redesign job assignments in order to facilitate the introduction of the new machines without encountering labor resistance. As Smith concludes in his detailed study (p. 137), "the past basis of industrial relations thus determines the rate at which management can progress in making a labor saving installation without causing unrest."

Managers also sought to achieve much greater regularity of employment, placing increasing reliance on offering stability of work to their employees and reducing reliance on outright discharges. Contemporary observers' accounts suggest, moreover, that these efforts at stabilizing employment were directed not only at reducing costly labor turnover but also at limiting the power of informal work groups. The famous Hawthorne experiments at Western Electric intended to contribute to this process through a systematic analysis of methods for improving productivity and reducing workers' resistance (see summaries in Roethlisberger and Dickson, 1969). As Mathewson concluded in general (1931, p. 68), "Time study ... owes its origin largely to the feeling of working people ... that they must hide from their employers their real capacity for work."

Many large corporations eliminated the high-cost departments and plants that could not be made consonant with their new efforts at systematic labor management. Average plant size in manufacturing declined slightly during the 1920s (National Industrial Conference Board, 1933). Jerome emphasizes (1934, pp. 237 ff.) the importance of this elimination of inefficient plants and its connection with the decline in average employment per establishment in manufacturing.

Corporation leaders also moved to remedy the shortage of skilled labor created by their own earlier assaults on the craft system. Craft shops had been the principal source of skilled workers throughout the nineteenth century. As a consequence of homogenization, however, fewer and fewer skilled workers were generated through the craft system itself. As Stone notes (1975), some large steel firms began to pay attention to this problem as early as the turn of the century. Indeed, vocational training institutes were set up as early as 1894 in the textile industry, which had experienced the earliest degradation of craft work. Until the 1920s, however, neither corporate planners nor educational planners had systematically attended to the problem of generating a greater supply of skilled workers (Douglas, 1921). Building upon ideas born at the turn of the century, corporations in the 1920s both created their own private vocational training institutes and encouraged the development of vocational training through the public school systems. Thus, the rapid growth of the engineering profession dates from World War I and the 1920s (*Historical Statistics*, 1975, series D-255; see Bowles and Gintis, 1976, ch. 7, and Noble, 1977, for further discussion of this development).

Finally, many large corporations began to embed their new efforts in systematic functional divisions among departments and offices. Under the drive system, as we noted in Chapter 4, most corporations had tended to move employees around from department to department and to alternate hiring and firing among workers from different ethnic and racial groups. During the 1920s, some employers began to experiment with the systematic allocation of different groups of workers to different plant divisions in order to embed job segregation into the job structure itself. Ford began to allocate blacks to the foundry in the early 1920s (Reich, 1981a, ch. 6), U.S. Steel began to channel black workers into specific shops in its steel plants (Greer, 1979), and rubber companies also began to make similar use of black employees (Jeszeck, 1981). Davies argues similarly about the "feminization of clerical employment" (1975), contending that employers began to segregate female employees into specific categories of clerical work in order to facilitate their degradation and the routinization of many clerical jobs.

We should emphasize that these early exploratory efforts were limited primarily to large corporations. The accounts by Feldman (1925) mention the prominent role played, for example, by General Electric, Westinghouse, Procter and Gamble, International Harvester, Ford, and U.S. Rubber. Edwards's more recent analysis (1979) also demonstrates the important exploratory role played by large corporations during the 1920s and early 1930s (see also Jacoby, 1981, chs. 5-6).

Indeed, it would be surprising if small firms could even have joined in the experiments. Few small firms could afford centralized personnel planning. Without such planning capacity, few small firms were likely to be able to pursue the job redivision, labor allocation, and redistribution of production among plants that characterized this early exploration. Small firms were also unlikely to be able to afford separate vocational institutes or to operate on a scale that would facilitate systematic segregation of various ethnic, racial, and sexual groups among different departments and offices.[2]

We should also emphasize the clearly experimental character of these early explorations. Many people in the personnel relations movement had begun to advocate what they called more "liberal" labor-management policies as early as World War I. Spurred by these proposals, some corporations followed a variety of the experimental paths we have described in the preceding paragraphs. These early explorations were not widespread during the 1920s, however, because the consolidation of homogenization was still bearing such bountiful fruit. Jacoby (1981, ch. 6) provides a persuasive argument, indeed, that the appeal and influence of these more sophisticated policies actually declined during the 1920s; at that time the drive system was working so well that corporations found little reason to regard changes in their labor-management practices as either necessary or useful.

Despite these temporary setbacks, however, the proponents of these new policies understood the ultimate necessity of a transformation of the drive system because of the class character of the frictions it generated. They understood these experiments as aimed in large part at increasing corporations' general control over the production process in order to permit and facilitate subsequent efforts at cost reduction. Slichter argued clearly (1919, pp. 426, 427) that new labor policies were necessary primarily to benefit the class of employers as a whole rather than any individual employers by themselves:

> The pursuit of a niggardly and drastic policy toward labor
> may profit a few employers but be unprofitable if practiced by
> employers in general ... The pursuit of a liberal labor
> policy ... benefits capital just as does an increase in the
> number of laborers. The profitableness of the policy, how-
> ever, depends upon its pursuit by employers in general. To a
> single employer or a few employers, the policy may be un-
> profitable because the advantages accrue to employers in
> general rather than only to those particular employers who
> incurred the cost of the policy ... When ... a 'drive' policy is

175

practiced by employers in general, affecting the entire working class, widespread and dangerous animosity may be aroused against employers. Although single employers may find a 'drive' policy practical, the interests of employers as a class may demand the pursuit of a liberal policy.

The Great Depression. Once the Depression had struck U.S. business in 1929, corporations no longer had the luxury of harvesting the fruits of homogenization. Two effects of the Depression immediately focused serious attention on the need for new systems of labor management. First, the collapse of profits itself pressured corporations to consider whatever methods were available which might restore profitability and improve their control over the labor process. Second, the Depression led fairly quickly to worker dissatisfaction – and ultimately, of course, to the emergence of industrial unions. The industrial union movement constituted a new force with which large employers had to contend, directly challenging some of the most important elements of both the drive system and the early explorations of more sophisticated policies.

These two effects cannot easily be separated, particularly since the two developments occurred more or less simultaneously. We trace their impact first by summarizing evidence on the spread of corporate explorations, then by tracing the growth of worker unrest and unionization, and finally by exploring the connections between the two.

The rapid exploration of new personnel policies seems to date from the early 1930s and particularly from the years following the passage of the National Recovery Act and the first thrust of strike activity after 1933. Jacoby (1981, ch. 7) documents the change: Between 1929 and 1935, the percentage of large firms (over 250 employees) with personnel departments nearly doubled; the proportion of large firms with centralized employment hiring and selection increased by half; and the percentage of large firms applying formal rating systems for internal promotion grew by nearly three-quarters. What seems most striking, as Jacoby notes, is that this rapid rate of diffusion of the new personnel policies contrasts so sharply with the stagnation – and in a few cases, actual contraction – of those policies during the late 1920s. This acceleration seems especially illustrative of the broader analytic hypotheses we have applied throughout this book: It took a period of real crisis, and of working-class response to that crisis, to induce employers actively and intensively to explore and apply new systems of labor management.

The working-class response could certainly not be ignored; the na-

ture and extent of the movement toward unionization during the
1930s has been amply documented. The frequency of strikes provides
a first index. The number of strikes per year jumped from an average
of 753 a year in 1927-1932 to an annual average of 2,542 a year from
1933 to 1938, reaching a peak of 4,740 strikes in 1937. The proportion of workers involved in strikes as a percentage of total employment increased from an annual average of 1.35 percent in 1927-1932
to an annual average of 5.3 percent in 1933-1938 (calculated from
Historical Statistics, 1975, series D-972, D-975).

Equally important, the focus of workers' strikes changed as the
industrial union movement grew in force. The percentage of striking
workers involved in strikes aimed at union recognition rose fairly
steadily, from only 13.9 percent in 1927 to peaks of 51.5 percent, 51.4
percent, and 59.8 percent in 1934, 1935, and 1937, respectively (*Historical Statistics*, 1975, series D-982, D-984). Strikes also acquired a
broader scope as unions organized on an industry-wide basis. The
percentage of striking workers involved in strikes affecting eleven or
more establishments (per strike) increased from 34.4 percent in 1929
to 65 percent in 1934 and 66 percent in 1935. Furthermore, the
effectiveness of strikes also increased. The percentage of strikes that
resulted in "substantial gains to workers" increased from an average
of 16.5 percent in 1927-1928 to an average of 27.4 percent in 1935-
1936 (based on data reported in Peterson, 1938, pp. 49, 68).

The form of strikes also changed, as industrial workers turned to
the sit-down strike to advance the effectiveness of their protests. According to Bureau of Labor Statistics data, nearly 400,000 workers
participated in sit-down strikes at their peak in 1936-1937 (cited in
Bernstein, 1971, p. 500).

The results of this spreading labor rebellion are clearly reflected in
the data on labor union membership. Union membership had remained constant at roughly 3.6 million between 1923 and 1930.
Unions were hit hard by the first years of the Depression, with membership dropping to 2.86 million in 1933.[3] But as strikes spread and
working-class organization increased, union membership soared.
Total union membership climbed to 7.28 million in 1940. Much of
this 4.4 million increase in seven years reflected the birth of the CIO
industrial unions. Membership in unions affiliated with the AFL increased from 3.0 million in 1930 to 4.2 million in 1940; the CIO
unions, accounting for none of the union total in 1930-1936, accounted for 3.6 million by 1940 (*Historical Statistics*, 1975, series
D-929, D-931, D-943). According to Wolman's estimates, the percentage of manufacturing workers organized in labor unions increased
from 9 percent in 1930 to 34 percent in 1940 (Wolman, 1952).

Most labor historians have emphasized the struggle for the right to form industrial unions as the principal focus of the organizing drives of the 1930s and the passage of the Wagner Act as the key step that legitimated labor's right to organize. We would supplement that analysis with some additional hypotheses. Labor organizing during the Depression, particularly as the CIO movement gained force after 1933, represented a worker response both to the drive system institutionalized by the process of homogenization and the more recent strands of experimentation pursued by large corporations; moreover, unions were most successful in work places where the drive system achieved a technological basis. The character of work and union activity and the location of organizing efforts in this period supports these hypotheses.

Workers in many industries in the 1930s were responding to the pace and character of mechanization characteristic of the period of homogenization. This concern appeared not only among the craft workers whose job security and status were jeopardized by the first wave of homogenization but also among the operatives whose pace of work was regulated by mechanized technology and whose job tasks were being recomposed around new technology. Workers were concerned with what Edwards (1979) terms "technical control," the way in which technology was used to define and alter the employer–worker relation.

Many contemporary observers noted this type of activity. Smith (1939, pp. 39 ff.) emphasizes that workers resisted technological change in those situations where they not only feared for their jobs but also anticipated disruption in their working routines and in the informal work group relationships upon which they depended. (He also emphasizes [p. 59] that these reactions were just as prevalent even in nonunion shops.) Riegel concludes (1942, p. 27) that worker resentment of technological change was "noticeably much more marked among workers in large and prosperous firms than among employees in small, competitively vulnerable companies," apparently because workers in those plants were more vulnerable to changes in the social relations surrounding their job tasks. "Accordingly," he argues (p. 118), "when the union movement experienced rapid expansion in 1933 and the following years, the control of technological change was one problem to which unions, and particularly the new industrial unions, gave much consideration." Slichter (1941, pp. 242 ff.) also emphasizes that the industrial unions were much more likely than traditional craft unions to seek to control and monitor technological change than to oppose it completely. They were more concerned with the way new machines affected the allocation of workers among jobs than with the destructive impact of the machines on the job privileges of the particular workers directly affected. While craft workers tended to resist the initial process of homogenization, workers forming industrial unions tended to resist further changes in work assignments after the initial process of homogenization had already transformed the production process.

The organizing drives of the 1930s also focused much attention on regaining leverage over working conditions. This concern was prompted both by the harshness of the drive system and by the emphasis placed on employer discretion and control over task definition in the new experimental methods of labor management. Brody (1968, pp. 177–178) and Slichter (1941, ch. 6) emphasize that worker and union protests during the Depression focused not just on wage cuts but also on management discretion over the pace and quality of work. This concern emerged through union focus on the necessity of *grievance procedures,* an organizing demand that articulated workers' concern about their lack of influence over working conditions. Indeed, Derber (1975) argues that workers' demands for grievance procedures constituted the most important organizing objective after the basic drive for union recognition. Until the Depression, only workers in printing, the mines, the railroads, and the needle trades had any institutionalized grievance procedures (p. 116). By the end of the Depression, almost all the industrial unions had won some kind of grievance procedure. Bernstein concludes (1971, pp. 775–776):

> Perhaps the most significant accomplishment of the new unions was to establish grievance procedures . . . While these procedures for the most part admitted grievances over the whole range of shop issues, their most significant immediate impact was in the area of discipline and discharge. The employer was now required to show cause for taking such action, and the worker who appealed to the grievance procedure was afforded representation and many other elements of due process. Here again, management's power was narrowed. Workers won protection against arbitrary or discriminatory punishment.

Finally, workers in the 1930s also objected to employers' use of promotion and job allocation. The explorations of the 1920s, as we noted above, sought to extend management discretion in promotion as a way of dividing workers, encouraging competition, and systematically regulating the allocation of labor within individual departments and plants. Workers responded by complaining about arbitrary promotional standards and supervisory favoritism (see Slichter, 1941, chs. 3–6; and Brody, 1968, p. 177). These complaints led to spreading demands for seniority systems. Millis and Montgomery reported (1945, p. 456) that seniority rules had been "rather exceptional" before the 1930s, limited largely to the printing trades and the railroads. Increasingly during the 1930s, they conclude, "the desire for recognition of seniority became strong."

Comparing union contracts negotiated during the 1920s with union contracts negotiated during the 1930s, Slichter found (1941, pp. 105–107) that while only 33 percent of his sample of contracts from 1923 to 1929 had some kind of contractual restriction on management hiring and layoff prerogatives, 72 percent of (sampled) contracts negotiated between 1933 and 1939 provided for some kind of limitation on those prerogatives. Of the 290 contracts with restrictions on management in the later sample, 252 contained clauses explicitly relying on the seniority principle in some variant or another. As Bernstein concludes (1971, p. 775), the seniority systems were not aimed only at providing "job security for employees with longer service." At least as importantly, the unions wanted "to restrict management's discretion both in selecting the worker considered best qualified for the job and in making arbitrary or discriminatory choices."

The loci of successful industrial union organizing drives in the 1930s also indicate an important connection between large corporations' recent explorations with new systems of management and the appearance of mass production unionism. Although we have not been able to compile a comprehensive catalog of the corporations that explored new labor systems most intensively in the 1920s, it appears that these corporations were concentrated in precisely those industries in which the most dramatic explosions of industrial unionism occurred after 1933.

During the 1920s, judging from the accounts provided by Feldman (1925, passim), Bernstein (1960, pp. 171 ff.), and Edwards (1979), what Slichter calls "liberal labor policies" were concentrated in large corporations in the following manufacturing industries: oil (Standard of New Jersey); agricultural implements (International Harvester); electrical equipment (General Electric and Westinghouse); automobiles (Ford); rubber (Goodyear and U.S. Rubber); meat-packing (Swift and Armour); and, to a lesser extent, textiles (scattered) and steel (several companies before and after the 1919 strike). Procter and Gamble, Kodak, Hills Brothers, and several arms manufacturers represent other important examples in either smaller industries or industries where those "liberal" firms seemed less typical of the rest of the industry. Of the nine industries that appear on our list of "consolidated" industries for both 1903 and 1919, eight are represented in this list of loci of labor management exploration[4] (only railroad equipment is missing). Of the other nine "nonconsolidated" two-digit industries, only textiles provides instances of exploration with the new labor-management policies during this period.

Through 1933, most of the important union organizing was not concentrated in these industries but rather continued the earlier efforts of craft workers to protect their job privileges and resist the degradation of their trades. In the early years of the Depression the International Ladies' Garment Workers Union, the Amalgamated Clothing Workers Union, and the various mine worker unions were the only significant industrial unions. As we noted in Chapter 4, the textile, apparel, and mining industries were relatively competitive and largely utilized older methods of labor management. As of 1934, according to Lester and Robie (1946), the only industrial unions with wage bargaining on a national basis were located among the garment workers (since the 1920s) and the flat glass and the West Coast pulp and paper workers (each dating from 1934).

After 1935, in marked contrast, almost all of the major organizing drives developed in industries characterized by exploration of "liberal" labor policies during the 1920s. We have compared our list of "exploring" corporations with the industrial composition of the list of major strikes for union recognition in manufacturing provided by Peterson (1938, pp. 125–151). Somewhat arbitrarily designating a major organizing drive as one involving 10,000 or more workers in strikes for union recognition in any one year between 1933 and 1936,[5] we find that the following industries from our list of "liberal" corporations all experienced major industrial union strikes during those years: iron and steel (including the other basic metals industries); machinery (principally electrical machinery and excluding transport); transportation equipment, principally automobiles; the garment industries (which had already acquired industrial unions); food, principally meat-packing; oil and chemicals; and rubber. All the major industrial union organizing drives in industries that do *not* appear to have experimented with "liberal" labor-management policies developed in industries with much more competitive product market structures: lumber and furniture, leather (primarily the fur trades), and boots and shoes.

Thus it appears that the probability of industrial unionism in U.S. manufacturing in the 1930s was greater in industrial sectors that were consolidated industries dominated by large corporations or industries that had experimented significantly with systematic methods of labor management from World War I through the early 1930s. Further research would be necessary to substantiate determinate hypotheses concerning causal connections between the earlier corporate explorations and the industrial union drives in the 1930s. Here, based on our general understanding of this period, we can only propose a relatively loose hypothesis: It is likely that production workers were responding not only to the harshness of the drive system but also to some of the greater discretionary authority portended by more recent experiments in labor-management policy. It may also be that the new liberal experiments raised expectations among workers which they *then* found it necessary to pursue through collective bargaining. We expect that further research on this critical period will help clarify both of these possible connections.

It is critical to emphasize, finally, that the rapid spread of new personnel policies did not occur only in those firms or industries that were directly experiencing industrial unionization. It was precisely the general and evidently class-based character of the rapid drive toward industrial unionism which prompted widespread employer exploration *whether or not* their companies were directly affected. One illustration of this effect comes from the data compiled by Jacoby (1981, ch. 7) on the spread of central personnel departments. He compares the proportions of workers in large firms (over 250 employees) employed by companies with personnel departments to the proportions of the entire industrial work force covered by a personnel department. The latter proportion was much lower during the 1920s – see Chapter 4 – but increased much more rapidly during the early 1930s and actually appears to have reached a higher proportion by 1935. The small unorganized firms were running scared. As the head of personnel at Sears, Roebuck later acknowledged (quoted in Jacoby, 1981, ch. 7), "The union movement has had a profound influence on personnel administration [even in unorganized firms] ... It has given personnel a function of great importance in management's eyes, and has therefore been a means for helping elevate its status."

The importance of World War II. The struggle between corporations and workers over the terms of resolution of the economic crisis did not halt suddenly in 1940. The period from 1941 to 1945, dominated by the war effort, was just as important for the ultimate shape of the new structure of labor management as the period from 1936 to 1940.

From the corporate side, corporations took major strides during the war that proved critical in later years. Many employers used the advantage of wartime discipline after 1941 to seek to regain some of the initiative and control they had surrendered to industrial unions at the end of the Depression. They encouraged arbitration of many grievance disputes, hoping to get the new grievance machinery off the shop floor. They increased dramatically the number of supervisory personnel, hoping to counter the unions' new prerogatives with respect to grievances and seniority with more intensive supervisory labor. Many employers used the opportunity provided by the War Time Labor Disputes Act and the War Labor Board to centralize the machinery that mediated production disputes between companies and unions. And many firms stepped up the pace of production, taking advantage of the war effort to justify the speedup.[6]

Many companies also used the war situation to pressure unions and the government to rid unions of radicals. From the first years of heavy wartime production in 1940–1941, companies, the media, and even government officials branded wildcat strikes as "red-inspired" and "Communist-led." Many observers have treated the purge of the unions purely as a postwar phenomenon. In fact, as Piven and Cloward argue (1977, pp. 164–165), "the red purge in the CIO that is ordinarily located in the post-war McCarthy period actually began in 1938."

Perhaps more important for the postwar consolidation era, the unions themselves moved toward accommodation with business and government during the years from 1940 to 1945. Although this accommodation occurred on a terrain favorable to labor by historical standards, labor's gains were accompanied by significant costs.

During the war the labor movement was able to press for broader union recognition, higher wages, and protection from speedup. The average number of strikes per year between 1941 and 1945 was 60 percent higher than during the peak Depression strike years, from 1933 to 1938. Although strikes were shorter during the war, nearly as high a percentage of workers was involved in strikes as during the peak organizing drives of the mid-1930s. The composition of strikes shifted, with a much higher percentage focused on wage and hour demands than during the Depression years. Still, union membership continued to climb, rising from 8.9 million in 1940 to 14.8 million in 1945. The percentage of total nonagricultural employment represented by unions, which had grown from 13.2 percent in 1935 to 26.9 percent in 1940, rose to 35.5 percent by 1945, a gain of another 9.4 percentage points (*Historical Statistics*, 1975, series D-970, D-972, D-975, D-981, D-946, and D-950, respectively). Much of this membership gain resulted from new dues-checkoff and membership maintenance procedures obtained by the unions in exchange for agreement with the wartime no-strike pledge.

The CIO leadership supported accommodation with business by opposing wildcat strikes and militant union activity. The leaders agreed to Roosevelt's no-strike pledge and sought to enforce it. Union

shop stewards also began to play a more active role in taking grievances off the shop floor and centralizing grievance adjudication machinery. Union commitment to arbitration and multistep grievance
procedures dates essentially from the war years. As a result, the gulf
between paid union leaders and the rank-and-file that had begun to
appear by 1938–1939 widened rapidly after 1941.

The union leadership also shares responsibility for the red-baiting
during the war. Piven and Cloward (1977, p. 171) provide several
examples:

> When the CIO woodworkers struck in 1941, Philip Murray,
> who had taken Lewis' place as head of the CIO, denounced
> the woodworkers' leadership, echoed press charges of com-
> munism, and demanded that the strike be called off. When
> the UAW workers struck North American Aviation the same
> year, UAW's Aviation Director Richard Frankensteen called
> the strike "communist-inspired" on national radio and later
> addressed a meeting of strikers to order them back to work. It
> was after the workers booed Frankensteen and ignored his
> order that Roosevelt called out the troops, apparently with
> the approval of Sidney Hillman. When Roosevelt seized the
> mines during the 1943 UMW strike to break the 'little steel'
> formula, the executive board of the CIO repudiated Lewis
> and the UMW and congratulated Roosevelt for his veto of the
> Smith-Connally Act despite the fact that the legislation re-
> flected Roosevelt's own public proposals.

Why did union leadership turn in these cooperative directions? The
widely popular desire to further the war effort against the Axis powers undoubtedly provided a predominant immediate cause. After the
German invasion of the Soviet Union in 1941, the American Communist Party adopted a policy of full support for the war effort. The
many organizers and local officials who belonged to the party actively
promoted union cooperation with business and government and actively opposed wildcat strikes and rank-and-file initiatives (Lichtenstein, 1975; Cochran, 1977; Green, 1980, ch. 6). These circumstantial
strategic decisions had an important effect on the subsequent course
of union strategy. Equally important, however, the dues-checkoff
procedures constituted a major concession to the unions, giving them
the opportunity to consolidate their power during the war to an extent unimaginable a decade earlier (Brody, 1980, p. 112).

The period of consolidation: World War II to 1970s
The consolidation of the process of labor segmentation began immediately after World War II. We present our argument about the
development of divergent job structures and labor markets in three
stages, focusing first on the necessary conditions for the consolidation
of new structures in the labor process and labor markets; second,
discussing the growth of structured internal labor markets in many
large corporations; and third, tracing the actual patterns of divergent
development in the labor process and labor markets.

Necessary conditions for consolidation. The consolidation of the period of
segmentation coincided with a reconstitution of the world economy at
the beginning of this new stage of capitalist development. Two necessary conditions for that reconstitution seem most important as background for our analysis.

First, large U.S. corporations emerged from World War II with
more power than ever. U.S. corporations now saw the world as their
oyster and developed internal corporate structures that would permit
planning on a global scale. Their size, their dominance in product
markets, and their planning capacity was qualitatively greater than it
had been after World War I, permitting extraordinary leverage and
flexibility in the fashioning and implementing of new labor-
management structures.

At the same time, the Cold War fever from 1946 through the Ko-
rean War signaled the end of an era of progressive reforms and the
containment of the trade union movement. In response to massive
postwar strikes in late 1945 and 1946, President Truman seized oil
refineries, railroads, mines, and packing-houses and proposed legislation to draft strikers in key industries into the army. Congress countered with the Taft-Hartley Act. This legislation, drafted largely by
the National Association of Manufacturers, dramatically curbed
unions' power. And the "most important phase" in the taming of the
labor movement, according to Caute (1978, p. 352) "was the anti-
Communist purge of the CIO between 1946 and 1950." The story of
the purge of radicals and communists from the unions is familiar (see
Bernstein, 1971; Cochran, 1977; and Caute, 1978; among others).
Business and many union leaders accused anyone who opposed
cooperative collective bargaining policies of having a communist
orientation. This purge not only robbed the CIO unions of much of
their lower-level leadership but also circumscribed much union militancy. Consequently, in these years business regained considerable

leverage against labor and was able to institutionalize a qualitatively different system of labor management in many U.S. industries.

Structured internal labor markets. Taking advantage of their power and flexibility, large corporations undertook a comprehensive and sustained effort to plan the labor process and develop a relatively more integrated approach to labor management. This approach combined some of the newer policies charted during the 1920s with the more advantageous aspects of the drive system of earlier years. Lester summarizes this period (1958, pp. 40, 39):

> During the 1930's and 1940's, labor and employee relations received increasing attention at higher levels of management. The staffs and programs of industrial relations departments absorbed a growing proportion of company budgets and labor costs, as new techniques were tried... Supervisory selection, training, and practices have improved. In the plant, persuasion and participation have been displacing authoritarian methods of management, as companies have experimented with human relations techniques... In addition, managements have gained a much better understanding of unions, and, consequently, are in a position to anticipate union actions and reactions.

Perhaps most important for the hypotheses we advance about segmentation, many corporations were forced by the necessity of relating to the new industrial unions to systematize their collective bargaining strategies. As Rees notes (1962), during this period U.S. collective bargaining assumed a different character from that of typical European systems. In Europe the government much more specifically stipulated the rules and outcomes of the bargaining process. In the United States, judicial and legislative precedent established a general framework within which bargaining took place, and corporations and unions were left to establish the specific agreements on virtually all issues. Business apparently preferred this approach, in the years after World War II, in order to preserve as much initiative and flexibility for their own planning departments as possible. (For more on the rise of corporate planning during this period, see de Kadt, 1976; Noble, 1977; and Edwards, 1979).

Corporate planning focused in part on technology. Corporations continued to mechanize, following the patterns of previous periods. In this period more than before, however, technology tended to effect a qualitatively greater degree of control over the activities of production workers. Technical control expanded beyond the industries in which it had been pioneered. Where it emerged, it reduced the degree of independent leverage that workers could still maintain over the pace and quality of their work. New technologies increasingly determined the direction of work tasks and the pace of work. Even in the automobile industry, where the form of assembly operations had remained essentially constant since the first assembly line was installed in 1913, new technical innovations after World War II, first installed in 1946 at River Rouge, linked machine tools operations into a kind of assembly operation. The new technology substantially reduced the independence in production of workers in the skilled trades. (On the automotive example, see Bright, 1958; Lichtenstein, 1980; on technical control in general, see Braverman, 1974; Bright, 1958; Leone, 1967; and Edwards, 1979, ch. 7.)

Corporations paid equal attention to improving what Edwards (1979) calls "bureaucratic control" – improving the structured design and management of job systems and rules to ensure the greatest possible worker compliance and productivity. In both union and nonunion shops, corporations instituted a vast array of formal rules for production activity. The rules were intended not only to specify the actual production tasks that workers would perform but also to ensure much more general worker compliance with the norms and standards of labor-management systems. Nonunion employers like Polaroid and International Business Machines were able to pioneer some of these techniques of bureaucratic control precisely because they were able to install the basic structure of the systems without union interference (see Edwards, 1979, ch. 9).

As with earlier efforts at mechanization, neither technical nor bureaucratic control was determined purely by technical or bureaucratic "laws." In both cases, corporations made their plans contingent upon the requirements of labor control and conformity with the general logic of the structured internal labor processes. As Doeringer and Piore argue (1971, ch. 4), engineers designed machine installation to conform to the job structure, by and large, and not the other way around. And as Weir (1977) has pointed out, job design was frequently altered in order to provide corporations with the maximum possible leverage over informal work groups. Job tasks would be arranged to isolate workers from each other, thereby minimizing during working hours the social contact that would permit continuing social relations. In the automobile industry, for example, Faunce's case study (1958) indicates that workers in a newly designed Chrysler engine plant in the mid-1950s engaged in much less social interaction during working hours than they had in a plant of older construction.

These corporate strategies reflected an effort to regain the initiative that corporations had lost in the late 1930s and during World War II. Unions had acquired enough new power in the 1940s to contest corporate efforts to increase their leverage over production. Strike activity during the late 1940s indicates that unions were still prepared to wage militant battle; strike activity soared to its highest levels ever (*Historical Statistics*, 1975, series D-970). But these indices mask a new accommodationist impulse among industrial unions.

From 1946 through the early 1950s, most U.S. industrial unions moved to policies of explicit cooperation with corporate labor-management strategies. Many unions agreed to sweeping "management rights" clauses in their contracts, following the model of the General Motors–United Automobile Workers contract in 1946. Following a pattern established with the United Mine Workers in the late 1940s, many unions agreed to what has often been called "unemployment by attrition," in which management is free not to fill union jobs when they are vacated. They agreed to institutionalize the grievance procedure, thereby removing it further from the shop floor (Brody, 1980, pp. 184–200). They also agreed to a system of "productivity bargaining," in which collective bargaining over wages would take the previous distribution of income as a foundation and would focus exclusively on the division of the income "dividend" resulting from increasing worker productivity. This bargaining pattern placed a premium on workers' improving their own productivity in order to expand the pie from which their wage increases would be drawn. In addition, many unions became more involved in administering the rules of production by cooperating in the application of grievance procedures and work norms. (For a general summary of union practice and collective bargaining procedures, see Dunlop, 1958, and Doeringer and Piore, 1971.)

In retrospect, the speed and comprehensiveness of unions' postwar accommodation with management in the new system of labor management appear quite remarkable. As we have seen, several factors were probably at work. Corporate profits soared during and immediately after the war, providing the financial margin within which unions could obtain real economic gains and consolidate earlier victories. The Cold War purges deprived the unions of much of their militant leadership. And many union leaders may not have appreciated the significance of their ceding so much managerial authority over the organization of work.

By the early 1950s, large corporations had succeeded in shaping and applying an essentially new structure of labor management. Nonunion employers in both manufacturing and nonmanufacturing industries followed similar patterns, led by the coherence of management theory and the similarity of production work in many blue-collar and white-collar settings. Corporations that negotiated with unions were able to organize the labor process along lines similar to those pursued by nonunion employers because they were able to win union agreement to the new systems of control (see also Brody, 1980, ch. 5.

The logic of the new system can be easily summarized. (For more detailed accounts, see Doeringer and Piore, 1971, chs. 2–4; and Edwards, 1979, chs. 8–9.) Jobs were finely divided, frequently situated within detailed job ladders and internal promotional systems. Technology not only effected substantial regulation of the pace and quality of work but also served the broader objectives of labor-management policy. Hiring, promotion, and firing were regularized, with corporations seeking to smooth employment over their inventory and investment cycles through the use of overtime and labor hoarding. Bargaining focused increasingly on wages and fringe benefits, leaving the determination of working conditions to the engineers and labor relations experts. As Edwards emphasizes (1979, ch. 9), labor management came more and more to rely on the logic and operations of a full system of rules and procedures rather than the direct and haphazard intervention of the supervisor's authority.

It is important to emphasize that this new system of labor management reflected a compromise between labor and capital. Corporate planning departments helped fashion the new system. Having gained path-breaking victories in the late 1930s and during World War II, unions participated in the early 1950s only after winning certain gains. The industrial union movement had forced upon management not only basic collective bargaining but also procedures, such as grievance and seniority systems, that limited management's discretion in the allocation of labor. The new system of labor management that emerged after World War II incorporated and transformed those initial victories; management was forced to accommodate itself to workers' gains and to change its practices in response. Its success in so doing does not indicate the futility of the workers' struggles.

Although large firms and industrial union organization tended to go together in this new system, the correspondence was not complete. For example, large firms that forestalled industrial unionism retained the possibility of maintaining the more primitive labor systems of the previous periods. The tobacco industry illustrates this alternative possibility. The large tobacco firms had stabilized their demand curves and their market power by the beginning of World War II; an industrial union of tobacco workers had obtained a foothold in 1944. Taking advantage of racial tensions in the Carolinas, the tobacco companies were able to break the union in 1946–1948. Because the union was sufficiently short-lived, the tobacco companies were not forced to transform their labor management practices. Throughout the 1950s and 1960s, the labor process in the tobacco industry continued to resemble the pattern established in most large firms during the stage dominated by the homogenization of labor (see Korstad, 1980).

Unions were able to transform their working conditions, to pick another example, in some situations in which employers were not large and did not otherwise possess the advantages of stable industries because their employers were not "footloose" and could not, like garment and textile employers, escape from the unions' influence. Kahn (1975) demonstrates that West Coast longshoremen were able to effect a "regularization" of employment on the docks, despite the competitive structure of the industry, and Thompson (1979) traces a similar history in the Appalachian minefields. Neither the shipping companies nor the mine companies could easily flee from the industrial unions confronting them.

Divergence between primary and secondary jobs. In general, reflecting these dynamics, a characteristic kind of large corporation emerged after World War II. Following others, we call this a *core* firm (see Averitt, 1968; Edwards, 1979, ch. 5; and Bowring, 1982). As Edwards (pp. 82–83) shows, large firm size was by itself insufficient to transform corporate profitability and planning capacity, but large firm size *coupled* with industry concentration produced substantially higher profit rates. Core firms also enjoyed appreciably reduced risks of failure. Taking advantage of these higher profits and reduced risks, core firms were those most likely to be able to afford new systems of labor control and those most inclined to appreciate their necessity. Where these firms faced a unionized workforce, the corporations and unions shaped these new systems through the bargaining process. In those cases where core firms did not face unions, the organization of the labor process nonetheless bore the imprint of the new system, to a substantial degree, because companies hoped to demonstrate to their employees that unionization was not necessary to achieve many of its benefits.

These large corporations came to constitute a "core" of the economy, dominating key industrial sectors, capturing rapidly expanding markets, and initiating innovative technical change. As this core economy grew, large corporations became increasingly differentiated from the small firms that remained on the periphery. These small firms continued to resemble the entrepreneurial firms of the late nineteenth century. Averitt (1968, p. 7) summarizes some of their essential characteristics:

> These enterprises are the ones usually dominated by a single individual or a family. The firm's sales are realized in restricted markets. Profits and retained earnings are commonly below those in the center; long-term borrowing is difficult. Economic crises often result in bankruptcy or severe financial retrenchment. Techniques of production and marketing are rarely as up to date as those in the center. These firms are often, though not always, technological followers, sometimes trailing at some distance behind the industry leaders.

Many such peripheral firms were taken over and transformed by the corporate center, but many survived or were replaced by others, with the result that the periphery still constitutes an important part of the U.S. economy.

Why did the peripheral firms survive? Why did the expansion of the corporate center fail to absorb the weak, poorly financed firms of the periphery? The periphery survives because the central corporations find the remaining periphery unprofitable for direct investment; at the same time, the existence of a periphery enhances the profitability of the corporations at the center. Center firms find several advantages in avoiding actual acquisition of periphery firms: In those product areas where demand is least susceptible of stabilization, business risks can be transferred to the periphery; the option of subcontracting to the periphery increases the potential flexibility of operations; the periphery provides a low-cost alternative for the maintenance of excess productive capacity in slack periods; center firms can circumvent potential union problems and save on employee fringe benefits by "indirectly" employing peripheral workers; and center firms can avoid products that are difficult to standardize and that would therefore create difficulties in the supervision of workers. Moreover, peripheral industries tend to have low barriers to entry; they therefore tend to be overcrowded, and this competition leaves many small firms vulnerable to monopolistic exploitation by center corporations.

The machine tools industry provides a classic example of the persistence of peripheral industrial structure. Having first arisen during the nineteenth century, machine tools firms were never able to consolidate. The demand for the products of the machine tools industry is highly cyclically sensitive, because the demand for the capital goods grows rapidly during upswings and plummets during recessions. The industry's largest customer is the auto industry; with cyclical variations in that and other industries, machine tools, as Averitt (1968, p. 96) notes, "is overrun with orders during a boom but severely depressed during a recession." Replacement sales, the most stable component of demand, comprise only about 10 to 15 percent of industry sales. Averitt (p. 96) concludes, "For this reason alone, center firms find other investment outlets more conducive to their long-run goals."

This process of divergence in corporate structure between core and peripheral firms had begun after 1900; as we noted in Chapter 4, large corporations had been able to homogenize the labor process and begin exploring more "liberal" policies of labor management in the 1920s. But we hypothesize that divergence in the labor process and in labor markets did not begin until the systematization of the new systems of labor management after World War II. It is possible to provide some provisional tests of this hypothesis for the manufacturing sector. In the next several pages we present the results of these tests.

Evidence for the segmentation hypothesis

A variety of institutional and econometric studies have explored the existence of segmentation between primary and secondary labor markets for a single point of time or over roughly five-year periods. These studies have focused on the specification of the boundaries separating the segments, the differing behavioral characteristics within each segment, and the extent of mobility between segments (for useful review, see Rosenberg, 1979; and Ryan, 1980). These studies have yielded mixed results, neither confirming fully the segmentation hypothesis nor indicating the superiority of the neoclassical model over the segmentation alternative.

Since our concern in this book is primarily historical, we cannot enter here into a detailed critique of this literature. It will suffice to state that tests of divergence between sectors should involve substantially longer time periods than five years. Time series data provide a preferable means of evaluating the theory. We undertake such an effort in this section. In view of previous controversies, we present the results in some detail.

To conduct tests of the segmentation hypothesis we have allocated detailed manufacturing sectors into core and periphery sectors. The allocation is based on the work of Oster (1979), whose factor analytic tests for structural differentiation of industrial characteristics yielded a dual core–periphery partitioning of the economy. Oster's statistical procedures showed that a core–periphery dualism not only correctly described a predominant pattern of industrial stratification in the U.S. economy; they also permitted the assignment of detailed industries, with twenty-eight industries designated as core and fifty-five as periphery.

Using this empirical definition of the core and periphery, one can test for divergence in key economic indicators of labor process and labor market outcomes. Although data are not available for many variables reflecting the qualitative character of structured internal labor markets, the available quantitative variables do permit approximate tests of the divergence between core and periphery sectors in general. These variables include value added per production worker, wages, number of production workers, total employment, and separation rates.

Before turning to the specific tests, we should note two of their limitations. First, our theory of dualism between core and periphery refers to units of capital, not to whole industries. Many industries contain both core and periphery firms; consequently, data on individual firms would be preferable to data based on two-digit or three-digit industries. Moreover, as we explain below, secondary labor processes are often present within core firms, rendering industry-based data a further step away from the economic units in our theory. We use industry data only because of limitations of the available data.

Second, again because of data limitations, we cannot test directly for divergence in qualitative differences, such as the existence of structured internal labor markets. The quantitative tests provide only a limited approximation of the qualitative tests we would prefer to conduct. Both of these limitations suggest that our tests capture only a fraction of the actual patterns of divergence in jobs.[7]

Keeping these considerations in mind, our discussion of core-periphery divergence leads to the following testable hypotheses:

1. Value added per production worker in the core manufacturing sector increases relative to that in the periphery. The higher profit rates and capital resources of core firms permit a higher rate of continuing technological innovation and investment. Moreover, the bargaining power of industrial unions in core firms raises wage costs, creating an incentive to substitute labor-saving technology for workers.

2. Production workers' earnings in the core increase relative to those in the periphery as capital/labor ratios in the core sector rise (relatively) and as labor unions apply their bargaining power in core industries.

3. The ratio of production workers to total employees in the core declines relative to that ratio for the periphery as core firms devote relatively rising proportions of their resources to planning, supervision, and sales functions.

4. The ratio of total layoffs per 100 workers falls in the core relative to the periphery as core firms place increasing emphasis on promotion ladders and continuous employment within the firm, giving core workers greater protection from layoffs, relative to the periphery.

These hypotheses concern long-term trends. We would also expect to observe deviations from these trends to correlate with short-term fluctuations in the business cycle. During cyclical expansions, when the short-term growth rate lies above the long-term trend, core firms remain concerned with long-term expansion and allow periphery firms increased market shares. Hence, we hypothesize that long-term divergent trends between core and periphery become attenuated during cyclical expansions. Analogously, with core firms more sheltered from recessions than periphery firms, divergence between core and periphery will become exacerbated during cyclical downturns.

For the first two hypotheses we can compare long-term trends between the pre- and post–World War II periods. Surveys by the National Industrial Conference Board (1933) provide data on average value added per worker and average hourly wages for 1914 to 1930. Data from the Commerce Department's *Census of Manufacturers* and from the Bureau of Labor Statistics trace value added per worker and average weekly earnings for selected years in the postwar period. Data for the third and fourth hypotheses on production workers' share of employment and on separation rates are available for the postwar years only.

Table 5.1 traces value added per production worker in core and periphery manufacturing sectors for selected years between 1914 and 1930; column 3 presents the ratio of this index between the core and periphery. This column shows a general constancy between 1914 and 1929 in the core–periphery ratio of value added per production worker. Except for a one-time rapid increase in periphery value added per worker during World War I (which the underlying data suggest is accounted for by the rapid expansion of food and textile production during the war), no trend toward divergence between the core and periphery sectors is visible through 1929.

Table 5.2 presents average hourly wages of core and periphery workers for the period 1914–1930. Column 3 indicates that the ratio of hourly wages between core and periphery sectors remained essentially constant in these years. The only exception occurs in 1921 to 1922, when the core–periphery ratio dropped sharply. But these years were unusual, marked by both deep recession and an aggressive antiunion offensive by core employers. The overall trend in this table indicates no clear differences in trend between core and periphery

Table 5.1. *Value added per production worker in core and periphery manufacturing, 1914–1929*

Year	(1) Core ($)	(2) Periphery ($)	(3) Ratio:(1)/(2)
1914	3,783	3,622	1.04
1919	6,579	7,419	0.89
1921	6,150	6,271	0.98
1923	7,532	6,844	1.10
1925	8,168	7,341	1.11
1927	8,127	7,418	1.10
1929	8,662	7,539	1.13

Source: Calculated from data contained in National Industrial Conference Board (1933) by applying the core–periphery distinction developed in Oster (1979).

Table 5.2. *Wages in core and periphery manufacturing, 1914–1930*

Year	(1) Core ($)	(2) Periphery ($)	(3) Ratio:(1)/(2)
1914	0.26	0.22	1.18
1920	0.67	0.56	1.21
1921	0.52	0.48	1.08
1922	0.51	0.46	1.12
1923	0.60	0.51	1.18
1924	0.61	0.51	1.19
1925	0.61	0.51	1.19
1926	0.62	0.52	1.18
1927	0.63	0.53	1.19
1928	0.63	0.53	1.19
1929	0.64	0.54	1.19
1930	0.64	0.54	1.19

Source: Calculated from data contained in National Industrial Conference Board (1933) by applying the core–periphery distinction developed in Oster (1979).

wage rates through 1930, providing support for our hypothesis that an institutionalized divergence between core and periphery had not yet developed.

Turning next to the data for the postwar period, Table 5.3 and Figures 5.1 and 5.2 present several different computations for trends in these years.

Table 5.3. *Value added per production worker in core and periphery manufacturing, 1947–1977*

Year	(1) Core ($ thousand)	(2) Periphery ($ thousand)	(3) Ratio (1)/(2)
1947	6.78	5.97	1.14
1954	11.46	8.01	1.36
1958	15.07	10.59	1.42
1963	20.14	13.27	1.52
1967	23.39	16.15	1.45
1972	31.64	21.03	1.50
1977	52.05	33.42	1.56

See text for method of allocation of industries between core and periphery. Current employment weights are utilized in these calculations.
Source: U.S. Bureau of the Census, *Census of Manufacturing,* various years, summary volumes.

Table 5.3 summarizes trends in value added per production worker in core and periphery manufacturing, covering those years from 1947 to 1977 in which the Commerce Department conducted its detailed survey of manufacturing industries. As hypothesized, value added per production worker rose more rapidly in the core over this period, particularly during the early years of consolidation. The expected cyclical pattern is also evident in Table 5.3. The burden of cyclical downturn falls disproportionately on the periphery industries; however, the core industries grow less rapidly than the periphery during cyclical business expansions – like the long boom of the 1960s.

Figure 5.1A presents the trend in the core–periphery ratio of average weekly wages (of production and nonsupervisory workers) in manufacturing between 1947 and 1979.[8] Figure 5.1B presents the trend in the core–periphery ratio of the share of production workers in total employment. The movement of the core–periphery ratios for these two variables again indicates a clear divergent trend in the postwar period. As expected, average weekly wages rose much more rapidly in the core than in the periphery; this trend accelerated in the early 1970s. The ratio of production workers to total employment fell more rapidly in the core than in the periphery, but most of this decrease occurred before 1960. The expected cyclical variation, superimposed upon the trend, is also evident in these figures (and is confirmed in further analysis, relying on multiple regression estimates

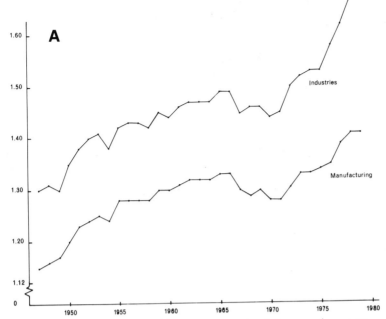

Figure 5.1A. Average weekly wages, core/periphery ratio, 1947–1979.

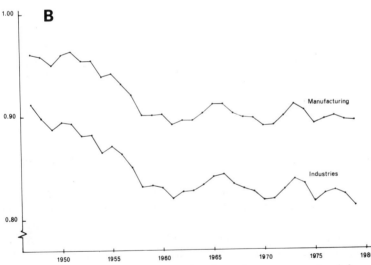

Figure 5.1B. Production workers/total employment, core/periphery ratio, 1947–1979. The industries curves in these figures differ from the manufacturing curves in the addition of wholesale and retail industries to the periphery. See text for explanation.

(*Sources:* U.S. Department of Labor, 1979, tables 42–45, 96, 97; U.S. Department of Labor, 1980, tables B-1, B-2, C-1, C-2.)

Table 5.4. *Layoffs, core and periphery manufacturing, 1958–1979*

Year	Core	Periphery	Ratio
1958	2.4	2.8	.860
1959	1.7	2.3	.708
1960	2.1	2.7	.802
1969	1.9	2.6	.701
1962	1.6	2.4	.662
1963	1.5	2.2	.654
1964	1.2	2.1	.595
1965	1.1	1.8	.606
1966	0.9	1.6	.544
1967	1.1	1.7	.661
1968	1.0	1.5	.605
1969	0.9	1.5	.623
1970	1.8	1.9	.924
1971	1.5	1.8	.920
1972	0.9	1.4	.589
1973	0.6	1.3	.483
1974	1.3	1.9	.671
1975	1.9	2.3	.825
1976	1.0	1.7	.590
1977	0.9	1.6	.568
1978	0.6	1.3	.470
1979	0.8	1.5	.556

Per hundred employees. Data are available only for manufacturing since 1958. See text for method of allocation of industries between core and periphery. Employment weights for 1963 used in calculating sectoral means.
Sources: U.S. Department of Labor, Bureau of Labor Statistics, (1979, table 55, and 1980, table D-2).

reported in Reich, 1981b; see Howell, 1982, for much more detailed evidence on wage divergence within manufacturing).

Table 5.4 presents trends on layoff rates for core and periphery manufacturing; unfortunately, these data are available only since 1958. The results are consistent with our hypotheses, although less clearly than with the other indices. The stage of the business cycle predominates in influencing both the level of layoffs per hundred employees in core and periphery and the core–periphery layoff ratio. Nonetheless, the hypothesized downward trend in the ratio is visible. (It appears, albeit weakly, in multiple regression estimates as well; see Reich, 1981b.)

We have also calculated unionization rates for core and periphery manufacturing. These figures are presented in Table 5.5. Systematic

The segmentation of labor

Table 5.5. *Unionization rates among production workers in core and periphery manufacturing*

Year	(1) Core (%)	(2) Periphery (%)	(3) Ratio (1)/(2)
1958[a]	76.6	58.4	1.31
1968-1972[a]	70.0	52.3	1.34
1973-1975[b]	56.7	39.7	1.43

Weights are 1963 employment ratios. See text for allocation of industries to core and periphery.

[a]Calculated from unionization estimates for two-digit industries, based on Bureau of Labor Statistics surveys of establishments. These surveys report establishment employment and percentage of establishments with a majority of factory employees covered by labor-management contracts. Data for 1958 from Douty (1960); 1968-1972 data from Freeman and Medoff (1979a), table 9.

[b]Calculated from union membership estimates for two-digit industries, based on Census Bureau household surveys. See Freeman and Medoff (1979a). These authors estimate that about 44 percent of the difference in estimates between 1968-1972 and 1973-1975 result from differences in survey concepts and about 38 percent of the decline represents an actual reduction in union membership.

data on unionization by detailed industry are available for only a few scattered postwar years. The results in Table 5.5 indicate that unionism is much more extensive in the core than in the periphery. However, union coverage has been declining within both core and periphery sectors in recent years.

Finally, we have also extended the tests of core–periphery divergence beyond the manufacturing sector. However, for nonmanufacturing, additional problems arise in allocating industries between the core and the periphery. For manufacturing, the use of firm and industrial characteristics to categorize core and periphery produced considerable homogeneity within the core and within the periphery. A consistent application of these same criteria would suggest that all of mining, construction, transportation, wholesale and retail trade, and some of public utilities and communication should be allocated to the periphery. But this result conflicts with other evidence, casting doubt upon the validity of the methodology for these cases (see Gordon, 1982, for detailed discussion).

One important heterogeneity among these nonmanufacturing industries consists in the conditions affecting union power. For example, according to the industrial criteria for firms, mining, construction, and transportation fall in the periphery. Yet workers in these industries have been able to form strong unions. For this reason, despite the peripheral structure of their industries, mineworkers, construction workers, and truck drivers have been able to increase their wages much more rapidly than workers in other peripheral sectors. (Kerr, 1979, provides parallel cross-sectional results.) In order to clarify the patterns of divergence that derive primarily from firm and industrial characteristics, we have therefore included in the periphery only a selected set of nonmanufacturing sectors, excluding mining, construction, and transportation.

Figures 5.1A and B review the trends for the expanded core and periphery sets for two variables: the average weekly wages and the ratio of production workers to total employment. The divergence in these indices over the postwar period is substantially greater than we found in manufacturing by itself.

Secondary labor processes in core firms. Small peripheral firms have not been the only enterprises maintaining secondary labor processes during recent decades. Large corporations have also organized a portion of their internal operations within the secondary labor market. Their size permits the flexibility to operate in both labor markets, depending on their circumstances, and many companies have chosen to take advantage of both markets simultaneously.

In some industries that are dominated by large corporations, industrial unions never succeeded in organizing a strong base. In such industries the large corporations have less impetus to transform the structure of the internal labor market. Both electronics assembly and watch assembly, for instance, still rely on intensified operative work and for the most part employ unskilled women. In these industries both the level and rate of increase of average weekly earnings fall substantially below the average for all core industries. Value added per production worker has increased much less rapidly in these industries as well. These industries are frequently labor intensive and geographically mobile, able to transfer operations easily either to the lower-wage South or, more recently, overseas. Other large corporations, such as the tobacco giants, have operated in industries traditionally tied to the South and have escaped strong unions. In tobacco, as in watches and electrical machinery, wages have remained far below those in other core industries (Howell, 1982).

Large corporations in many of the core industries have also located some of their production activities in the secondary labor market in order to avoid many of the costs that result from highly structured labor markets. In some core industries, such as defense and electronics, substantial subcontracting permits corporations to transfer some of the risks of unpredictable investments to smaller enterprises (Galbraith, 1967). Subcontracting is also prevalent in cyclically sensitive industries, such as steel and motor vehicles. As Doeringer and Piore (1971, p. 173) point out, "small job and specialty shops bear the brunt of the cyclical instability in these industries." In shipping and longshoring, as well, the decasualization of work accompanying unionization has also been accompanied by "the formal recognition of a permanent pool of casual workers with little or no attachment to the industry and only residual employment rights" (p. 173).

In most large corporations, moreover, the rapid growth of administrative functions has led many firms to organize some of their administrative operations along secondary labor market lines. For example, many corporations have relegated much of their standardized typing work to typing pools organized by secondary labor process principles; few opportunitites for promotion exist, turnover can be high, and virtually no on-the-job training takes place. Part of the impetus leading to the typing pool, as Lockwood (1958) notes, has been the desire to separate those clerical activities that do not require on-the-job experience to achieve maximum productivity from other tasks, such as personal secretarial work, in which incentives to promote longer tenure are necessary for high productivity. Some of the growth of temporary clerical services has also resulted from the same impetus.

Finally, large corporations have a range of choices about when and how to provide business and repair services for themselves. Many choose to subcontract for various business services, thereby sustaining some of the small firms in the secondary labor market. Others choose to provide such services internally within the corporations. In a study of the business repair service industries in New York, Joffe (1975) found that firms of relatively comparable size engage in both internal and external provision of services and that a dual labor market has evolved within the business repair occupations.

It is difficult to develop data for testing divergence of labor processes within and between firms in the service sectors. Here, we hypothesize that divergence takes place as much or more between occupational groupings within industries as between particular sectors. Industry data do not adequately reflect this pattern of occupational divergence, and time series on occupations by industry do not permit proper comparisons. However, several industry case studies indicate that structured internal markets have emerged in key service sectors and that these structured jobs have become more clearly differentiated from unstructured jobs in those same firms and industries. (See Kraft, 1977, and Greenbaum, 1979, on the computer industry; Ehrenreich and Ehrenreich, 1972, on hospital services; and de Kadt, 1976, on insurance.)

Segmentation within the primary sector. As the primary labor market itself has developed, a division has emerged between an "independent primary" and a "subordinate primary" segment. Jobs in both these segments share many of the general characteristics of the primary market: They are increasingly dominated by large corporations; they pay relatively higher wages and salaries than secondary work; they feature some job security; and they offer opportunities for advancement. They differ largely in the behavioral rules governing their task performance, the mechanisms through which their requisite skills are acquired and applied, and the labor market mechanisms mediating the allocation of workers among jobs (Buchele, 1976; Edwards, 1979, ch. 9; Rumberger and Carnoy, 1980).

The independent primary sector includes many professional, managerial, and technical jobs. (See Gordon, 1982, for definitions and listings of occupations by labor segment.) Professional standards tend to govern work performance; employees in these jobs are often free of specific instructions and authority. Independent primary workers tend to acquire general skills through formal education and to apply those general rules and capacities to variable individual situations they encounter in their work. They receive greater returns to schooling and experience, and they tend to internalize the formal objectives of their organizations. They often experience substantial job mobility, both within and between enterprises. Gordon (1982) finds that 70 percent of independent primary workers are white males (see also Buchele, 1976).

The growth of the independent primary segment can be traced to changes in employers' control over the production of skills and over technological innovation. During most of the nineteenth century, technological innovation was usually developed outside the productive sector or by the tinkering of artisans at the point of production. But by the 1920s, and in some cases earlier, corporations were increasingly seeking to control the directions of innovation and to stimulate new inventions by harnessing science and research to their own ends. Corporations developed research and development departments, sponsored scientific institutes, and helped stimulate the growth of engineering schools and professional engineering standards. More and more, technological innovations resulted from the efforts of professionals who worked increasingly as salaried employees within the corporations.

Corporations also sought new mechanisms for developing the technical skills involved in management and design. Under the craft system, artisans had acquired the broad expertise necessary to understand the production process and to perform its technically sophisticated tasks. As the craft tradition was broken and semiskilled operatives became more common, fewer production workers acquired technical skills through their own on-the-job experience. Corporations faced a problem; they needed technically skilled workers but did not want to form a dependence upon the craft system for their training. To resolve this problem, corporations moved to help establish vocational training institutes, either internally or nominally independent of the industry. These institutes sought to train workers with some generalized skills and to impart respect for the imperatives of the corporate form of employment (Douglas, 1921; Stone, 1975). In contrast to those who emphasize only deskilling, we would emphasize that this process involved substantial reskilling as well.

These self-conscious corporate efforts to create groups of workers with general skills, whose applications the corporations could control, were influenced by the efforts of these workers themselves. Periodically throughout the years since the 1920s and 1930s, previously independent professional and technical workers tried to resist the increasing corporate and organizational control over their work activities. In resisting that encroachment, they often turned to the formation of professional associations to protect the integrity of their work. More recently, professional associations of technical workers have also emerged, at least partly in response to a similar dynamic. These efforts also segmented independent primary workers from the subordinate primary labor force.

The subordinate primary sector includes many semiskilled, primary sector blue-collar jobs and many semiskilled white-collar jobs. In contrast to the independent primary segment, subordinate primary jobs usually involve routinized, relatively repetitive tasks oriented around and governed by specific supervision and formalized work rules within the enterprise. Many subordinate primary workers acquire specific job skills on the job, within the enterprise. They rarely learn general skills. As a result of firm rules and union provisions, subordinate primary workers are more likely to remain either within a single firm or within a single industry.

It is possible to test for the statistical significance of differences between independent primary and subordinate primary occupations and also to test our hypothesis of divergence between these segments for the postwar period. Relying on the listings developed by Gordon (1982), we have divided all three-digit occupations into the three principal labor market segments and analyzed data on median annual earnings (by detailed three-digit occupation) available from the 1950, 1960, and 1970 decennial censuses. We have applied standard analysis of variance techniques to these data, testing for the statistical significance of between-segment variance in annual earnings with respect to within-segment variance.

The results (presented in detail in Reich, 1981b) indicate not only that between-segment differences in earnings between the independent primary and subordinate primary segments were already statistically significant in 1950 but also that the between-segment variations in earnings were much greater than the within-segment variations. This suggests that empirical attention to the segment in which a worker is employed is critical for understanding the forces affecting his or her earnings. The tests also indicate that the ratio of between- to within-segment variations increased both from 1950 to 1960 and from 1960 to 1970, providing direct confirmation of our hypothesis concerning the growing importance of segments during this period of consolidation and the trend toward divergence between them. Similar results obtain when the analysis of variance is conducted to include the secondary segment occupations as a third group (Reich, 1981b).

Segmentation by sex. After World War II, women and members of various racial and ethnic groups entered the U.S. labor force in growing numbers. The development of tendencies toward segmentation interacted with growing participation by these groups in the labor force. In one direction, labor segmentation influenced and limited employment opportunities for women and minority workers. In the other direction, the mechanisms reproducing discrimination and occupational segregation helped reproduce segmentation; it was easier to maintain differences between jobs within a firm when the job differences were matched by differences in workers' ascriptive characteristics. We summarize some of the main dimensions of the historical relation between segregation and segmentation in the paragraphs that follow.

After a period of stagnation during the 1920s and 1930s, the rate of participation of women in the labor force has more than doubled since 1940. Married women began to enter the labor force in unprecedented numbers. The resulting patterns of female employment reflected both the patterns already established during the earlier period of exploration and the continuing effects of segmentation in the period of its consolidation. Four developments seem noteworthy.

First, as corporate demand for clerical workers continued to soar, corporations turned to women to fill clerical jobs. Total clerical employment grew from 3.4 million in 1920 to 12.6 million in 1970, whereas total female clerical employment grew from 1.6 million in 1920 to 9.5 million in 1970. The female share of clerical employment rose from 47 percent to 75 percent during those years. Both absolute employment levels and the percentages increased more rapidly after 1940 than in the earlier period of exploration.

More important than these quantitative trends, however, was the corporations' systematic segregation of men and women within the white-collar occupations. As Davies (1975) points out, employers recognized that the segmentation of white-collar work could be facilitated by channeling women into the lower-level clerical occupations. Large numbers of female workers were shunted into both the emerging secondary white-collar occupations and the subordinate primary clerical occupations. The increasing employment of married women permitted the growth of subordinate primary occupations in the clerical sector, as their turnover rates were lower than those of younger and single female workers. The segmentation of corporate office work foreclosed much of the potential movement of women into better-paying office jobs with better promotional opportunities.

Second, the number of service jobs in the economy grew extraordinarily rapidly. In many of these areas, women had already secured a traditional hold on certain occupations. For example, as the health and education sectors expanded with quantum leaps between 1945 and 1970, women increased their employment as nurses, health technicians, and teachers dramatically. In 1920, approximately 800,000 women worked as teachers and trained nurses (Hutchins, 1934, p. 32). By 1970, the number of women employed as teachers, nurses, and health technicians had increased to almost 6 million.

Although some women were able to take advantage of this greater service employment to expand their opportunities in the professional and technical fields, they were prevented, as they had been in the office sector, from moving beyond a limited set of jobs. For example, few women entered the educational field at the college and university level. Women as a percentage of college teachers actually declined during this period, particularly up to 1960. The percentage of women among graduate degree recipients declined from 1930 to 1950; more recent gains have only begun to make up for those losses. In health, as in teaching, women were often limited to traditional female roles. As the large hospital complexes grew, the stratification of the hospital labor force grew apace (see Ehrenreich and Ehrenreich, 1972). Although many women were able to enter the independent primary segment in the health field, they remained subordinate to the doctors and managers, who had ultimate power in the organization. In response, professional associations with quasi-union status began to spring up in those health occupations.

Third, as the primary labor segment left the secondary labor segment behind, both in manufacturing and in trade, peripheral employers were more frequently forced to turn to women as potential low-wage employees. Women increased their share of the labor force in the peripheral goods-producing sector – noncore industries in mining, construction, manufacturing, transportation, communication, and utilities – from 19.7 percent in 1950 to 24.3 percent in 1970 (Gordon, 1982).

Fourth, in much the same way, peripheral employers in some of the services and particularly in retail trade were forced to turn to female employees. While total employment in retail trade increased from 4.5 million to 11.1 million between 1920 and 1970, female employment in retail trade increased from 0.7 million to 5.1 million during those years. Two-thirds of the increase in retail employment occurred by hiring women, and the percentage of retail trade employees who were female increased from 15.5 percent to 45.9 percent. With wage rates in retail trade lagging behind primary labor market levels, many women found their earnings falling farther and farther behind those of many men (Gordon, 1982).

These four developments account for an astonishing proportion of current female employment. Four categories of female workers – those in the peripheral manufacturing industries, in retail trade, in clerical occupations, and in the health and educational sectors, accounted for 95 percent of all female employment in 1970 (Gordon, 1982).

Segmentation by race. The more recent patterns of economic life for black workers began to crystallize during and after World War II. Black migration from the South accelerated during wartime as a result of the labor shortages and continued when mechanization of agriculture pushed blacks off Southern farms in the late 1940s and the 1950s. The number of blacks soon exceeded the job opportunities traditionally or newly available to them. Consequently, blacks augmented the reserve army of labor in the Northern cities and became concentrated in the secondary labor market. Black employment came mainly to consist in low-wage jobs in the secondary market, mainly in peripheral industries; some jobs in the primary labor market, largely in the core industries into which blacks had already gained access before World War II; and jobs in the rapidly expanding service sectors, most of them in the secondary labor market.

The migration of blacks from the South to the North increased during the war. The percentage of blacks living in the North increased from 23.0 percent in 1940 to 40.1 percent in 1960; the percentage of blacks living in Northern cities increased from roughly 20 percent to roughly 38 percent over the same period. By 1970, those proportions had reached 38.4 percent and 39.8 percent, respectively (Reich, 1981a, ch. 2).

The first stage of the movement was dominated by the pull of new manufacturing opportunities during World War II. After the war, the migration was dominated by the push out of Southern agriculture. The capitalization of cotton agriculture, first with the introduction of tractors and herbicides and later, in the 1960s, with the introduction of mechanical harvesters, pushed millions of blacks off the land and into the cities (Piore, 1979a). Many of those who did first settle in the North moved into the rapidly growing cities of the South. Today, three-fourths of U.S. blacks live in metropolitan areas, making them more urbanized than whites.

Although blacks had lived in segregated enclaves in Northern cities well before World War II, the degree of segregation now became more intense. The ghettos spread, as did racial segregation in housing in the large cities (Reich, 1981a, ch. 2). Following traditional channels of northward migration, many blacks moved into the older northeastern and midwestern industrial cities. In those cities especially, the decentralization of many manufacturing jobs and the suburbanization of the white population accelerated. At the same time, the housing stocks of the older cities, largely antedating the 1920s, began to deteriorate. A declining structural dynamic began to develop in many American cities, trapping blacks in the regions that were deteriorating most rapidly, thereby isolating them from many of the better economic opportunities in the primary labor market.

Industry and service employment in both the North and the South grew during the 1950s and 1960s. But the demand for black labor in industries that had traditionally employed blacks could not entirely absorb the rapidly expanding supply. During the 1950s, in particular, after the wartime recovery of manufacturing from the Depression had slowed, few new job opportunities opened in the primary sector. While employment of blacks in manufacturing rose from 479,000 to 998,000 between 1940 and 1950, it had increased to only 1,306,000 by 1960.

For peripheral employers, often lagging in comparison to the dynamic core industries, and relatively more concentrated in the older central cities, the black labor reserve became an important source of low-wage labor. In this period blacks entered many peripheral manufacturing industries from which they had been excluded before the war. For example, black employment in the clothing, food processing, and meat product industries all grew rapidly between 1940 and 1960. The black share of the secondary labor market in manufacturing increased as a result. In these peripheral industries, as we have noted, average weekly earnings rose more slowly than in the core industries throughout the post–World War II period. Blacks had been shunted into lower-paying jobs in the North since their arrival in the 1920s and even earlier; now they became trapped in those jobs simply by the dynamics of industrial composition and growth. Between 1950 and 1970 blacks as a percentage of peripheral manufacturing employment increased from 7 to 10 percent (Gordon, 1982).

Some of the same factors affected blacks in the service sectors. As in the peripheral industries, many service employers operate small enterprises and cannot afford to pay high wages. Blacks became a significant low-wage labor supply for those employers, too. For example, blacks moved out of the declining domestic service and personal service occupations (newsboys, maids, draymen, bootblacks, elevator operators), into expanding service occupations (hospital orderlies, nursing aides, food counter and fountain workers).

In many of these service industries, black workers were additionally affected by the reorganization and stratification of production occurring in the larger institutions. In many large corporations and hospitals, for instance, the growing number of service jobs were allocated among the respective segments of the labor process. In corporations, many office jobs, such as that of file clerk, janitor, and office machine operator, were separated, filled from the secondary labor market, and isolated from other ladders of promotion. In hospitals, the growing orderly, kitchen, and cleaning occupations became more rooted in the secondary labor market. Blacks entered these jobs, as into the peripheral manufacturing industries, in large numbers.

Some blacks continued to work in the core manufacturing industries. For example, black employment in steel, automobiles, and mining increased from 142,000 in 1940 to 204,000 in 1960. As before the war, however, blacks were unable to gain access to many other primary manufacturing industries. The number of black males employed in core goods sectors decreased from 506,000 in 1950 to 502,000 in 1960. And within those core industries, the pattern of occupational segregation tended to persist. Blacks tended to stay in the lower-skilled, lower-paying jobs at the bottom of the occupational hierarchy. Opportunities for blacks to earn higher wages were opening quite slowly, retarded by the slow growth of employment and by barriers to promotion. Employment in automobiles, steel, tobacco, and mining fell by 12 percent during the 1950s; separate seniority ladders in industries such as shipbuilding and steel retarded the occupational upgrading of black workers (Gordon, 1982; Reich, 1981a, ch. 6).

During the 1960s some of these patterns began to change slightly. First, both the prosperity of the 1960s and the success of many black protests concerning employment discrimination expanded primary labor market opportunities in the core manufacturing industries. Consequently, black male employment in the core goods industries increased from 502,000 in 1960 to 682,000 in 1970 (Gordon, 1982).

Second, also largely as a result of black protest, blacks began to gain some access to the jobs in the independent primary sector from which they had been long excluded. For instance, the proportion of black males employed as managers rose from 2.1 to 3.5 percent.

Third, the rapid expansion of welfare payments during the 1960s began to provide an alternative to low-wage employment for many blacks in the reserve army of labor. The number of black households receiving Aid for Dependent Children or General Assistance payments increased from nearly 300,000 to close to 700,000 between 1961 and 1969. This development began to force some peripheral employers to search for new sources of low-wage labor; the patterns of labor supply to which they had become accustomed during the 1940s and 1950s were changing. Puerto Ricans, Chicanos, and immigrants from Mexico and the Caribbean provided some of the alternative labor supply for many of those employers.

Finally, many blacks, as we noted above, became increasingly intolerant of low-wage labor and the lack of opportunities for advancement characteristic of the secondary labor market. The black protests of the 1960s and the rapid turnover among many younger black workers reflected this development. As a result, at least in the short run, the problems of labor discipline for many secondary employers were exacerbated. Piore (1979a) notes that this qualitative phenomenon was as influential as the quantitative decline in the supply of low-wage black workers in prompting many secondary Boston employers to begin to search for new sources of low-wage labor in the mid- and late-1960s.

The net result of these several forces (Gordon, 1982) was that

Table 5.6. *Unemployment rates and unemployment segmentation index*

Year[a]	All workers	White males	Nonwhite males	White females	Nonwhite females	Segmentation index[b]
1949	5.9	5.6	9.6	5.7	7.9	2.5
1954	5.5	4.8	10.3	5.6	9.3	4.8
1959	5.5	4.6	11.5	5.3	9.4	5.9
1964	5.2	4.1	8.9	5.5	10.6	7.5
1971	5.9	4.9	9.1	6.3	10.8	5.3
1974	5.6	4.3	9.1	6.1	10.7	8.6
1979	5.8	4.4	10.3	5.9	12.3	8.8

Unemployment rates refer to percentage of civilian labor force, 16 years or older, in specified group.
[a]Data are displayed for years with approximately equal overall unemployment rates, as the first column shows.
[b]The segmentation index is defined as the product of the ratios of the unemployment rates of nonwhite males, white females, and nonwhite females to the white male unemployment rate: $I = (U_{NWM}/U_{WM}) \cdot (U_{WF}/U_{WM}) \cdot (U_{NWF}/U_{WM})$.
Source: U.S. President (1980a, tables B-29, B-30).

blacks were disproportionately confined to secondary jobs: 60 percent of black workers in 1970 were employed in secondary jobs. Similar forces affected Hispanic workers, of whom 50 percent were concentrated in secondary work.

The segmentation of the labor force by sex and race is also visible in the continuing differences in unemployment rates among sex and race groups. We have calculated a convenient ordinal statistic of unemployment rate differentials by multiplying the ratios of the unemployment rates of nonwhite males, white females, and nonwhite females to the white male unemployment rate. The trends for this segmentation index are presented in Table 5.6; the index more than tripled over the postwar period. Further calculations (not included in the table) indicate that the worsening of unemployment among black youth accounts for much of the increase in the segmentation index. However, the index increases even when it is calculated for 25-34 year olds or 35-44 year olds only, indicating the persistence of segmentation by sex and race in the postwar period.

The size and composition of segments. To provide a final check on the segmentation hypothesis, we have also estimated the size and composition of each labor segment for the years 1950 and 1970. These

Table 5.7. *Distribution of employment among labor market segments, 1950*

	Male		Female		Total	
	N	%	N	%	N	%
Independent primary	10.6	34.0	2.1	14.6	12.7	27.8
Salaried	2.9	9.2	1.3	9.1	4.2	9.1
Craft	5.4	17.4	.5	3.5	5.9	13.0
Control workers	2.3	7.4	.3	2.0	2.6	5.7
Subordinate primary	10.2	32.8	6.8	46.6	17.0	37.2
Secondary	10.4	33.2	5.6	38.9	16.0	35.0
Totals	31.2	100.0	14.5	100.0	45.7	100.0

Nonagricultural employment only. *N* in millions.
Source: Gordon (1982), based on decennial census data.

Table 5.8. *Distribution of employment among labor market segments, 1970*

	Male		Female		Total	
	N	%	N	%	N	%
Independent primary	17.3	42.7	5.1	18.2	22.4	32.8
Salaried	7.1	17.4	3.5	12.8	10.6	15.5
Craft	6.2	15.4	.9	3.1	7.1	10.4
Control workers	4.0	9.9	.6	2.3	4.7	6.9
Subordinate primary	10.0	24.8	11.1	40.0	21.1	31.0
Secondary	13.1	32.5	11.6	41.8	24.7	36.2
Totals	40.5	100.0	27.8	100.0	68.2	100.0

Nonagricultural employment only. *N* in millions.
Source: Gordon (1982), based on decennial census data.

estimates, presented in Tables 5.7 and 5.8, are based on both industry and occupational categorizations. The industry categorization follows the factor-analytic method of Oster (1979), as discussed earlier in this section. The occupational categorization is based on detailed factor and descriptive statistical analysis of key variables from the *Dictionary of Occupational Titles* (DOT). Neither the underlying industry nor the DOT variables includes any information on the characteristics of workers in those jobs; consequently, the segment categories presented in these tables reflect *job*, not *worker*, characteristics. Because none of the variables include wage data, further, they are not tautological with previously presented indices of wage inequalities among labor segments. However, the categories in these tables do differ from previously presented categories in one respect: "control" workers – salaried managers and supervisors – have been separated from the other categories within the independent primary segment in order to trace their particular movements (see Gordon, 1982, for further details on the derivation of these estimates). The tables exclude others in the labor force who were "self-employed."

Several main conclusions stand out from the data in these two tables. The size of the segments in 1970 corresponds approximately to related estimates by Buchele (1976) and Rumberger and Carnoy (1980). In 1970 the independent primary segment accounted for about a third of total nonagricultural employment, the subordinate primary segment for a little less than a third, and secondary workers for a bit more than a third. Similar estimates appear in Edwards's (1979, ch. 9) review of a larger number of similar studies.

The overall segment structure remained relatively stable between 1950 and 1970. This stability is to be expected; given our periodization, major changes in these decades would be uncomfortable for our analysis. Nonetheless, some changes are visible. The most notable trend concerns the relative decline in employment among subordinate primary and craft workers, especially among males. This trend is also to be expected. As the labor movement was contained, firms hired relatively more (salaried) independent primary employees and secondary workers, taking advantage of those areas of the labor process where the relative power of workers was lower than in the industrial unions. The tables also indicate that the distribution of women among labor segments remained relatively stable in these two decades, despite an increase of over 90 percent in the number of female workers in this period.

We note, finally, that separate data for the private sector (from Gordon, 1982) provide two further qualifications of the general portrait for 1970 revealed by Table 5.8. First, the percentage of secondary workers in the private sector is higher than for the economy as a whole; nearly 40 percent of private workers are employed in secondary jobs in the private sector, compared to 36 percent in the public and private sectors combined. Second, much of the growth in (salaried) independent primary employment revealed by the changes from 1950 to 1970 is accounted for by the growth in public employment; more than 40 percent of noncontrol workers in the public sector hold independent primary jobs, whereas only 31 percent of noncontrol workers in the private sector are employed in the independent primary segment.

The effects of labor segmentation. We hypothesized in Chapter 1 that the segmentation of labor provides a principal explanation of recent divisions within the American working class. What are the connections between our analysis of the transformation of labor and our hypotheses about its impact on the relative disunity of the working class?

We suspect that the emergence of segmentation affected the relative unity of the U.S. working class through three related transmission channels. First, workers in different segments eventually experienced very different relations of production – with their employers, with their co-workers, and with their unions. These differences in working experiences would be likely, other things being equal, to contribute to divergent attitudes and political orientations. Second, as we have already seen in previous sections, the segmentation of labor significantly affected the development of differences among workers by race and by sex, thus conditioning the ways in which these historically crucial divisions developed and were reproduced. Third, some analysts have hypothesized that differences in the structures of heterogeneous family, schooling, and community institutions in the postwar period came increasingly to correspond to some of the qualitative differences among labor segments.[9]

Whether or not all of these transmission mechanisms had a determinate effect, we think that there was a close parallel between workers' (and their households') positions among segments and their respective political orientations. We summarize here some of the predominant political inclinations that, in our view, characterized the politics of each segment of the working-class population during the postwar period:

Independent primary workers and their households were particularly likely to focus on political issues concerning the quality of life and individual autonomy – at least partly as a result, we think, of their relative autonomy on the job and the space within which they were able, at least during the 1950s and 1960s, to enjoy a differentiably higher quality of work. This led, for example, toward a focus on issues concerning the environment, civil liberties, and personal rights, and to demands for freedom from political and social oppression.

Subordinate primary workers and their households, following up on their recent ability to achieve relative security and stability of income and employment, were likely to emphasize the importance of economic growth (to preserve the conditions permitting real wages to rise); the U.S. international dominance upon which American growth partly depended; full employment; and the integrity of the institutions (of the social structure of accumulation) within which their stability and security were rooted.

Secondary workers and their households were likely to place particular importance on access to government services and income support, given their lower and less stable earnings from employment. Their relatively lower returns from participation in the established economic institutions were likely to translate into relatively lower participation in established political institutions as well – and therefore, into lower rates of voter participation, for example.

All these hypotheses need to be tested carefully and developed much more fully. Their ultimate political implications should nonetheless be fairly evident. We would argue that labor segmentation retarded the movement toward an increasingly class-conscious working class, with its own political presence, and that it helped create the splintered set of political forces, based on class fractions, that have dominated U.S. politics since the 1940s. Thus, although segmentation did not eliminate class politics, it did fragment, reshape, and channel them. In so doing, segmentation dramatically weakened the working class as a whole (see Edwards, Ch. 10, 11; and Reich and Edwards, 1978).

The development of class-fraction rather than class-wide politics stands in clear contrast to the trajectory of American working-class movements in the 1930s. Then, a growing class-wide perspective seemed to portend the emergence of a class-wide political organization. Notwithstanding the many unresolved questions – would such an organization grow out of or replace the Democratic party? would it be socialist or social-democratic? – it appeared that the unionization of the mass industries, the legal and political victories gained in the 1930s, and the cultural and ideological self-confidence of the working class would ensure a fundamental political realignment and that such a realignment would reflect and accommodate these profound class changes.

The growth of a working-class-based political party would also have placed the United States more squarely in line with other advanced capitalist countries, where labor parties, Socialists, Communists, and others have been central political forces. Yet neither the events of the 1930s nor the familiar examples of capitalist development elsewhere are by themselves sufficient to explain the constellation of class forces in the postwar United States. Of course, a number of factors beyond the scope of this study – the Cold War, American nuclear supremacy, and more – intervened as well. Nonetheless, it seems clear that the emerging domestic politics was profoundly affected by the system of labor segmentation.

The net result was that segmentation generated a splintered working-class politics rooted in class fractions. Indeed, the labor–

capital accord that emerged in the new social structure of accumulation – see the discussion on consolidation earlier in this section – was itself founded upon the presumption of class fraction politics: It had no place for general strikes, class-wide bargaining, or a renewal of the unionization offensive. The postwar accord worked effectively only as long as working-class demands could be constrained to reflect the interests of particular class fractions.

In all these respects, therefore, labor segmentation constitutes a fundamental and, we think, inescapable answer to the questions that initially motivated this book: Why have American workers been so quiescent during the current crisis and why has the achievement of a working-class agenda remained so distant? We conclude that the present weakness of the American working class can be traced directly to the splintering and subsequent weakness caused by the postwar system of labor segmentation. In order to understand both the evolution of the current crisis and the workers' responses to it, it seems to us essential that one view these recent events at least partly through the lenses provided by this analysis of segmentation and its effects.

The period of decay: 1970s to the present

We have already noted that the world economy began sliding into sustained economic crisis in the early 1970s. Our analytical framework would therefore lead us to expect a corresponding decay in the prevailing structures of labor management, gradually eroding the organization of the labor process and labor markets that characterized the post–World War II U.S. economy. Recent developments seem to support this expectation.[10]

We are hardly the first to highlight initial evidence of decay. Many journalists and social scientists have been trumpeting slowdowns in productivity growth, growing worker dissatisfaction, and rapid shifts in at least the location if not also the organization of production. These recent accounts have even included unprecedented and serious doubts about the ability and creativity of U.S. corporate management. (See, for example, the influential summary that appeared in the *New York Times Magazine:* Lohr, 1981.)

Many of these accounts have revealed considerable surprise at the phenomena they trace. This surprise arises from a widespread failure to relate recent evidence *of* decay to the analysis of the actual structures *in* decay, particularly in those labor-management structures that formerly predominated in the U.S. economy. In contrast, our analysis of the postwar processes of segmentation helps clarify, we believe, the character of the current period of decay. It not only points toward some emergent corporate exploration of new methods for organizing the labor process and labor markets; it also suggests that restructuring efforts are likely to involve the other elements of the social structure of accumulation, particularly in the role of the state and relations among the major capitalist nations (see Bowles and Gintis, 1982, and Rosenberg and Weisskopf, 1981, for related discussions).

The breakdown of the postwar social structure of accumulation has squeezed relations within each of the three main labor segments. We develop this final part of our analysis by reviewing recent developments in each of the three labor segments of the postwar economy. In each case we present evidence both of decay of the labor process and labor markets and of initial exploration in each of those respective sectors.

The subordinate primary segment. We begin with the subordinate primary segment because its consolidation played such a critical role in restructuring the postwar U.S. economy.

From hindsight, it seems fairly clear that the postwar truce between large corporations and their workers, particularly those represented by large industrial unions, rested on a fairly explicit quid pro quo. In one direction, many unions and workers ceded to corporate management a relatively unbridled discretion over the organization of production; this "management prerogative" permitted corporations to shape the internal organization of production and increase their relative leverage over workers. In the other direction, corporations bought worker cooperation by promising to deliver on three important conditions: rising real wages, reliable employment security, and improving working conditions. At the same time, the government sought to solidify the truce both through legislation regulating union–management relations and social welfare programs that ameliorated labor–capital conflict. This accord effectively provided the framework, at least through the late 1960s, within which stable conditions of production fueled prosperity and expansion.

Corporations took continuous advantage of their prerogatives over production to increase their relative administrative leverage fairly dramatically (see Edwards, 1979, ch. 8). Gordon (1981a) estimates the ratio of supervisory to nonsupervisory employees (in the private nonfarm economy) as a proximate measure of the intensity of corporate supervisory and administrative effort. This ratio rose from 13 supervisory employees per 100 nonsupervisory workers in the late 1940s to 23 per 100 in the late 1960s, an increase of more than 75 percent.[11]

Subordinate primary workers were able to enjoy improvement along each of the three critical dimensions of the postwar bargain.

Between 1947 and 1967, the real (average weekly) wages of workers in core manufacturing industries increased substantially, rising by more than 3 percent per year (these figures are based on the series reported in Table 5.3). Average unemployment rates among adult male workers fell to below 2 percent at the height of the mid-sixties boom (U.S. Department of Labor, 1980b, table A-20), and many workers had begun to take for granted the employment protections embodied in the seniority systems of the postwar period. Working conditions also appear to have improved; for example, the index of accidents in manufacturing declined steadily after World War II, falling by 40 percent from 1946 to 1963 (*Historical Statistics*, 1975, series D-1029).

With both sides to the bargain enjoying the promised fruits of compromise, labor peace spread. Workdays lost through strikes declined fairly steadily through the mid-1960s (*Historical Statistics*, 1975, series D-1013), and labor unions appear to have slowed their organizing activities, apparently contributing to a declining union share of the nonagricultural labor force.

We suggest that the terms of this labor peace no longer hold. Although we do not in this chapter provide a year-by-year account of the accord's unraveling, we shall review structured evidence indicating that the foundations of peace in the subordinate primary segment have been dissolving.

Many workers no longer seem to be able to realize *any* of the three conditions for their cooperation with corporate management. Through the mid-1960s, as we saw, workers enjoyed a trend toward rising real wages, employment security, and improving working conditions. Since the late 1960s and the early 1970s, these trends have essentially been reversed. Table 5.9 provides data indicating some rough measures of this reversal. The table divides the postwar period into three distinct time periods (with the end-points representing comparable years in the short-term business cycle): expansion through 1966, slowdown until 1973, and spreading instability through 1978. (Rosenberg and Weisskopf, 1981, develop a similar periodization in their analysis of inflation.) Column 1 tabulates rates of change of real wages for production workers in the core manufacturing sector; column 2 traces the change in the adult male unemployment rate of production workers in manufacturing; and column 3 shows the rate of change in a standardized index of industrial accidents.[12] All three columns indicate the extent of reversal for subordinate primary workers since the onset of crisis in the late 1960s.

Have corporations acknowledged these reversals and sought to restore the postwar truce by relinquishing some of their prerogatives

Table 5.9. *Postwar trends in wages, unemployment, and working conditions in the subordinate primary segment*

Years[a]	Average annual percentage change in real wages[b]	Average annual percentage change in unemployment rates[c]	Average annual percentage change in accident rates[d]
1948–1966	+3.52	−6.02	−1.54
1966–1973	+1.14	+4.22	+2.94
1973–1979	+0.26	+8.77	+3.33

[a]The endpoints are the years in which the rate of growth of aggregate output peaked before a business cycle downturn (the 1966 peak preceded a very short downturn).
[b]This series measures the average annual (arithmetic) changes in average weekly earnings adjusted by the consumer price index for production workers in core manufacturing industries.
[c]This column measures the average annual (arithmetic) change in the unemployment rate for experienced blue-collar operatives, with the first period for the years from 1959 to 1966.
[d]This column traces the average annual (arithmetic) change in the index of industrial accidents for manufacturing; see note 12 to text for details on adjustment of series for years before and after 1970.
Sources: Wage data from series reported in table 5.3; unemployment rates from U.S. President, 1980b, table A-23; accident rates from *Historical Statistics,* 1975, series D-1025; and U.S. Department of Commerce, 1975, 1980.

and easing the blow for workers? Quite the contrary, corporate managers have adopted a more aggressive and offensive strategy toward their production workers. This strategy features four main prongs of attack.

1. After a pause from 1968 to 1973, corporations have resumed their previous increases in the intensity of supervision and management. The ratio of supervisory to nonsupervisory workers (in the private nonfarm economy) has been rising since 1974 at rates roughly comparable to its growth through 1968 (Gordon, 1981a).

2. Corporations have accelerated their relocation of fixed capital in manufacturing, disinvesting in the Northeast and expanding rapidly in the Sunbelt and overseas. A recent study by Varaiya and Wiseman (1980, tables 1, 2) confirms, for example, that declining relative employment and investment in the northeastern and northcentral regions began to accelerate after 1968. Bluestone and Harrison (1980), building in part on data developed by Birch (1979), show clearly that the bulk of this regional disinvestment is attributable to location decisions by large corporations with multiunit operations; large firms are shifting around their resources, in other words, rather than smaller

(single-unit) firms picking up and running away. A number of studies have confirmed, finally, that regional differentials in workers' power, measured by both relative wages and relative unionization, dominate such other factors as energy costs and state/local tax and subsidy benefits, in "explaining" the recent locational shifts of corporations (see Vaughan, 1979, and Bluestone and Harrison, 1980).

3. Corporations have complemented these first two strategies with intensified antiunion activity. Although it is extremely difficult to develop reliable aggregate data on this trend, several indices suggest the shift that has occurred. First, it appears that corporations have turned increasingly to private management consulting firms that specialize in union-breaking and union prevention. Second, such corporate groups as the Business Roundtable have intensified their hostility to labor-oriented reform of labor legislation. Third, many unionized corporations have resisted extending unionism to workers in their new Southern plants. This aggressive stance has succeeded, contributing to a rapid increase in the frequency both of decertification elections and of union losses in those elections (see Brody, 1980, pp. 248 ff.).

4. All these weapons in the corporate arsenal have enhanced the bargaining leverage of corporations over even the most established unions. Many national and local unions are being asked more and more frequently to "give back" wage, benefit, pension, and seniority gains; and many unions, feeling themselves under the gun, have complied. Once again, it is extremely difficult to provide quantitative documentation of this trend; however, recent journalistic reports confirm that this give-back phenomenon has spread fairly widely (Brody, 1980, p. 248).

None of these developments necessarily imply an actual "decay" in production relations. They could imply, much more simply, some shifts in the relative bargaining power of corporations and workers and some compositional shifts in the structure and location of production.

We incline toward a stronger conclusion, however. We propose that the gradual erosion of the postwar labor truce has already begun to undercut the stability and effectiveness of the structured production relations in the subordinate primary segment and that this erosion constitutes a principal source of the well-known slowdown in productivity growth in the U.S. economy.

Some fairly direct evidence, first of all, indicates that workers have become increasingly dissatisfied with their jobs and their union representatives. Absenteeism has increased steadily since the early 1960s (Naples, 1981). The Quality of Work Life Surveys conducted by the

219

University of Michigan Survey Research Center indicate, moreover, that workers' concern over their working conditions also rose steadily from 1969 to 1977. Those surveys also suggest that workers now evince considerable dissatisfaction with the effectiveness of their union representation over issues involving wages, working conditions, and employment security (see Staines, 1979, for a summary, and *Quality of Work Life,* 1979, for detailed results).

Some of this growing dissatisfaction has manifested itself in militant protest by workers. Total strike activity rose between 1966 and 1974 but has since diminished, presumably because of the disciplinary effect of higher unemployment rates and the growing threat of layoffs and plant shutdowns. However, some significant measures of worker militance have increased, suggesting that the character of workers' protests has changed substantially. The following indicators of this shift in the focus of worker militance have all increased significantly in mining and manufacturing since the mid-1960s: the proportion of all strikes concerning working conditions; the proportion of strikes that are not authorized by the union (wildcats); the proportion of wildcats concerning working conditions; and the proportion of proposed contract settlements rejected by the rank-and-file union membership (Naples, 1981; see also Flaherty, 1981). These increases apparently reflect growing concern about those aspects of production, such as working conditions, that were formerly regarded as the purview of management. Drawing on both quantitative and qualitative evidence, Naples argues (1981, 1982) that these changing dimensions of worker militance reflect an unraveling of the postwar truce and an increasing inclination among many workers to channel protest outside the previous boundaries of that truce.

A final argument seems especially critical, although we must still advance it very tentatively. It appears that the declining effectiveness of the postwar system of bureaucratic control has contributed significantly to the slowdown in the growth of labor productivity in the U.S. economy. Suggested by Edwards (1979), this hypothesis gains provisional econometric support in Gordon's (1981a) analysis of the private nonfarm economy; proxies for the effectiveness of bureaucratic control explain far more of the productivity slowdown since 1974 than such technical factors as a slowdown in the growth of capital per worker or rising energy prices. An analysis of the manufacturing sector by Berndt (1980), who also disaggregates labor inputs into production and nonproduction components, also seems consistent with this hypothesis.[13]

If there has been decay, then "exploration" should not be far behind. It is always extremely difficult to project future trends in any kind of institutional structure; the organization of production is certainly no exception. It is far too early to predict the future organization of production in the subordinate primary segment, particularly since, as our analytical framework emphasizes, future outcomes will be determined in large part by a process of conflict between capitalists and workers.

For our current purposes it is sufficient to highlight some of the emergent indications that corporations have already begun to explore new methods of organizing production. At least some of these dimensions of exploration will centrally affect, in ways we cannot yet clearly foresee, the restructuring of the U.S. economy over the next decade or two.

1. The organization of production will be deeply affected by recent developments in technology. Although it is still difficult to discern the implications for the social relations of production, it is clear that recent technical innovations, such as robotization and the proliferation of microelectronic equipment, carry profound potential implications for the organization of work and the relative power of managers and workers.

2. Corporate leaders have experimented with diverse forms of worker "participation" in management (see Mares and Simmons, 1982). Although capitalists have been leery of the potential disruptions and further loss of management prerogatives that such new relations might bring, they have been driven to explore these new production relations by the pressure of increasing competition and more slowly growing markets.

3. Many corporate managers appear to display growing interest in the "Japanese system" of labor management, with its close and almost paternalistic relationship between employer and employee. Everyone recognizes that the "Japanese model" could not possibly be transplanted to the United States without major adjustments and modifications, given the profound historical and cultural differences between the two countries. Indeed, Japanese firms that have opened plants in the United States in recent years have demonstrated an extreme hostility to unions. But many managers are becoming increasingly interested in exploring the kinds of changes that would be required in the United States in order to capture some of the perceived benefits of production relations in Japan.

4. Large corporations are apparently involved in a mounting debate over the future role of unions. One side of that debate blames unions for many of the problems that U.S. corporations have recently experienced. Another approach recognizes that unions cannot be eliminated and that some kind of future accommodation will be

necessary and perhaps even profitable (see Freeman and Medoff, 1979b). Where and how corporations and unions resolve their current differences is beyond the scope of anyone's crystal ball.

5. The exploratory efforts also extend beyond the domain of the managers of individual corporations. National discussions concerning new forms of wage determination through incomes policies indicate the attempt underway to restructure capital–labor relations through governmental intervention. The on-and-off flirtation with governmental industrial policy and planning based on the French and Japanese models also indicates the scope of the present exploratory efforts.

The independent primary segment. Corporations pursued the consolidation of this segment, we have argued, in order to solve problems created by the decline of the old craft system of production. Like the stabilization of subordinate primary work, the success of this consolidation depended on a kind of implicit contract. Considerable evidence suggests that this contract has at least partly ruptured and that the structured relations organizing production in this segment have also begun to decay.

Corporations have sought independent primary workers who would exercise initiative and solve problems and at the same time ultimately respect corporate authority. Corporate success in creating and maintaining this delicate balance depended on management's ability to provide certain guarantees and satisfactions to independent primary workers in return for their loyal respect for corporate authority. Three dimensions of independent primary jobs held the greatest appeal and played the most important role in this bargain: widening relative earnings differentials, at least with respect to subordinate primary workers; opportunities for skills development and relatively autonomous job control; and some combination of stable employment and opportunities for job advancement. However fragmentary, evidence is mounting that independent primary workers are suffering reversals along each of these three dimensions.

First, the relative earnings position of primary workers is eroding. As we saw in the previous section, the income gap between independent primary and subordinate primary workers was statistically significant and widening from 1950 to 1970. Data on median occupational earnings during the 1970s suggest that this trend has reversed. Indeed, the table compiled by Blumberg (1980) suggests that many independent primary workers, particularly those like university faculty who earn straight salaries rather than commissions or negotiable fees, have suffered the greatest recent declines in real earnings among a wide range of occupations and that the earnings differential between the independent primary and the subordinate primary segments of employees has probably narrowed.

Second, data based on the *Dictionary of Occupational Titles* indicate that the most important changes in the occupational skill requirements from the mid-1960s to the mid-1970s involved significant declines in the number of jobs demanding the highest general educational development and the highest specific vocational preparation time (Rumberger, 1981a). These changes have reduced skill development opportunities for many independent primary workers. In addition, a number of qualitative studies have traced erosion in the relative autonomy of many independent primary jobs: Greenbaum (1979) and Kraft (1977) both document dramatic deterioration in the autonomy and independence of computer systems analysts' work. Nurses and some other health technicians have experienced substantial standardization of many job functions (Brown, 1980). Although we have not seen any detailed studies, journalists have presented repeated accounts of engineers' complaints about the standardization of their work. We suspect that these pockets of evidence reflect a relatively general trend: routinization of many jobs within the traditional boundaries of the independent primary segment.

Third, job insecurity is no longer the exclusive preserve of secondary or even subordinate primary workers. Unemployment rates of professional, technical, and managerial employees have all risen relative to those of blue-collar workers (U.S. Department of Labor, 1980b, table A-23). The aggregate demand for college-educated workers has slowed so dramatically, it appears, that promising opportunities for college graduates have declined in many sectors; the clearest evidence of this shift in relative demand lies in the dramatic recent diminution of the relative income returns to a college degree (see Freeman, 1976, and Rumberger, 1981b, for detailed studies). While corporate management remains one of the fastest growing occupational categories, demand in many health and education professions has shrunk as a result of stagflation and the fiscal crisis of the state.

These developments have begun to take their toll. Work dissatisfaction is mounting among many occupational groups within the independent primary segment. In the detailed data provided through the *Quality of Work Life* survey (1979), for example, professional, technical, and managerial employees display the most rapid increases in job dissatisfaction along several important dimensions. Perhaps more surprisingly, union organizing drives among some groups of independent primary workers have proved especially successful during the 1970s. Unionization has grown particularly rapidly among teachers, nurses, and other health technicians, and several miscellaneous groups, such as museum curators and publishing professionals. The very notion of unionization begins to contradict, of course, the original corporate conception of the independent primary segment and of corporate hopes for ultimate control over independent primary workers.

How have these elements of decay begun to affect the basic performance of independent primary workers? Since it is difficult to perform detailed studies of productivity by occupational groups, we cannot judge the effects of decay in this segment with any precision. Recent studies by Medoff and Abraham (1979, 1980) nonetheless point to an interesting contradiction of hierarchical job structures within this segment. Through detailed microstudies of middle-level managerial personnel in large corporations, Medoff and Abraham find that earnings *rise* with employee experience on the job but that employee performance, based on independent supervisors' evaluations, *declines* with continued experience. The longer these employees work, apparently, the less productive they become. This finding suggests that the effectiveness of traditional incentive structures within corporate hierarchies has probably decayed and that these workers do not derive independent stimulus from the structure of their jobs to improve their performance continually while they work.[14]

Are there signs of exploration in this segment? Future developments will depend primarily on the resolution of two conflicting tendencies that seem increasingly evident in current managerial discussions. On the one hand, managers have been exploring means of breaking down and routinizing many independent jobs – in computers, health care, data processing, engineering, and business services. Alongside these developments, one hears recurrent discussion about the inflexibilities of structured internal systems providing job security, including both tenure systems in universities and the civil service system in the public sector. On the other hand, top-level management has been devoting considerable attention to systems of group management and team work, moving away from pyramidal hierarchies toward more collegial systems of decision making and job assignment.

These two countertendencies reflect the contradiction, embodied in independent primary work, between corporate desires to ensure some independent creativity and corporate desires to reproduce continuing internalization of firm objectives. The future of independent primary work will undoubtedly depend not only on the technical evolution of the demand for high-skilled, problem-solving labor but also on the initiatives that both employers and employees take about the organization of work in this segment.

The secondary segment. The organization of production changed relatively little in the secondary segment, as we have argued above, from the pre- to the post–World War II period. Firms in this segment continued to rely on the structures of labor management first developed during the period of labor homogenization. Consequently, it is not surprising that data on working conditions and relative earnings provide the least evidence of decay for this segment since the early 1970s.

Working conditions have not deteriorated as much among secondary workers as in the subordinate primary segment, largely because they had never improved as much during the earlier period of postwar expansion. Disaggregated data on industrial accidents during the 1960s suggest, for instance, that accident rates in peripheral manufacturing industries remained relatively constant while core accident rates first declined and then increased (*U.S. President's Report on Occupational Safety and Health*, 1972, appendix B).

Because workers in the secondary segment have always suffered from relatively weak bargaining power, they have felt the effect of inflation on their real earnings more sharply than subordinate primary workers. Our data indicate, for example, that the real (average weekly) earnings of peripheral workers in manufacturing declined by almost 5 percent between 1973 and 1979 (cf. Table 5.9 for the comparable figures for core workers).

And yet, critical changes appear to be affecting secondary work during the current period of decay. One such change involves a shift in the labor supply. During the late 1960s and early 1970s many native-born minority workers appear to have become less tolerant of secondary wages and working conditions. This development helped accelerate an apparent shift in the labor supply of secondary workers toward immigrant workers from the Caribbean and Mexico. It is difficult to measure the effects of this supply shift on the organization of production in the secondary segment, partly because of the virtually subterranean character of many enterprises employing immigrant workers. We are inclined to assume, however, that some important changes have occurred; the lack of citizens' rights among many of these workers must have undercut their relative power and therefore influenced production relations in this segment.

A second change in secondary work involves increasing foreign competition. Many peripheral industries in manufacturing are especially susceptible to foreign competition because they are relatively labor-intensive and their products have low transportation costs per value of shipment. As is well known, the international division of labor has shifted rapidly in recent years (see, for example, Fröbel et al., 1979). These international adjustments make it likely that rapid domestic shifts in the relative viability of many peripheral industries will also continue. The future of secondary work in many areas within the United States will reflect the manner in which the world economy is being restructured.

Conclusion. Our discussion suggests that the structure of segmentation has begun to decay and that explorations are under way that will significantly alter existing institutions in each of the three principal labor segments. Given the pressures on each segment, it would be easy to move from this conclusion to a prediction that the decay of segmentation will be followed by a new period of homogenization. However, such a prediction would be justified neither by our analysis nor by our evidence. Rather than a return to homogenization, our discussion suggests that a reshuffling of the boundaries of the different labor segments and changes in their internal structures are taking place.

The persistence of some continuing segmentation is evident in several of the indices that we have already presented. For example, earnings of workers in the secondary segment have continued to deteriorate relative to earnings of subordinate primary workers, while some independent primary workers continue to maintain their relative position. The ratio of union members' earnings to those of nonunion members has increased substantially during the 1970s (Johnson, 1981). The occupational segregation of women continues unabated (see Blau and Hendricks, 1979, for a careful study), and the growth in the proportion of women in some professions does not carry sufficient numerical weight to upset this conclusion. The position of racial minorities in the subordinate primary segment has strengthened somewhat (again, the numbers in the professions carry little overall significance), but the gap between minority workers in the primary and secondary segments has widened. These trends augur continuing, but not inevitable, differences among U.S. workers.

Our analysis does not, of course, provide us with perfect foresight or prescience. We can offer a much more modest final conclusion: Postwar prosperity depended upon and reinforced a specific institutional structure that generated segmentation of the labor process and labor markets. Spreading instability and economic crisis, as in earlier historical periods, have begun to erode those postwar institutional structures. Corporate exploration appears to have begun amid the spreading signs of decay. The future of work in the United States will depend on the relative power and strategic initiatives of corporations, workers, and other groups with influence over the organization of production. The more American workers can become aware of the structural determinants of these changes and of the structural bases of the divisions among labor segments, the more they will be able to overcome their weaknesses and the more influence they will exercise over the future of their own work.

6

A recapitulation

We argue in this book that three major structural transformations have shaped the labor process and labor markets in the United States. These structural changes have consolidated successive tendencies toward the initial proletarianization, homogenization, and segmentation of labor. In Chapters 3 through 5 we have presented a wide variety of historical evidence that lends plausibility to our principal hypotheses.

The analysis in those chapters is historically complex and not easily summarized. And yet, because we recognize that the detailed nature of the analysis may make it difficult for many readers to digest its major conclusions and implications, some review seems useful. In this brief concluding chapter we recapitulate and highlight the most important dimensions of our historical argument. Where possible, we have linked our qualitative analyses to specific quantitative indicators that illustrate those analyses most clearly. We rely heavily on these indicators in this summary, neither because we believe that numbers adequately express the qualitative complexity of our argument nor because we think that these numbers somehow "prove" that the analysis holds. Much more modestly, we use these numbers in this recapitulation as some approximate benchmarks by which readers can help keep track of and focus more clearly on the major implications of our argument.

We have combined these benchmark numbers into a single summary chart, Table 6.1. The table is organized to mirror the analytical framework first presented in Table 1.2. In the following pages we review the three historical transformations of labor in the United States by proceeding through the schema and data of Table 6.1.

Initial proletarianization. An initial proletarianization of labor accompanied the original development of capitalist production in the United States. As line 1 in Table 6.1 shows, the extension of wage labor has continued to the present. However, the fifty years of exploration and consolidation between 1820 and 1870 mark the initial acceleration of proletarianization. According to the rates of change presented in line 1a, in these years the percentage of wage workers increased more rapidly than in any other period in the history of U.S. capitalism.

The emergence of capitalism involves a rapid growth of capitalist production in industry. Line 2 traces this aspect of the stage of initial proletarianization, showing that the percentage of the labor force employed in "goods production" – defined for the purposes of this table as the manufacturing, mining, and construction sectors – increased by roughly two-thirds between 1820 and 1870. That share of employment has remained essentially constant ever since, rising slightly in the contraction phases of long swings, when productivity growth falls and more employees are required to produce goods, and falling slightly during periods of expansion, when productivity growth in the goods-producing sector correspondingly rises.

Although wage labor became predominant in the United States between 1820 and 1870, as we argued in detail in Chapter 3, the stage of initial proletarianization did not yet involve a qualitative transformation of the labor process. A wage-labor force emerged, but the labor process remained relatively untransformed. As a result, industrial output could increase only when employment increased in industry; there were not yet any reliable mechanisms available to employers for increasing output *per* worker employed. Line 3 reviews some data that dramatize this characteristic of the stage of initial proletarianization. The figures in line 3 reflect the additional amount of manufacturing output (measured in real prices) attributable to an additional employed production worker, on average, during the decades represented in the table. If a given figure in line 3 exceeds 1.0, then average production worker productivity has increased in manufacturing.

The patterns reflected in this row of Table 6.1 support an important conclusion of our analysis. The period of consolidation of initial proletarianization between the 1840s and the 1870s – with the labor process still untransformed – represents the period of consolidation (or expansion) in the measurable history of U.S. industrial capitalism when average labor productivity increased *most slowly*. Line 3 also provides some additional confirmation of our hypotheses about the impact of long swings on average productivity in manufacturing. After 1870, the two subsequent periods of consolidation each shows a greater elasticity of output (with respect to production worker employment) than does the previous period of decay and exploration.

Homogenization. The crisis of the 1870s and 1880s clearly revealed for capitalists the insufficiency of their untransformed labor processes.

Table 6.1. *The historical transformation of labor in the United States*

	Initial proletarianization		Initial proletarianization / Homogenization	Homogenization		Segmentation	
	Exploration	Consolidation	Decay / Exploration	Consolidation	Decay	Exploration	Consolidation
	1820	1850	1870	1900	1930	1950	1970
Proletarianization							
1. Wage labor as percentage of free labor force	31*	42*	52*	61.8	75.8	82.1	90.1
a. Average annual percentage change		+1.18	+1.19	+0.53	+0.76	+0.41	+0.49
2. Goods employment as percentage of labor force	11.6	20.8	26.5	28.2	26.4	29.9	27.2
3. Increase in manufacturing output ÷ increase in mfg. production employment			1.29	1.78	2.06	1.50	4.20
Homogenization							
4. Surplus as percentage of manufacturing value added		48.9	55.5	52.6 (51.4)	53.3	48.0	52.7
a. Average annual percentage change			+0.67	−0.17	+0.12	−0.50	+0.45

5. Real capital/labor ratio in manufacturing (1929 = 100)	18.4	50.9	100.0	88.3	136.0
a. Average annual percentage change		+5.8	+4.8	−5.8	+2.7
6. Male operatives and laborers as percentage of male manufacturing employment	38.6	42.0	55.0		
7. Nonproduction employees ÷ production employment in manufacturing		.077	.154	.231	.334
a. Average annual percentage change			+3.3	+2.5	+2.2
8. Percentage change in ratio of unskilled/skilled hourly wage	−8.3	+5.4	−9.3	+6.8	
Segmentation					
9. Union membership as percentage of total nonagricultural employment		5.2	11.6	31.5	27.4
10. Total engineers ÷ total craft workers		.014	.040	.063	.111
11. Average annual percentage growth in manufacturing "total factor productivity"		+1.60	+2.85	+2.02	+3.24
12. Segmentation of jobs					
a. Independent primary jobs as percentage of nonagricultural employment				27.8	32.7

(*continued*)

Table 6.1. (Cont.)

	Initial proletarianization			Homogenization			Segmentation		
	Exploration	Consolidation	Decay	Exploration	Consolidation	Decay	Exploration	Consolidation	
	1820	1850	1870	1900		1930		1950	1970
b. Subordinate primary jobs as percentage of nonagricultural employment								37.2	31.0
c. Secondary jobs as percentage of nonagricultural employment								35.0	36.2
13. Fragmentation of labor force: women and black males as percentage of labor force						29.4		34.6	43.8
14. Index of income inequality by labor market segment								8.4	13.2
15. Index of unemployment segmentation by demographic group								2.5	5.3

*Indicates rough estimate.

Sources and Notes for Table 6.1: Row 1: Figures for 1900 and 1930 from Lebergott (1964, tables A-3, A-4). Figures for 1950 and 1970 from Reich (1978). Figures for 1820, 1850, and 1870 derived by using 1780 estimate from Reich (1978) and 1880 estimate based on Bell (1940, p. 10) and Lebergott (1964, tables A-3, A-4), in the following manner: Although Bell and Lebergott agree on the percentage of the labor force who are self-employed farmers for 1900 to 1940, they disagree slightly on the percentage of non-farm self-employed. We take the more careful Lebergott estimates and use these to correct Bell's figure for 1880, arriving at an estimate of 57 percent for 1880. Interpolation between 1780 and 1880, relying on compound growth rate projections, yields the rough estimates for 1820, 1850, and 1870. Row 2: See note 17 in Chapter 3. Row 3: Data are based on production worker employment and value added in manufacturing (*Historical Statistics*, 1975, series P-5, P-10). Value added is deflated by the wholesale price index (*Historical Statistics*, 1975, series E-52). The first two figures in the row are estimated for 1849–1879 and 1879–1899 in order to correspond more closely to the dating of these two phases of the long swing delineated in Table 2.1. (The problem with 1869, in part, is that the real value-added figures are distorted by the substantial swing in wholesale prices during and after the Civil War.) The figure itself is the ratio of the exponential rate of growth of value added to the exponential rate of growth of employment. Row 4: Based on data for manufacturing from *Historical Statistics*, 1975, series P-7-10. The figure for net surplus is calculated as $(VA_1 - W_1/VA_1$ where VA_1 measures current value added in manufacturing and W_1 measures compensation paid to wage-and-salary employees. The two figures for 1900 reflect the different bases for the series before and after 1899. The figure in parentheses corresponds to the post-1900 sample. Row 5: Based on Kendrick (1961, table D-I), and Kendrick and Grossman (1980, appendix, p. 118). Row 6: See note 8 in Chapter 4. Row 7: Based on *Historical Statistics*, 1975, series P-5-6. Row 8: Based on the inverse of Lindert and Williamson (1977, table A3). Row 9: Based on *Historical Statistics*, 1975, series D-127, D-940, D-951. Row 10: Based on *Historical Statistics*, 1975, series D-152 ff. Row 11: Derived from Kendrick (1961, table D-I) and Kendrick and Grossman (1980, appendix, p. 118). Row 12a–c: See Table 5.8 for sources and derivation. Row 13: This series is equal to the sum of the estimated labor force for women, from *Historical Statistics*, 1975, series D-49; and a series for black males from Bancroft (1958, table D-1); the 1970 figure for black males is calculated from the *Historical Statistics* figures for the black male population, series A-123–133, and the figure for labor force participation, Series D-23. Row 14: Ratio of between- to within-group variance in earnings inequality by segment; see Chapter 5, under "Period of consolidation." Row 15: See Table 5.6.

233

Average labor productivity increased, but it did not increase enough. Although prices were falling in the 1880s, workers were able to maintain the level of money wages; as a result, labor costs rose relative to workers' output. Between 1869 and 1889, during the period of spreading stagnation, we estimate that unit labor costs increased by an average of 1.5 percent per year.[1] In consequence, as we saw in Chapters 3 and 4, a crisis developed for capitalists. Unless they could do something either about labor productivity or about workers' wages (they could not yet do anything about prices), their profits would continue to feel the squeeze.

Line 4 traces the approximate impact of this crisis on entrepreneurial profitability. It measures the trends in relative "surplus" in manufacturing – calculated as the amount of revenue from value added that manufacturers were able to retain after covering wage-and-salary compensation. The figures in line 4 confirm important conclusions of our analysis of the period of homogenization. First, net surplus fell between 1870 and 1900, after a rise during the earlier period of consolidation between 1850 and 1870.[2] This fall in the surplus reflects the squeeze on entrepreneurial profits in manufacturing that we discussed both above and in Chapters 3 and 4. Second, to follow this simple strand of our story across line 4a into the twentieth century, the trends in net manufacturing surplus provide a second summary confirmation of our hypotheses about the impact of long swings on U.S. industrial capitalism: the surplus consistently rises during periods of consolidation of a new structure of labor management and falls with comparable consistency during periods of long-swing contraction.

As we argued in Chapter 4, employers responded to crisis by beginning to explore and ultimately to consolidate a homogenization of the labor process. One important and relatively immediate dimension of this emergent homogenization involved the process of mechanization. This mechanization quickly transformed the labor process, as we saw in Chapter 4, and began to confront workers with more and more capital equipment on their jobs. Line 5 traces this development through an index of the capital/labor ratio for manufacturing (with the index pegged at 100.0 for 1929). This index in line 5 shows a dramatic increase in the capital/labor ratio between 1870 and 1900 and again from 1900 through 1930.[3] The decline in the capital/labor ratio between 1930 and 1950 apparently reflects both the abandonment of considerable (and relatively less productive) capital plant and equipment during the Depression and the equally considerable public bequest to private capital after World War II of huge stocks of capital goods constructed by the government during the war (see Gordon,

1967). The historic significance of mechanization in the period of homogenization is nonetheless revealed by the numbers in line 5 and the rates of change in 5a. Even during the rapid technological advances after 1950, the capital/labor ratio did not increase as rapidly (on an average annual basis) as during the period of either exploration or consolidation of homogenization.

Mechanization and a simultaneous expansion of the supply of surplus labor helped foster a homogenization of jobs in the industrial labor process; craft skills were undermined and more and more jobs were reduced to a common, semiskilled operative/labor denominator. Since occupational data are relatively scanty on the years before 1900, one must assess evidence on the homogenization of jobs in the labor process with some caution. Line 6 compiles the share of male manufacturing employment represented by operative and labor occupations between 1870 and 1930. This index is calculated from Alba Edwards's summary of occupational data from the *Census of Manufactures* during those six decades. As one would expect from our historical analysis, this index shows a slow rise in relative operative-and-laborer employment during the period of exploration and a much more rapid rise during the period of consolidation.[4]

We also noted in Chapter 5 that large corporations began after the mergers at the turn of the century to take advantage of their consolidated scale and to pursue new labor-management policies designed to reinforce the impact of homogenization and to undercut the increasingly unified workers' opposition that the early exploration of homogenization appear to have provoked. As a principal correlate of this initiative, many corporations installed progressively larger systems of control within their own administrations. This development was reflected in a rapid growth in the ratio of nonproduction to production workers in manufacturing. Line 7 shows this central tendency in U.S. industry: The relative weight of nonproduction workers in manufacturing nearly doubled between 1900 and 1930 and continued to rise through the next phase of segmentation.[5] Line 7a, tracking average annual rates of change, shows further that the most rapid relative increase in this index of administrative personnel occurred during the years of the consolidation of homogenization. After World War II, new systems of bureaucratic control relied relatively more on the extension of *rules* and managed, as a result, with less rapid relative increases in nonproduction employment.

The dynamics of the homogenization phase produced some evident effects upon the wage structure in the capitalist sector. Many historians have already noted the fragmentary quality of the data, so we need not repeat our concerns for those problems here. The best available data, shown in line 8, provide a confirming commentary on the logic of homogenization, however, and provide one final measure of the impact of homogenization.

As we noted in Chapter 4, the early period of exploration of homogenization, from the 1870s through the 1890s, produced an increase in the unskilled/skilled hourly wage ratio, shown in line 8; both the rapidly increasing demand for unskilled labor and the uncertain fate of craft unions during this period made these trends relatively plausible. In contrast, the unskilled/skilled wage ratio fell after 1900. We suspect that this reversal reflects both the acceleration of immigration after the mid-1890s – generating a rapid augmentation of the reserve pool of unskilled labor – and the growing cooperation (and consequently cozier bargaining relationships) between large corporations and the craft unions.

The other figures in line 8 also seem consistent with our more general historical account. The data suggest a decline between 1850 and 1870 in the unskilled/skilled wage ratio during the consolidation of initial proletarianization; production conditions had not yet generated a fluid mechanism of "competitive" labor market wage determination, and, as a result, trade unions were still able to take advantage of local and regional monopolies. Analogously, we suspect that the unskilled/skilled wage ratio rose between 1930 and 1950 because industrial unions had already begun to exert decisive effects on the relative wages of millions of relatively less-skilled industrial workers.[6]

Segmentation. The emergent decay of the drive system of labor management accelerated in the 1930s, as workers were able to organize industrial unions that dramatically advanced their struggles to resist corporate control over the production process (see Chapter 5). Corporations responded to this challenge from labor by pursuing the implications of some of their early explorations of new "internal labor market" structures and by encouraging an integration of the industrial unions into a new collective bargaining structure. This corporate initiative – and the ultimately cooperative industrial union response – established the foundation upon which the process of labor segmentation was established. A new labor-management structure managed to curb the spread of industrial unionism and also to channel some of the impulses that the CIO movement had initially tapped.

Line 9 traces both the initial union imperatives to which the new labor-management system responded and the success of labor segmentation in containing the spread of industrial unions. Unions had managed to increase their members' share of nonagricultural employment by a small but significant margin during the period of compromise between corporations and craft unions from 1900 through the 1920s. But these gains soon paled beside the quantum gains that unions achieved between 1930 and 1950. By the time union membership had reached its historic peak in 1950–1954, the relative growth of union membership had more than doubled its earlier expansion.

And then, of course, it stopped. After 1954, the unions' share of nonagricultural employment declined continuously through 1970, and this decline accelerated during the subsequent period of decay (see Chapter 5). Lines 4 and 9 should be reviewed together. Just as the decline of relative union membership after the early 1950s reflects a moderation of workers' relative power, so the rapid increase in capitalists' net surplus in manufacturing suggests a dramatic improvement in employers' bargaining power and relative well-being.

Early in the phase of homogenization, corporations had begun to seek substitutes for the general skill-training mechanisms that craft unions had provided earlier. This development led to the growth of private vocational institutes, as we saw in Chapter 5, and to the more general spread of the engineering profession and related occupations. Employers used these sources to seek generally skilled workers who would be likely to internalize the broad goals of the corporations. Line 6 indicates that relative craft numbers began to decline early in the phase of homogenization. Line 10 traces the corollary rise in the relative importance of engineers in the U.S. economy, indicating that the ratio of engineers to craft workers had risen by 1970 to nearly eight times its level in 1900.

The growth of large corporations and their eventual consolidation of segmentation after World War II both reflected and facilitated a much more effective use of factor inputs than had been possible in either of the two earlier phases of labor transformation. Corporations could expand administration, labor, or capital (not to speak of energy) inputs with much greater flexibility than before. (Line 3 indicates that the effectiveness of continually increasing labor inputs had decreased, controlling for phases of the long swing, after 1930, and, according to the evidence provided by line 5, capitalists moderated the rate of increase of capital inputs after World War II.)

This flexibility suggests a look at measures of "total factor productivity" to assess the impact of segmentation. Line 11 summarizes data from the study by Kendrick and Grossman (1980) of manufacturing productivity. Their data indicate that total factor productivity increased faster between 1950 and 1970 than in any of the three previous long-swing phases since the late-nineteenth century.

The rapid increase in total factor productivity during the period of consolidation of segmentation helps to clarify the success of the postwar integration of new structures of labor management and the moderation of capital–labor struggle after the early 1950s.

The new structure of segmentation helped reverse earlier tendencies affecting the structure of jobs in the U.S. economy. As we saw in line 7, the process of homogenization had helped promote a leveling of the occupational structure, undercutting craft requirements and continually generalizing the semiskilled conditions of work in modern industry.

As we saw in Chapter 5, the process of segmentation eventually had the opposite effect. Although industrial and other workers resisted the effects of homogenization, employers eventually achieved a reduction in the relative numerical strength and effective bargaining power of those workers.

This development affected the aggregate composition of the labor force. Lines 12a to 12c summarize the occupational effects of segmentation. Despite the complexity of the analysis of data underlying these rows, the main conclusions seem fairly straightforward. The jobs that had grown most rapidly in the earlier phase of homogenization had been transformed into a subordinate primary segment; this segment was now losing relative weight within the occupational structure. In contrast, both the independent primary segment and the secondary segment increased their relative importance after World War II. Yet it is in these two segments that capital holds relatively greater power: in the independent primary segment, from the low degree of unionization and the greater flexibility of work rules; and in the secondary segment, from the myriad disadvantages that secondary workers confront in facing their employers. Consequently, we can conclude that capital had substantially consolidated its power through the evolution of the structure of segmentation after 1950. The figures on net surplus in line 4 also support this impression.

Workers experienced not only greater segmentation after World War II but also greater fragmentation among themselves. Line 13 measures in a fairly simple manner this dimension of twentieth-century labor market history. Increasingly after 1930, females and black males composed a growing portion of the U.S. labor force. This growing heterogeneity afforded many employers an opportunity to play upon race and sex divisions within their work forces and to enhance their relative bargaining power over workers in their establishments. As line 13 shows, the growth of this index of fragmentation accelerated between 1950 and 1970.

A recapitulation

Finally, lines 14 and 15 summarize the consequences of this segmentation for divisions among workers. They report the indices for earnings inequality by segment and for unemployment segmentation by demographic group. Both show a substantial increase during the period of consolidation from 1950 to 1970.

Epilogue

The U.S. economy entered a new period of crisis at the beginning of the 1970s, a period of long-swing stagnation that continues to the present. This change is reflected in the temper of the time: There was a dramatic switch from the optimism and confidence of the 1950s and 1960s, as the prevailing mood became one of insecurity and pessimism about the future.

The economic troubles of the 1970s and 1980s cannot be attributed to any single "cause" such as OPEC, declining productivity, too much deficit spending by government, or an excessive money supply. These putative causes, and others that have been blamed as well, are but symptoms of the crisis. Each appears to contribute to the poor economic performance. But like the pain and incontinence of the cancer victim, they make matters worse without themselves constituting the essential cause of the problem.

The postwar boom grew out of that integrated complex of law, institutions, and customary arrangements that we have labeled the "postwar accord." This social structure of accumulation was rooted in the Wagner Act, Social Security, Taft-Hartley, the Employment Act of 1946, and the Bretton Woods system and encompassed segmented labor markets, diverse (simple, technical, and bureaucratic) systems of control of the labor process, class conflict channeled into the governmental arena, an extensive economic role for government, and the maintenance of a hegemonic military posture to protect the opportunity for American corporations to invest abroad. These institutional arrangements have all begun to decay.

The present crisis, no less than those of the late nineteenth century and the 1930s, stems from the deterioration of a social structure of accumulation. By the end of the 1960s, the postwar accord provided a less and less favorable and more unstable climate for investment. The successful period of rapid growth had produced, or developed alongside, internal contradictions that now pushed the system toward stagnation. The channeling of class conflict into contestation over governmental policy had produced a dramatic increase in the role

240

(and costs) of the state. The attempt to police the world capitalist market ran into disaster in Vietnam, weakening U.S. ability to deal with the oil-producing countries and anticapitalist insurgencies in the Third World. The growth of capitalist competitors in Europe and East Asia eroded the dominant and privileged economic position of the United States, undermining the basis of the Bretton Woods arrangements.

Most importantly, the specific institutions and arrangements that provide the focus for this book – the diversified systems of control in the labor process and the segmentation of labor markets – no longer provided an adequate basis for continued rapid growth. In the labor process itself, bureaucratic control had depended upon stable employment and (with rising productivity) industrial expansion; the maintenance of technical control in the subordinate primary sector, where it was jointly (management–union) administered, required the acceptance by management of unions and real (productivity-based) wage increases; yet industrial expansion, acceptance of unions, and real wage increases all deteriorated with the onset of hard times in the 1970s.

The bases of segmentation in labor markets eroded as well. Race and sex segregation, legally permitted and formally embraced by virtually all employers at the beginning of the segmentation period, were legally prohibited and delegitimized by the end of the boom period, even though the pattern of job segregation persists. The unions have suffered successive losses in their ability to defend the structural elements (and real benefits) in the primary subordinate market. Primary independent workers, mostly without union protection and more susceptible to fluctuations in the public sector budget, have seen their wages and working conditions deteriorate.

As growth slowed, employers increasingly directed investment to regions, countries, and industries where the terms of the postwar accord did not obtain. The great Northeast–Midwest industrial belt, heartland of the postwar boom, showed the greatest decline.

Within this general decline, as in prior crises, exceptions stand out. The oil companies, for example, have achieved exceptionally high profits: Petroleum firms accounted for fully 40 percent of all manufacturing profits in 1980, and Exxon alone captured over $5 billion in profits. Engineers and unionized steelworkers have experienced real wage gains. Parts of the Sunbelt are witnessing boom conditions. Yet despite this uneven development, the general condition has been growing stagflation.

If past patterns hold true, the resolution of this crisis will require the construction of a new social structure of accumulation. Minor

changes in policy, better fiscal or monetary management, and gim-
micks such as tax-based incomes policies may be implemented. But
such tinkering will not, individually or even in sum, amount to a
successful reconstruction program.

Moreover, the construction of a new social structure of accumulation will require (again, if past patterns hold true) the creation of a
new political constituency to effect the necessary changes. The Republican program, as it emerged from the watershed election of 1896 and
was elaborated by Presidents Roosevelt, Taft, Harding, Coolidge, and
Hoover, represents one example. The New Deal coalition, established
in the 1930s and held together until the Vietnam War, reflects
another. The process is evident: Construction of a new social structure of accumulation requires major institutional innovations, and
such innovations require for their implementation a new political
agenda and new sources of support – in other words, the creation of a
new political coalition.

The onset of a long-swing boom is accompanied by the emergence
of a new dominant political force, and their joint appearance is significant. The new political group (electoral party or wing of an established party) proposes the needed institutional innovations and, if it is
successful in implementing them and if the reforms are in turn successful in stimulating the boom, the new political force reaps the
credit. Its ideology becomes the "dominant" ideology ("the business
of America is business" or "mixed capitalism" in the welfare/warfare
state), and the political faction becomes the dominant political force.

Thus, the crisis that began in the early 1970s can only be resolved
by the construction of a new social structure of accumulation. That
construction requires a new political coalition, and the political group
that proposes and implements a successful reconstruction program
is likely to become the dominant political force for the duration of
the long-swing boom – that is, for a generation or longer.

In the early 1980s the program that appears to match these criteria
most closely belongs to the conservative "New Right," a movement
culminating in the election of Ronald Reagan as president of the
United States. Moreover, the 1980 election was widely interpreted as
establishing exactly the kind of new political constituency always associated with the construction of a new social structure of accumulation.

The Reagan program addresses the causes of slow growth in terms
of a systemic diagnosis and systemic prescriptions. Indeed, its vision is
to reestablish the conditions that existed in 1947: a relatively small
nonmilitary public sector; a "social safety net" consisting primarily of
Social Security and associated programs; and a dominant military

presence, "dominant" at least in the non-Communist world. The Reagan program thus seeks to revive the boom by rolling back the gains achieved by working-class groups under the postwar accord, as though the years of postwar prosperity could be run through again once environmental laws, health and safety regulations, income maintenance programs, and the rest of the welfare state apparatus have been dismantled.

Whether the Reagan program will succeed requires speculation far beyond the scope of this study. We might note, however, that there is no guarantee that the program of a newly ascendant coalition will indeed provide the basis for a new burst of growth; recall the failure of the first New Deal (1932–1935). More importantly, the early Roosevelt years also suggest that when no plausible alternative exists – and the Republicans in 1934 and 1936 offered no new ideas – the new political group may have a considerable length of time in which to change its analysis, sort out its strategy, and maneuver or bungle its way into a successful program.

The most crucial issue with regard to the Reagan program, therefore, may well be whether or not its opposition is able to put forward a coherent alternative plan. To put the matter more directly, in order for the present crisis to be resolved in a way favorable to the working class, the Left must advance a plan for the construction of a new social structure of accumulation. Articulating a reconstruction program must become a top priority for all who believe that following the New Right ensures widespread hardship and risks social catastrophe. This kind of opportunity for restructuring comes only once a generation.

Notes

1. The historical transformation of labor: an overview

1. In this brief summary we do not attempt a detailed discussion of the comparative merits of each approach, but rather situate our analysis in relation to others.
2. Bell (1960) provides one of the most important early statements of this view, later developed more fully in Bell (1976). Young (1954) brilliantly satirized the internal logic of the meritocratic perspective. Kerr et al. (1960) presented a related and influential synthetic analysis. In mainstream economics, human capital theory provided a rigorous microeconomic foundation for this view; see Becker (1964) for the first fully developed elaborations. By the late 1960s this perspective was typically applied to most social problems involving the allocation of "human resources." For a Marxian approach to postindustrial analysis, see Block and Hirschhorn (1979); see also Plotke (1980).
3. Later critiques also revealed some serious flaws in the logic of the meritocratic view. See Bowles and Gintis (1976, chs. 3–5) and Carnoy and Levin (in press) for analysis of hypotheses about the relation between skills and economic success.
4. Some of the proponents of Braverman's analysis have subsequently criticized earlier versions of our own work; see Geller (1979), Zimbalist (1979, ch. 1), and Clawson (1980). We respond to some of their specific criticisms in the process of developing our argument throughout succeeding chapters.
5. See, for example, Gutman (1976). Davis (1980) and Montgomery (1980) provide a synthesis of much of this literature; see also Aronowitz (1973), Brody (1979), and Green (1980). Both Brody (1979) and Montgomery (1980) call for a theoretical framework within which to interpret the concrete studies.
6. See Dunlop (1958) for a general statement of the industrial relations perspective. Kerr's essays have been compiled in a valuable collection (Kerr, 1977). Doeringer and Piore (1971) worked with Dunlop and two of us (Gordon and Reich). Further elaborations by Piore are presented in Piore (1979b) and Berger and Piore (1981).
7. Two comments about our analysis of initial proletarianization may be useful at this point.
   First, we should offer a word of explanation about the term itself. *Proletarianization* refers to the process through which people become dependent on wage labor for their survival. Our analysis of the phase of initial proletarianization focuses on the institutional changes that proved

244

necessary to establish the *first* critical mass of wage labor in the United States. Proletarianization continues throughout the course of capitalist economies, but its subsequent history in the United States became interwoven with the institutional changes necessary to resolve the periodic problems and struggles that the capitalist production system itself had created.

Second, we should repeat our earlier caution that this book focuses on the capitalist sector of the economy. Many of the important national political–economic issues of the nineteenth century – the conflicts over the extension of the transportation system, tariffs, slavery and Reconstruction in the South, and the position of the farmers – involved the expansion of the capitalist system into noncapitalist areas. Despite their evident significance for U.S. history as a whole, these events lie outside our perimeter here. Thus, for example, we touch only tangentially on the emancipation of the slaves and the Civil War in our discussion of nineteenth-century crises and structural changes.

2. Long swings and stages of capitalism

1. For analytical development of the necessary conditions for the reproduction of capitalist economies, see, for example, Harris (1978) or Roemer (1981). The condition focusing on the household and the state was not normally stressed in earlier Marxian work but has received substantially greater focus in the recent Marxian tradition. See, for example, Gough (1979) and Bowles and Gintis (in press).
2. This list of five tendencies should be read as our distillation of the most illuminating components of the historical materialist framework. Other elements of the Marxian literature have proved less illuminating. As we note below, we believe that much of the traditional Marxian analysis requires, and has undergone, considerable reformulation; some of these reformulations remain controversial. However, this book is not the place to debate these issues.
3. Marglin (in press, ch. 3) has clarified the theoretical importance of this dynamic, arguing that the differential between the average rate of growth of capital, g, and the average rate of growth of the labor force, n, determines whether or not the capitalist economy tends continuously to extend its boundaries. If $(g - n)$ is greater than zero (in "steady state"), the relative power of workers inside the previous boundaries of the capitalist economy is likely to increase; this pressure forces capitalists to expand beyond those boundaries.
4. There has been relatively little formal theoretical Marxian work on this tendency toward collective working-class activity. See Hyman (1975) and Gordon (1981b) for two such efforts.
5. See Gordon (1980) for a related theoretical discussion of many of the arguments outlined in this section and for a brief critical review of earlier literature on stages of capitalism.
6. Marglin (in press) provides a careful review of neoclassical, neo-Marxian, and neo-Keynesian theories of growth and investment.
7. For further discussion of the dynamics of capital accumulation, see Harris (1978) or Roemer (1981).
8. Gordon (1980) reviews the set of institutions constituent to a social struc-

ture of accumulation and provides one formal listing of these institutional requirements.

9. This relation between the financial rate of return and the rate of profit on industrial capital has not been carefully analyzed within the Marxian tradition. For one recent effort, see Panico (1980).

10. Plotke (1980) and Mandel (1980) have both recently criticized an earlier formulation of this analysis of stages of capitalism (in Gordon, 1980) as "economistic." The analysis appears to them to elevate "economic" forces arising from the accumulation process to a position of undue primacy in analyses of historical change. We do not intend such an elevation. We recognize that our analysis of stages of capitalism must be combined with cultural and political analyses for a fuller understanding of history, and we have tried in this book to link our analysis with other determinants of working-class movements. Our analysis of long swings and stages of capitalism provides only a starting point, albeit an absolutely necessary one, for a full theoretical and historical account of the important forces that have shaped production and the working class in U.S. capitalism.

11. Gordon (1980) hypothesizes that substantial infrastructural investment is concentrated at the beginning of a new stage of capitalism as a result of new productive structures and new systems of transportation and communication. Such bunching of infrastructural investment would impart a large stimulus to the economy at the beginning of a new social structure of accumulation.

12. Some further commentary on related literature seems useful at this stage in our introduction.

Two recent strands of literature have pursued parallel analyses of the impact of capitalist development on the labor process. First, Braverman (1974), Clawson (1980), and others following Braverman's lead have emphasized a continuous process of deskilling and a continual capitalist effort to seize control over production from relatively skilled and autonomous workers. These analytic efforts do not go far enough, we would argue, because they fail to analyze the effects of alternating rhythms of capital accumulation on capitalists' resources in their quest for control and also because they pay much more attention to what capitalists have sought to accomplish than what has actually happened. Second, Aglietta (1979, first published in French in 1976) pursues an analysis whose intentions seem very similar to ours, particularly in his effort to identify stages of "capitalist regulation." Aglietta pursues some interesting theoretical hypotheses about the effects of accumulation on the conditions of wage labor and intercapitalist competition. Like Braverman's, however, Aglietta's analysis remains limited because he also pays too much attention to what capitalists said they were trying to accomplish, essentially ignores workers' responses, and fails to present much evidence about what actually happened to the organization of work and working-class movements, whether or not it supports his analytic scheme. In particular, as we argue in Chapter 4, his special attention to "Fordism" seems misplaced and historically misleading.

Ironically, these criticisms echo Rubery's (1978) comments on our earlier work; she argued that we exaggerated the power of capitalists to achieve whatever they wanted and also neglected workers' response to capitalists' initiatives. We largely agree with those criticisms; the theory

246

and the history developed in this book begin to redress the one-sidedness of our prior formulations.

We note, finally, that Cronin (1979, 1980) pursues analyses of workers' strikes and insurgencies in Great Britain that parallel our approach in this book, although he pays much less attention to the organization of production than we have tried to pursue in this study. As in our analysis, Cronin finds that the dynamic of the long swing helps illuminate many aspects of the history of workers' insurgency in Britain that heretofore seemed inexplicable.

13. We summarize here the implications of our analysis for an understanding of historical changes in the institutional mechanisms for transmitting skills.

    In the initial proletarianization phase, skilled workers controlled the labor process. They hired apprentices or helpers who gained skills while working alongside the artisan or master. The transmission of skills from one cohort to another thus passed through the bottleneck of the skilled workers, who could regulate the terms and magnitude of the transmission process. Indeed, this bottleneck (and the control that skilled workers exercised over the level of output) constituted one of the main incentives for capitalists to enter the workplace and transform the labor process.

    In the homogenization phase, mechanization tended to downgrade the demand for skills, and employers sought ways to substitute less skilled for more skilled labor. Yet the demise of the old apprenticeship system created a vacuum, and in some industries at least (see, for example, Brody, 1960) the lack of training programs created problems. Some capitalists sought to fill this vacuum by establishing their own vocational or training schools – Henry Ford's school for boys was probably the best known. Others turned more directly to formal schooling, and it was in this period that Andrew Carnegie and others began looking to college graduates for foremen. Apprenticeship programs, even if drastically curtailed from the preceding years and no longer controlled solely by skilled workers, nonetheless remained important.

    In the segmentation period, the mechanism for transmittal of skills has become almost entirely removed from the control of the workers. Increasingly, employers rely on formal schooling (at all levels) and upon a new internal hierarchy established within the firm that provides opportunities for on-the-job learning. Schooling has thus replaced (in part) the old worker-dominated skilling process. Moreover, workers are hired into job ladders where advancement to higher paying jobs requires (among other things) learning new skills. But here the specification of the job ladder and the determination of the rate of advancement generally reside with the employer, not the skilled workers. An untrained worker learns skills for the next job while in his or her current job. Thus, the pattern of development described for the labor process and labor markets has had its impact on how skills are acquired, who governs access to skills, and whose interests the skilling process will expand or contract.

14. R. A. Gordon (1961) summarized the consensus view in his macroeconomics textbook (p. 238): "In the last 10 or 15 years, however, the existence of these 'Kondratieff' waves has been increasingly questioned." These doubts had been initially solidified by the influential article by Garvy (1943).

15. Maddison (1977), on whose data compilations we rely in Table 2.1, considers that the differences between phases IIB and IIIA are sufficiently small to include them both in a single period of expansion lasting from 1870 to 1913. Our periodizations differ from his because we derive our phases in the first instance from our analyses of qualitative changes in social structures of accumulation; we find it difficult to imagine that the structural changes in the advanced capitalist countries around 1900 are not sufficiently important to warrant the demarcation of a new stage of development. Moreover, our dating is at least as justified as Maddison's on the basis of the quantitative data: The difference in his tabulations between the weighted rates of output growth in 1870–1913, as one phase, and 1913–1950, as another, is only 0.6 percentage points (Maddison, 1977, table 6). Although the difference in Table 2.1 between our phases IIB and IIIA is slightly smaller than this (0.4 percentage points), the difference between our phases IIIA and IIIB is substantially larger (1.0 percentage points). If one wants to point toward long periods with substantially different rates of growth in output, Maddison's periodization seems to blur some important differences that ours appears to reveal. Kleinknecht (1981) provides data for Italy, Sweden, Denmark and Norway which also appear to fit the same periodization as ours.
16. We weighted the growth rates in Table 2.1 by the countries' respective shares of world trade rather than by their relative gross outputs. The trade connections among nations are the principal transmission mechanism through which the long swing spreads. For this reason, trade shares constitute a better measure of the relative impact of the respective economies on long swings in the world capitalist economy than total output.
17. These hypotheses have precedents in the earlier empirical literature on business-cycle behavior pioneered by Mitchell (1913). Thus, Burns (1929) mentions that Mitchell had observed quite early the differing short-term cyclical contours between the respective phases of the long swing, noted in our Table 2.2, well before economists began to formalize long-swing theories in the post-Kondratieff era.

3. Initial proletarianization: 1820s to 1890s

1. Our account of the timing of this boom is relatively consistent with recent mainstream estimates of the basic data for this period of "take-off." Gallman's (1975) downward revisions of the pre-1840 growth rates estimated by David (1967) render more plausible our view of the period from the 1820s through the early 1840s as a period of relatively slower growth. Gallman's (1966, table 6) estimates of the average quinquennial rates of growth in real GNP from 1839 to 1903 support both the notion of an acceleration in growth in the period covered by his estimate for 1839–1843 to 1844–1853 and a conclusion that rates of growth of real output declined steadily after the mid-1870s, falling rapidly through the four successive quinquennial comparisons leading up to the recovery of 1889–1898 to 1894–1903.
2. For an engaging and essentially correct interpretation of the early struggles over the monetary system, see Galbraith (1975, chs. 7 and 8). On the

tariff, see Edwards (1970). The essays in Williamson (1951, part 3) provide perhaps the best overall view of the creation of nonlabor institutions.

3. In this interpretation we take issue with those recent investigators, both of the left (e.g., Mandle, 1978) and the right (e.g., Reid, 1973), who see the development of (respectively) wage labor or voluntary exchange in the sharecropping system in the South. A more plausible interpretation, stressing the extensive land, credit, and political controls on the black laboring population, is given in Ransom and Sutch (1977).

4. Many of the young men who escaped wage labor in the East wound up working for wages in the West; Jensen (1950) ascribes much of the militancy of western workers – for example, the radicalism of the Western Federation of Miners – to their disillusionment over their failure to make a permanent escape. See also Shannon (1945).

5. This point appears to have been overlooked by those recent analyses that so emphasize the ethnic diversity of the nineteenth-century working class as to ignore the important elements of continuity with existing American society (see, for example, Cole, 1963; Greene, 1968; and even Gutman, 1976). These analyses allocate to ethnic groups not only all the foreign-born, no matter how early in life emigration occurred, but also the children of the foreign-born. For a more balanced view, see Montgomery (1967, ch. 1).

6. The earliest data for occupations by nativity, from the *Ninth Census* (1870), confirm the assertions in the text. For earlier but more qualitative evidence, see case studies by industry: Cole (1926), Cole and Williamson (1931), Ware (1931), Thistlewaite (1958), Modell (1971), and Hirsch (1978).

7. Modell (1971, pp. 82–83) notes that the push from land pressure was likely the dominant force, since those many migrants who moved short distances tended to take up jobs in great proportions at the very lowest levels in the urban hierarchy, even though their proximity should have equipped them with the knowledge of how little the city had to offer.

8. We ignore here two important nineteenth-century female occupations, domestic service and schoolteaching. Both are central to understanding women's employment prospects but are less crucial for our analysis of accumulation and the capitalist labor force.

9. This public sentiment crippled the first attempt at the establishment of factories by a General Humphrey in 1804. According to a late-nineteenth-century source (writing in 1887), "the prevailing opinion was so unfavorable to the factory system, the horrors of which were fully described in the English newspapers, that many parents refused to allow their children to accept employment in his works" (quoted in Ware, 1964, p. 71). The "Rhode Island" system was crippled, too. As Gitelman notes (1967, p. 231), "If the labor of children could not be used, the economic advantage of the family labor system was lost."

10. The mills in the 1820s and early 1830s seem to have provided real opportunities for women. As Gitelman (1967) has pointed out, mill wages appear to have been substantially higher than those afforded by other employment open to women (primarily schoolteaching and domestic work). The dormitories, frequently criticized for being overcrowded, were, in the words of one of the harshest critics, "far from being slum dwellings"

(Josephson, 1949, p. 70). Moreover, as the defenders of the system have rightly emphasized, the cultural, educational, and social aspects of the boardinghouses compared very favorably with the often boring life on the farms from which most of the women came; and the women's own creativity, poured out in publications and performances, can hardly be denied. Yet the system existed primarily to attract labor to the mills; consequently, the corporations' paternalism was shot through with less friendly aspects. The regulations were pervasive and no respecters of privacy. The employment contracts were one-sided, requiring the women to obey all the regulations, to remain at the mills for twelve months, and to give two weeks notice if they intended to leave; violations meant a dishonorable discharge and the employers' blacklist. Employers were not bound to provide employment for the twelve months and maintained the right to change the wages, hours, or conditions of work as they wished.

11. Shlakman (1934, pp. 99 ff.) provides some carefully compiled data on company profits. After brief recovery in the mid-1840s, she notes, profits settled down to "4 and 5 percent per annum" through the Civil War. See also McGouldrick (1968, ch. 4).

12. In the case of the textile industries, the fights for the ten-hour day during the 1820s and 1830s, although they had not overtaken the textile industry, limited the possibilities for extending the working day (see Commons et al., 1918, vol. 1). Based on extremely detailed surveys of the industry during this period, McGouldrick (1968, p. 39) concludes: "During these years, machinery technology was stagnant. The only two machine innovations of substance . . . were as much capital-saving as they were labor-saving." Deprived of those options, employers were forced to intensify labor as the profit squeeze continued.

13. If wages could be reduced, the urgency of labor intensification was obviously diminished. In general, employers sought both to reduce wages and to intensify work. For evidence of wage reduction, see Shlakman (1934, pp. 114 ff.). Shlakman disputes Caroline Ware's (1931) casual contention that the ownership of the companies changed hands. Even the owners originally responsible for the paternalism of the "Lowell System" were forced to assume an increasingly exploitive stance as profits declined during the 1840s (see also Josephson, 1949, pp. 208 ff.). The increase in the number of machines tended by each hand may have been partially compensated for by the greater reliability of the machinery.

14. The suddenness of the replacement by the Irish was partly explained by the severity of the depression from 1848 to 1851, which pushed more and more of the Yankee girls back to their family farms (see Ware, 1964, p. 150; and Shlakman, 1934, p. 150). Moreover, we should not overstate the extent to which native-born women left the mills. If they no longer provided sufficient labor for the quickening accumulation of the 1840s and 1850s, they nonetheless remained in the factories in large numbers. Gitleman (1967) found that as late as 1860 the non-Irish workforce, essentially Yankee women, constituted 53 percent of the labor force in the mills he studied. As Norman Ware (1964, p. 74) has observed, "as the New England farms disappeared, the freedom of the mill operatives contracted. They could no longer escape." Despite the speedup, the reduced wages, the long hours, and the collapse of a remaining pretense of "moral experiment," many women stayed.

15. For evidence on rising productivity, see Gitelman (1967, p. 243) and McGouldrick (1968, pp. 38–39). Technical change seems to have been minor, but the speedup was frequently accompanied by increased capital per worker (e.g., four spindles per operative instead of three).

16. The conventional view can be found in the essays in Williamson (1951) or, for the "new economic history," Davis et al. (1972). A slightly dissonant view, although one that still places primary reliance on technology, is given in Chandler (1977).

17. These numbers are based on *Historical Statistics* (1975, series D-172–174). The figure for 1820 is an approximate estimate because the same data series does not stipulate a separate figure for manufacturing; the figure 11.5 percent comes from the numbers for employment in construction and manufacturing reported in series D-156, D-157 and an assumption that mining employment in 1820, not reported separately, was as high as the 1840 figure. This estimate is therefore an upper bound on the figure for 1820.

18. See Davis et al. (1972) for the "consensus" view.

19. This analysis is open to three objections. First, it might be argued that changes in relative prices tend to bias the results by understating the real (physical) output growth in such industries. If declines in relative prices were most severe in industries with the greatest technical change – a reasonable assumption – then the effect of technical change would be underestimated. Second, a deterioration in labor quality would tend to make our measure an overstatement of the effective increases in labor and hence exaggerate its effects; a deterioration seems unlikely, but remains a possibility. Finally, the quantity of labor input may be poorly measured by "average number of workers employed"; most observers suggest, however, that the working day lengthened over this period, rather than shortened, and the pace of work probably increased also. These changes would tend to work in the opposite direction from the first two biases.

20. Although neoclassical economic historians have primarily fashioned the conventional view that we criticize in the text, scattered neoclassical studies provide evidence that adds further support to our interpretation of this period. For example, the study by Zevin (1972) of the textile industry, to quote Lee and Passell's review of this literature (1979, p. 93), "damages the conventional wisdom that technical change was the single important factor setting the stage for economic development."

21. Based on Freedley (1858, pp. 427–429). This comprehensive volume gives a remarkable view of manufacturing in 1857.

22. Figures on the foreign-born composition taken from *Ninth Census of the United States*, vol. 3, p. 826 and table 20.

23. Many females worked as domestic servants and as schoolteachers, two waged occupations that are not considered here.

24. Calculated from data kindly supplied (privately) by John Modell; see Modell (1971).

25. For useful discussions of labor struggles during this period, see Commons et al. (1918); Ware (1935); Ulman (1955); Grob (1964); Brecher (1972); and Foner (1972, vol. 1, Chapters 23–25).

4. The homogenization of labor: 1870s to World War II

1. The economic history literature has debated whether or not the period from the 1870s through the mid-1890s should be considered an "economic crisis." Those who express doubts about the depth of economic instability in the U.S. economy during this period have usually focused on aggregate growth rates. As we note in the appendix to Chapter 2, this criterion by itself does not distinguish dramatically between the last two decades of the nineteenth century and the first two decades of the twentieth. Instead, we argue that one should pay attention to a much wider variety of both quantitative and qualitative, economic and sociopolitical indicators of crisis. This broader perspective proves a persuasive basis for siding with the "crisis" interpretation. On some of the altered characteristics of business cycles during this period, see Mitchell (1913, pp. 410–411) and Burns (1929, pp. 731 ff.); see also Fels (1959). On some of the broader economic dimensions of this crisis, see, for example, Hoffmann (1956).

2. As we note later in this chapter, manufacturing employment increased fairly steadily throughout this period. Immigration behaved much less predictably, however, and peaked precisely when unemployment rates also reached relatively higher levels. After 1906, each of the years in which the unemployment rate exceeded 6 percent followed a year in which gross immigration exceeded one million. In addition, average annual immigration rates between 1903 and 1914 reached nearly one million, far higher than in any previous or succeeding period. Immigration flows are from *Historical Statistics*, 1975, series C-89. Unemployment rates are from the same source, series D-86.

3. Here we take issue with the interpretation of the Progressive Era offered by Gabriel Kolko (1963). We do not see the reforms as motivated by big capital to eliminate increasingly effective competition from small capital. Rather, it appears that the broad reform coalition created political conditions that required some reform, and in this sense reforms were *forced* upon big capital. Once such reforms had become necessary, big capital not surprisingly attempted to shape and distort the process of writing and enforcing the laws to suit its own interests. It is from this process that Kolko derives most of his evidence, thus leading to his incorrect conclusion that big capital *wanted* regulation. After 1915, of course, the reform movement collapsed.

4. We note, with appropriate self-criticism, that the forerunner to this essay (Reich et al., 1973) suffered precisely from its treatment of the entire twentieth century as one single stage of "monopoly capitalist" development. The abandonment of that perspective has permitted us to account for some of the major differences distinguishing the decades before World War II from those after the war.

5. One must be careful before jumping from these observations about mechanization to simple comparisons with the available empirical literature on the pace of "labor-saving" technical change. Most studies in this literature base their calculations on the rate of displacement of the most unskilled occupations. Our own hypotheses about homogenization – and most of the related institutional literature – affirm that mechanization during this period displaced skilled workers and tended to augment the demand for semiskilled labor. The impact on the least skilled grades is

less pertinent. Recent studies (see, for example, Williamson and Lindert, 1980, pp. 160 ff.) also rely on assumptions of constant relative skill intensities among industries in order to estimate the effect of uneven sectoral growth on aggregate skill composition. Our own analysis of this period raises serious doubts about this assumption, however, since the pace of early trends toward homogenization, with their consequent effects on the intraindustry composition of labor skills, was extremely uneven among industries. With all of these qualifications, the data presented by Williamson and Lindert (1980, table 7.2) are essentially consistent with our view of the timing of mechanization. We can compare the first fifteen years of expansion (in the stage of initial proletarianization), from 1844 to 1859, with the first fifteen years of decay, from 1879 to 1894, during which we argue that mechanization accelerated. The decline in "unskilled labor's share" was 60 percent more rapid from 1879 to 1894 than from 1844 to 1859, suggesting a more rapid rate of "labor-saving" mechanization, in their terms, during the early stages of homogenization.

6. It is difficult to disentangle the effects of "labor control" imperatives from more traditional cost-minimizing forces and to assess the relative importance of each. We do not propose that the three examples in the text fully support the weight of the theoretical argument. For substantial development of the theoretical proposition, see Braverman (1974), Marglin (1974), Gintis (1976), Gordon (1976), and Reich and Devine (1981).

7. As Ozanne points out (1967, pp. 22 ff.), the company could scarcely have been motivated by a simple calculus of cost reduction in the short run. The new equipment had never been tried; it broke down so frequently that both labor costs and capital costs increased after its adoption, and profits suffered for several years after its installation. The investment was justified, of course, because it helped rid the company of a long-term problem (see also Clawson [1980, pp. 196–198]).

8. The problem with the data for our purposes here is that, although the general category of "operatives, laborers, and allied occupations" in the 1940 Census tabulation includes many skilled occupations within several key industries, such as steel and meatpacking, the time series prior to 1900 do not permit an extraction of these skilled categories from the data. The amalgamated category for "iron and steel, machinery, and vehicle industries" includes within the operative line, for example, all of the following skilled occupations: "filers," "forgemen," "iron molders," "rollers," and "toolmakers." As a result, we cannot easily compare the growth in the operative category with the growth in skilled job categories such as butchers and iron molders and rollers. More disaggregated data, probably on an industry-by-industry case-study basis, will be necessary to provide a more meaningful account of these changes in occupational composition during this early period of homogenization.

Given those limitations, we chose a procedure for estimating the change from 1870 to 1900 which would understate the growth in actual employment within the operative and laborer categories. The data come from Edwards, 1943, table 9. The series for operatives and laborers is derived (1) by summing employment in those industries in which the 1930 employment share of the main craft category is less than half and (2) by subtracting the major craft occupation totals within industries on the basis of the detailed 1930 breakdowns. For 1870 and 1900, where details on craft categories are not available, we assumed that the share of industry employment in craft occupations in 1900 and 1870 equaled the 1930 share; this estimate establishes an upper bound for the share of craft workers in those industries in the earlier years. Given data for the later periods showing declining craft employment, our estimate therefore understates the growth in this index of homogenization.

9. Lindert and Williamson (1977, p. 95) agree that the "inequality of *real* income tended ... to ... rise to about 1873 [and] fall to about 1896" (emphasis in original). Our explanation seems to us consistent with the full context of economic development during this period. It is conceivable that the failure of the unskilled/skilled wage ratio to widen during these years may also be due to the reduced bargaining power of skilled workers in response to the attack on their industrial strongholds; a disaggregated comparison of the wage ratio among major industries might permit disentanglement of the alternative explanations. Pending such further analysis, we are inclined to treat the period from 1873 to 1896 as one of the moments in U.S. economic history when competitive labor market analysis makes the most sense, for reasons highlighted in the following paragraphs of text. As we note in the section on consolidation below, bargaining power factors become much more important as determinants of wage dynamics after the turn of the century.

    Williamson and Lindert (1980) provide more detailed analyses; for our comments on their conclusions, see the discussion in Chapter 6, note 6.

10. It is probably useful to reiterate here our argument that labor markets were relatively fragmented on a local and regional basis through the 1860s and early 1870s (see Ch. 3, under "The Period of Consolidation").

11. Independent estimates reported by Lindert and Williamson (1977, p. 90) also support these conclusions about regional wage differentials. Their data suggest a widening of regional differentials from 1840 to 1880, before this movement toward a more national market, and then a substantial narrowing (by 10 percent) from 1880 to 1900. It is possible that this narrowing is attributable primarily to rapid increases in the demand for labor in previously low-wage areas. Indeed, this did happen. But the demand for low-wage labor also increased very rapidly in more traditional industrial cities like New York and Philadelphia (see Gordon, 1978b, for this timing). Given the relative mobility of labor (Thernstrom and Knights, 1970) among cities during this period and independent evidence of the activities of labor contracting agencies (see, for example, Ehrlich, 1974), it seems unlikely that the scarcity of labor in the Midwest would have been sufficient to support a primarily demand-pull explanation of the narrowing of regional wage differentials.

12. Unless otherwise noted, all the data reported in this paragraph are taken from Edwards, 1943, tables 8 and 10. In order to retain consistency with later census tabulations of the domestic and personal service categories, boarding and lodging house keepers, hotelkeepers and managers, and restaurant, cafe, and lunchroom keepers were all subtracted from the aggregate totals for domestic and personal service for the purposes of these calculations.

13. Column 3 in table 4.3 is based on Peterson (1938, table 8, p. 33). "Noneconomic strikes" were defined as the sum of three strike

categories: strikes over "recognition, wages, hours"; "recognition, union rules, and other"; and "sympathy." (Since there was another category for just "wages and hours," the first item was presumably distinguished by its inclusion of recognition demands.) This definition may significantly understate the "noneconomic" strikes; Peterson reports that a large proportion of the "miscellaneous" category involved strikes over "demands for or against discharge of certain employees or foremen," etc. This miscellaneous category, which is not included in the series reported in Column (3), included another 16.1 percent of total strikes in 1902–1904.

14. See also Green (1980, ch. 2) and Foner (1955, vol. 2; 1964, vol. 3) for further detail about some of these movements.

15. For more on corporate attitudes during this period, see Hays (1957), and Kirkland (1967), as well as U.S. Industrial Commission (1901, passim).

16. The series on horsepower per worker (col. 4) (in many ways the most direct evidence of mechanization, since it relies on a physical rather than a value measure) shows the most stable rate of growth over the period, with an average annual increase of 3.3 percent per year between 1879 and 1899 and a corresponding increase of 3.3 percent per year from 1899 (second series) to 1914.

Our analysis of the effects of mechanization on the skill structure in this period is also consistent with the econometric literature on the rate of technical change. Morishima and Saito (1968) construct an index of the labor–capital ratio, holding factor prices constant for 1902–1955. The index declines rapidly until the late 1920s, indicating a rapid decrease, controlling for factor prices, in the amount of employment per unit of capital (p. 438). Strikingly, this index does *not* decline during the later period of the consolidation of segmentation – indicating that increases in productivity after World War II were achieved through changes in production relations which did not require a declining labor–capital ratio. (For further comparisons along this dimension, see our discussion in Chapter 6.) This study does not suffer from some of the problems cited in note 5 above, but see Williamson and Lindert (1980, p. 158) for other qualifications.

17. We defined *consolidated* and *nonconsolidated* industries in the following manner: Edwards (1975a, tables A.4, A.5) provides lists of the largest-ranking firms (by total assets) for 1903 and 1919. We tabulated the cumulative assets by two-digit industry of firms with assets exceeding $15 million in 1903 and assets exceeding $50 million in 1919 and then expressed that cumulative share of assets held by large firms as a percentage of total book value of assets (by two-digit industry) (*Historical Statistics,* 1975, series P-126–176). We considered an industry as "consolidated" if the large firms' share of total assets was 25 percent or greater. (There was a considerable break in the distribution between 15 percent and 25 percent.) Of eighteen two-digit industries for which comparable classifications and calculations could be performed, ten were counted as consolidated in 1903 and eleven in 1919; nine were labeled as consolidated in both years. The results correspond very closely to a parallel tabulation on combinations' share of total value of products by industry from the U.S. Bureau of the Census, 1903, table 26, p. lxxxi. We chose our method because we were able to work with a more standardized list of

two-digit industries; because it permitted comparisons between 1903 and 1919; and because the census tabulation includes combinations only up to 1900, two years before the end of the merger wave.

18. The data on establishment size by two-digit industry come from *Historical Statistics,* 1975, series P-58. For industries with full data, the average establishment size in 1899 stood at 66 workers per establishment for consolidated industries and 32 for nonconsolidated industries. Average establishment size for consolidated industries almost doubled to 128 in 1919, while the average for nonconsolidated industries remained virtually constant at 34 (the figures represent unweighted averages).

19. These figures do not solely reflect the added managerial personnel resulting from corporate consolidation. In 1900, there was one foremen for every two managers in manufacturing; by 1920, the ratio had risen to nearly three foremen for every four managers (*Historical Statistics,* 1975, series D-316, D-393). Unfortunately, it is impossible to compare the aggregate rate of increase in employment of foremen with the growth in the period *before* 1900, since the data prepared by Edwards (U.S. Bureau of the Census, 1943) lump foremen together with a wide variety of miscellaneous operatives in the years before 1900.

20. For further information on the rise of personnel departments, see Eilbert (1959), Korman (1967, pp. 64–81), Nelson (1975), Clawson (1980, pp. 184 ff.), and Jacoby (1981, chs. 5–7).

21. This argument obviously rests on several component hypotheses: (1) Data compiled by Bennett and Earle (1980, app. tables) confirm that a disproportionate number of strikes took place in the 1880s and early 1890s in the largest manufacturing cities: Between 1881 and 1894, "almost half of all strikes took place in just eight large urban counties" in just six cities – New York, Chicago, Philadelphia, Boston, Pittsburgh, and Cincinnati – even though those cities composed only one-quarter of the total urban population in 1890 (for population, see *Historical Statistics,* 1975, series A-57). (2) Employers moved at least partly because they consciously sought to escape workers' unrest and unionism. Taylor (1915, passim), Feldman (1925), and Jones (1925) all confirm this hypothesis; Feldman (1925, p. 346) concludes, for instance, that "firms wishing to avoid union conditions have also established small shops in the country." See Gordon (1978b, pp. 49 ff.) for further quotes and evidence. (3) Employers achieved greater freedom from union unrest once they set up shop in the suburbs. Taylor (1915, pp. 101 ff.) was quite confident that the moves had had such effects, particularly because of the greater fragmentation of worker communication it produced: "[Employee] contact with workers in other factories, with whom they might compare work conditions, is much less frequent" (p. 101).

22. Noble (1977) provides especially interesting evidence of the self-conscious attention paid by engineers to problems of capital–labor conflict in these years. With this background the hypothesis that industrial architects shared similar concerns becomes cogent.

23. It is important to note that these early experiments with piecework represent essentially prebureaucratic efforts to dissolve workers' "union of interest." See Edwards (1979, chs. 6–8) for discussion of some of the differences from the later period of "bureaucratic control."

24. See Commons et al. (1935) and Foner (1955, vol. 2) for some summary of this tendency. Commons et al. (1935, vol. 3, p. xxv) quotes a personnel officer in a meat-packing firm to this effect: "I visited the employment office of Swift and Company in 1904. I saw, seated on benches around the office, a sturdy group of blond-haired Nordics. I asked the employment agent, How comes it you are employing only Swedes? He answered, Well, you see, it is only for this week. Last week, we employed Slovaks. We change about among different nationalities and languages. It prevents them from getting together. We have the thing systematized. We have a luncheon each week of the employment managers of the large firms of the Chicago district. There we discuss our problems and exchange information. We have a number of men in the field, some of them officers of labor organizations. They keep us informed about what is going on. If agitators are coming in or expected, and there is considerable unrest among the labor population, we raise the wages all around about 10 percent. It is wonderful to watch the effect. The unrest stops and the agitators leave. Then when things quiet down we reduce the wages to where they were."

25. Korman (1967, pp. 66 ff.) and Higgs (1980) provide some corroborating support for this argument.

26. Green (1980, chs. 2, 3) provides a good general account of some of this history. See also Foner (1955, vol. 2; 1964, vol. 3).

27. Jacoby (1981, chs. 5–6) presents detailed evidence that supports this view, and we are particularly indebted to his insightful analysis of the 1920s. He shows that relatively few firms used job evaluations, fixed promotional criteria, or "welfare" plans during those years. He also presents data indicating that the spread of central personnel departments, after a brief burst during World War I, slowed to a snail's pace after 1920. Perhaps most strikingly, he documents a declining involvement of central personnel departments in discharge decisions during the 1920s. For reasons which we discuss in the section on decay in this chapter and which Jacoby discusses at length (ch. 6), the drive system was still too strong and workers still too weak during the 1920s for there to be strong evidence of decay in the dominant system or powerful imperatives toward its transformation.

28. Clawson (1980, passim) provides a recent rejoinder to this conclusion, arguing that scientific management had already become important by World War I and that it represented the dominant tendency in corporate management strategy during this period. Although we find his account useful for its exposition of the Taylorist perspective, we remain unconvinced by his argument. Clawson limits himself primarily to summaries of the views of managers and engineers and does not provide clear evidence of either the actual frequency of scientific management applications or the relative timing of implementation between the pre- and post–World War I periods. We find Jacoby's account (1981, chs. 5–7) more convincing.

29. The calculations are based on data for manufacturing from *Historical Statistics*, 1975, series P-7-10. The figure for gross surplus is calculated as $(VA_i - W_i / VA_i)$, where VA_i measures current value added in manufacturing and W_i measures wages paid to production workers. The figure

for 1869 is based on the assumption that the percentage of payroll paid in salaries (to nonproduction personnel) is the same as the average for 1889 and 1899. This seems reasonable and is unlikely to distort the results significantly, because the actual figures for (salaries/wages) remain roughly constant for 1890–1900 before the relative rise in the non-production salary share after 1900. In any case, we are concerned primarily with the rise from 1889 to 1929, and the data provide a separate breakdown for production workers' wages for both those years.

30. See note 8 above for the method of calculation and the source.

31. In the twenty years from 1881 to 1900, annual gross immigration averaged 446,000; in the 14 years from 1901 to 1914, annual flows averaged 923,000 (*Historical Statistics*, 1975, series C-85).

32. These calculations are based on the series compiled by Lindert and Williamson (1977), tables A.1, A.3. The unskilled workers' hourly wage series was deflated by a merged consumer price index from *Historical Statistics*, 1975, series E-183, E-185.

33. For our comments on Williamson and Lindert's (1980) analysis of these trends, see Chapter 6, note 6.

34. Some recomposition of female employment did occur, but within the five occupational categories mentioned in the text. The percentage of female nonagricultural employment accounted for by just the clothing and domestic and personal service categories fell from 87.4 percent in 1870 to 66.8 in 1900 and 40.4 percent in 1930. However, the percentage of female nonagricultural employment accounted for by all five occupational categories fell by much less – from 94.0 percent in 1870 to 84.2 percent in 1900 and 79.2 percent in 1930 – and the drop from 1900 to 1930 was much smaller than that for 1870 to 1900. Thus, although women moved (proportionately) out of clothing and service, they remained substantially concentrated in five occupations.

  The data cited here are calculated from Edwards (1943, table 10). To preserve consistency with later census occupational definitions, telephone operators were included in the clerical category.

35. For detailed evidence on the relatively different earnings patterns between men and women during this period, and for the relative dominance of sex discrimination over ethnic differentiation among female workers, see Blau (1980).

36. The data from which table 4.1 was drawn indicates that establishment size in the apparel industries grew relatively slowly before 1870 but increased rapidly thereafter, apparently because of relatively rapid mechanization. For a history of the clothing industry in this period that provides supporting evidence for homogenization before 1900, see Pope (1905).

37. These data measure the share of "industrial combinations" in total industry "value of product." By this measure, only lumber was more competitive than apparel (see U.S. Bureau of the Census, 1903, table 26).

38. Of the 2.2 million increase in union membership between 1916 and 1920, 1.6 million – or 73 percent – occurred in the construction trades, the machine industries, and transportation and communications (*Historical Statistics*, 1975, series D-952–969).

39. See Millis and Montgomery (1938) for a detailed history of the wartime spread of militance and unionization.

40. Although we have not performed detailed econometric studies of productivity during the 1920s, this argument gains at least superficial support from data available for the entire manufacturing sector. While employment growth ceased completely after 1919 and investment increased slightly, labor productivity increased nearly twice as rapidly as investment, producing a sudden and unprecedented decline in the capital/output ratio. This rather dramatic reversal cannot be entirely accounted for by short-term movements in capital per worker; nor is it likely that quality improvements in the capital stock could have had such sudden effects. Consequently, it seems plausible to propose that much of the rapid increase in labor productivity resulted from the sudden tilt toward employers in the capital–labor struggle. For basic data on manufacturing, see, Fabricant (1942); Creamer et al. (1960); and *Historical Statistics*, 1975, series D-130, P-110, W-30.

41. It is interesting to take note of developments at the Ford Motor Company during this period. Ford had developed extremely "liberal" personnel policies between 1914 and 1917, leading Gramsci (1971) and others more recently (Aglietta, 1979) to speak of "Fordism" as a new and more modern approach to labor management. The general triumph of employers and the drive system during the 1920s rendered many of Ford's innovations superfluous, however, and he shifted to much tougher policies, including industrial espionage and dismissal of dissidents. As Meyer (1977, ch. 9) documents in some detail, Ford essentially abandoned his velvet glove and displayed his iron fist. By the 1920s, Meyer concludes (p. 310), the "notorious Service Department and the network of factory spies proved the most efficient and effective method to control the Ford workforce."

5. *The segmentation of labor: 1920s to the present*

1. This point requires much further exploration. It may be, for example, that the declining rate of growth in supervisory personnel reflects the stagnation in the spread of personnel departments during the 1920s. It may also be, to suggest a different line of inquiry, that the increase in supervisors between 1900 and 1920 provided a sufficient critical mass to pursue effective consolidation of the drive system during the 1920s and that no additional foremen were necessary.

2. Jacoby (1981, ch. 6) cites several studies in support of the hypothesis that early explorations were concentrated in relatively large firms.

3. For the early 1930s the union membership series developed by Wolman (1936) differs slightly from that of the U.S. Bureau of Labor Statistics. We use the latter series here because it provides a consistent estimate through the 1960s.

4. See note 17 in Chapter 4 for a discussion of the method used to construct the category of consolidated industries.

5. We use this threshold in part because government strike data for the 1950s and 1960s define a "major strike" as one involving 10,000 or more workers.

6. See Lichtenstein (1975) for a detailed study of the war period.

7. There is cross-sectional evidence on qualitative differences in working conditions and attitudes among segments; the problem is simply that these data are not available over sufficiently long periods to permit tests of divergence in qualitative characteristics over time. For summaries of the cross-sectional evidence, see Gordon (1982).

8. Figures 5.1 and 5.2 were constructed using constant employment weights for 1963. The use of constant rather than current employment weights removes the effects of variations in sectoral size upon the movement of the index. The choice of 1963 as the base year reflects two considerations. First, 1963 is the midpoint of the 1953–1973 consolidation phase, and weights from midpoints of intervals are less likely to introduce bias into an index than are weights from initial or terminal points. Second, 1963 falls in neither the trough nor the peak of a business cycle and therefore does not introduce a cyclical bias. As a check on this procedure, Figures 5.1 and 5.2 were also constructed using current employment weights. The results proved to be remarkably similar.

9. See Bowles and Gintis (1976) for elaboration of the general hypothesis of correspondence between work and nonwork institutions. See Gordon (1982) for a review of specific hypotheses about the correspondence between differential working conditions among segments and the differential institutional relations of families, schools, and communities.

10. It is probably useful to reiterate here that the period of decay in the United States was itself rooted in important changes in the world economy and that deterioration of the social structure of accumulation partly reflected declining relative American power around the globe. The summaries that follow in this section are by no means meant to imply that the decay was *caused* by these various changes in labor relations in the United States. Rather, we view these changes as symptomatic of the decay of the underlying postwar social structure of accumulation on a world scale. For similar points, see Weisskopf (1981).

11. For the nongoods sector, the underlying data refer to "supervisory" and "nonsupervisory" personnel. For the goods-producing sectors, the data refer to "nonproduction" and "production" workers. The nonproduction category excludes many, but not all, clerical workers. In general, however imperfect the data, this series seems to reflect remarkably parallel movements across all industries in the growth of the administrative apparatus. See also Berndt (1980).

12. Because of the change in reporting practices after the Occupational Safety and Health Act of 1970, it is not possible precisely to compare the series before and after 1970. In this table, the figure for "1966–1973" represents the internally consistent annual rate of change between 1966 and 1970. The figure for "1973–1979" measures the frequency of disabilities resulting in workdays lost in order to maintain maximum consistency with the pre-1970 data; the major change after 1970 was to include accidents that did not result in workdays lost.

13. Gordon (1981a) argues more specifically that workers' responsiveness to intensified supervision is mediated by the inducements workers receive from corporations to cooperate with the system of bureaucratic control. Supervision became more intense during the period of consolidation but workers were well rewarded, as we have already seen in Table 5.9, and

they were therefore induced to cooperate. After 1973, corporations further intensified supervision, but workers did not receive commensurate inducements. A variable serving as a proxy for this effect in Gordon's econometric analysis accounts for nearly 90 percent of the difference in the rate of growth of labor productivity before and after 1973. Although the results are provisional (and far too aggregated), they nonetheless point away from capital-shortage explanations of the decline in productivity growth and toward the sort of explanation we discuss in the text. Berndt (1980) does not test our hypothesis directly, but he finds that almost all of the slowdown in labor productivity in manufacturing after 1973 has been due to "reduced productivity growth of nonproduction workers" (p. 68). Our hypothesis would explain this result by arguing that corporations continued to add supervisory workers after 1973 but that their effectiveness at eliciting greater effort from workers had eroded. In informal discussions, Berndt agrees that this interpretation is at least consistent with his results – about which he expresses some puzzlement in his published paper.

14. Since these studies were based on point-of-time cross-sectional surveys, we can only speculate whether their current results reflect some change from an earlier period. Edwards (1979, ch. 8) suggests that the original genesis of the hierarchical structure of independent primary work was consistent with continuing employee productivity on the job.

6. A recapitulation

1. This calculation is based on nominal unskilled hourly wages from Lindert and Williamson, 1977, table A.3; output per labor input from Kendrick, 1961, table D-1; and the index of producers' prices from *Historical Statistics*, 1975, series E-23.

2. We use figures for net surplus in this table, subtracting all employee compensation, because earlier data do not separate production-worker from nonproduction-worker compensation. In Chapter 4, we focus on what we call "gross surplus," separating out only production-worker compensation.

3. The index rises less rapidly through 1920, but, as Table 4.2 also showed, the employers' offensive after 1920 seems to have helped effect a rapid deceleration in the rate of capital investment necessary to generate increasing output.

4. See Chapter 5, "Period of consolidation," for another occupational index that confirms the movements reported here for the years 1900 to 1930.

5. As we noted in Chapter 4, the relative number of *foremen* per production worker grew more rapidly in the manufacturing sector than the ratio of *managers* to production workers; consequently, one cannot ascribe the increase in the nonproduction/production worker ratio solely to the growth of managerial personnel.

6. The substantial outmigration from the South between 1940 and 1950 more than offset any dampening effects of back-to-the-land migration during the Depression on the aggregate rate of increase of the supply of unskilled labor; this development leads us to our emphasis in the text

on industrial union bargaining effects (rather than pure labor supply effects).

In their recent book, Williamson and Lindert (1980) provide a detailed alternative interpretation of the alternating movements in the skilled/unskilled wage ratio. Their analyses rely on two major arguments – that the wage movements are closely related to movements in the relative rate of increase of labor supply (with more rapid increases in labor supply depressing unskilled workers' relative wages) and that a general equilibrium model of the demand for unskilled labor is best able to explain movements in this differential wage variable. We are not yet in a position to compare or argue between our interpretations and theirs, since we have not had time to translate our institutional analysis into a quantitative form that would be commensurable with their calculations. For the moment, we simply note the two alternative approaches – ours relying primarily on a bargaining power approach and theirs relying primarily on a more conventional neoclassical demand-and-supply framework.

Bibliography

Abbott, Edith. 1924. *Women in Industry: A Study in Economic History*. New York: Appleton.

Abramovitz, Moses. 1956. *Resource and Output Trends in the United States Since 1870*. New York: National Bureau of Economic Research.

Adams, Graham. 1966. *Age of Industrial Violence, 1910-15*. New York: Columbia University Press.

Adams, Henry. 1918. *The Education of Henry Adams*. New York: Scribner.

Aglietta, Michel. 1979. *A Theory of Capitalist Regulation: The U.S. Experience*. Translated by David Fernbach. London: New Left Books.

Aronowitz, Stanley. 1973. *False Promises: The Shaping of American Working-Class Consciousness*. New York: McGraw-Hill.

Atkins, Willard E., and Lasswell, Harold D. 1924. *Labor Attitudes and Problems*. New York: Prentice-Hall.

Averitt, Robert T. 1968. *The Dual Economy: The Dynamics of American Industry Structure*. New York: Norton.

Baker, Elizabeth Butler. 1964. *Technology and Women's Work*. New York: Columbia University Press.

Bancroft, Gertrude. 1958. *The American Labor Force: Its Growth and Changing Composition*. Baltimore: Johns Hopkins Press.

Baran, Paul, and Sweezy, Paul. 1966. *Monopoly Capital: An Essay on the American Economic and Social Order*. New York: Monthly Review Press.

Baritz, Loren. 1960. *Servants of Power: The Use of Social Science in Industrial Relations*. Middletown, Conn.: Wesleyan University Press.

Barnett, George E. 1926. *Chapters on Machinery and Labor*. Cambridge, Mass.: Harvard University Press.

Baron, Harold M. 1971. "The Demand for Black Labor: Historical Notes on the Political Economy of Racism." *Radical America* 5 (Mar.-Apr.):1-46.

Barr, Kenneth. 1979. "Long Waves: A Selective, Annotated Bibliography." *Review* 2 (Spring):675-718.

Becker, Gary. 1964. *Human Capital*. New York: National Bureau of Economic Research.

Bell, Daniel. 1960. *The End of Ideology*. Glencoe, Ill.: Free Press.

1976. *The Coming of Postindustrial Society*. New York: Basic Books.

Bell, Spurgeon. 1940. *Productivity, Wages and National Income*. Washington, D.C.: The Brookings Institution.

Bennett, Sari, and Carville, Earle. 1980. "The Geography of Strikes in the Northeastern United States, 1881-1894." Unpublished paper, University of Maryland, Baltimore County.

Berger, Suzanne, and Piore, Michael J. 1981. *Dualism and Discontinuity in Industrial Societies*. Cambridge University Press.

Bibliography

Berndt, Ernst. 1980. "Energy Price Increases and the Productivity Slowdown in United States Manufacturing." In *The Productivity Problem*. Conference Series No. 22. Boston: Federal Reserve Bank of Boston.

Bernstein, Irving. 1950. *The New Deal Collective Bargaining Policy*. Berkeley: University of California Press.

——— 1960. *The Lean Years: A History of the American Worker, 1920-1933*. Boston: Houghton Mifflin.

——— 1971. *Turbulent Years: A History of the American Worker, 1933-1941*. Boston: Houghton Mifflin.

Berthoff, Rowland. 1953. *British Immigrants in Industrial America, 1907-1950*. Cambridge, Mass.: Harvard University Press.

Birch, David L. 1979. *The Job Generation Process*. Cambridge, Mass.: MIT Program on Neighborhood and Regional Change.

Blau, Francine D. 1980. "Immigration and Labor Earnings in Early Twentieth-Century America." In *Research in Population Economics*, edited by J. Simon. Vol. 2. Westport, Conn.: JAI Press.

Blau, Francine D., and Hendricks, Wallace D. 1979. "Occupational Segregation by Sex: Trends and Prospects." *Journal of Human Resources* *14*(Spring):197-210.

Bloch, Louis. 1920. "Occupations of Immigrants Before and After Coming to the United States." *American Statistical Association Publications* *17*(Dec.):402-416.

Block, Fred. 1977. "The Ruling Class Does Not Rule: Notes on the Marxist Theory of the State." *Socialist Revolution* 7(May-June):6-28.

Block, Fred, and Hirschhorn, Larry. 1979. "New Productive Forces and the Contradictions of Contemporary Capitalism: A Post-Industrial Perspective." *Theory and Society* 5(May):363-396.

Bloomfield, Meyer, 1921. *Labor and Compensation*. New York: Industrial Extension Institute.

Bluestone, Barry. 1970. "The Tripartite Economy: Labor Markets and the Working Poor." *Poverty and Human Resources* 5(July-Aug.):15-36.

Bluestone, Barry, and Harrison, Bennett. 1980. *Capital and Communities: The Causes and Consequences of Private Disinvestment*. Washington, D.C.: Progressive Alliance.

Bluestone, Barry; Murphy, William M.; and Stevenson, Mary. 1973. *Low Wages and the Working Poor*. Ann Arbor, Mich.: Institute of Labor and Industrial Relations.

Blumberg, Paul. 1980. *Inequality in an Age of Decline*. New York: Oxford University Press.

Bodnar, John E. 1976. "The Impact of the 'New Immigration' on the Black Worker: Steelton, Pa., 1880-1920." *Labor History* *17*(Spring):214-229.

Bowles, Samuel, and Gintis, Herbert. 1976. *Schooling in Capitalist America*. New York: Basic Books.

——— 1977. "The Marxian Theory of Value and Heterogeneous Labor: A Critique and Reformulation." *Cambridge Journal of Economics* *1*(June):173-192.

——— In press. "The Crisis of Liberal Democratic Capitalism: The Case of the United States." *Politics and Society*.

Bowring, Joseph. 1982. "The Dual Economy: Core and Periphery in the Accumulation Process." Unpublished doctoral dissertation, University of Massachusetts, Amherst.

Braverman, Harry. 1974. *Labor and Monopoly Capital: The Degradation of Work in the Twentieth Century.* New York: Monthly Review Press.

Brecher, Jeremy. 1972. *Strike: The True History of Mass Insurgency from 1877 to the Present.* San Francisco: Straight Arrow Books.

Bright, James. 1958. *Automation and Management.* Cambridge, Mass.: Harvard University Press.

Brissenden, Paul F. 1923. "Occupational Incidence of Labor Mobility." *Journal of the American Statistical Association 18* (Dec.):978–992.

Brody, David. 1960. *Steelworkers in America: The Nonunion Era.* Cambridge, Mass.: Harvard University Press.

———. 1964. *The Butcher Workmen: A Study of Unionization.* Cambridge, Mass.: Harvard University Press.

———. 1968. "The Rise and Decline of Welfare Capitalism." In *Change and Continuity in Twentieth Century America: The 1920s,* edited by John Braeman, Robert H. Bremner, and David Brody. Columbus: Ohio State University Press.

———. 1979. "The Old Labor History and the New: In Search of an American Working Class." *Labor History 20*(Winter):111–126.

———. 1980. *Workers in Industrial America: Essays on the Twentieth Century Struggle.* New York: Oxford University Press.

Broehl, Wayne. 1964. *The Molly Maguires.* New York: Vintage Books.

Brown, Susan. 1980. "The Professionalization and Unionization of Nurses." Unpublished paper, University of South Carolina, Columbia.

Bruchey, Stuart (ed). 1980. *Small Business in American Life.* New York: Columbia University Press.

Buchele, Robert. 1976. "Jobs and Workers: A Labor Market Segmentation Perspective on the Work Experience of Middle-Aged Men." Unpublished paper. Smith College, Northampton, Mass.

Burns, Arthur. 1929. "The Duration of Business Cycles." *Quarterly Journal of Economics 43*(Aug.):726–733.

Burns, Arthur, and Mitchell, Wesley C. 1946. *Measuring Business Cycles.* New York: National Bureau of Economic Research.

Cain, Glen. 1975. "The Dual and Radical Challenge to Labor Economics." *American Economic Review 65*(May):16–22.

———. 1976. "The Challenge of Segmented Labor Market Theories to Orthodox Theory: A Survey." *Journal of Economic Literature 14*(Dec.):1215–1257.

Carnoy, Martin, and Levin, Henry M. In press. *The Dialectics of Education and Work.* Stanford, Calif.: Stanford University Press.

Carnoy, Martin; Levin, Henry M.; and King, Kenneth. 1980. *Education, Work, and Employment.* International Institute for Educational Planning, Vol. II. Paris: UNESCO.

Caute, David. 1978. *The Great Fear: The Anti-Communist Purge under Truman and Eisenhower.* New York: Simon and Schuster.

Center for International Business Cycle Research. 1981. "Growth Cycle Chronologies, 13 Countries." Unpublished table. New Brunswick, N.J.: Rutgers University.

Chandler, Alfred D., Jr. 1962. *Strategy and Structure: Chapters in the History of the Industrial Enterprise.* Cambridge, Mass.: MIT Press.

———. 1977. *The Visible Hand: The Managerial Revolution in American Business.* Cambridge, Mass.: Harvard University Press.

Bibliography

Clark, Victor S. 1929. *History of Manufactures in the United States.* Vol. I, 1607–1860; Vol. II, 1860–1893; Vol. III, 1893–1928. Washington, D.C.: Carnegie Institution.

Clawson, Dan. 1980. *Bureaucracy and the Labor Process.* New York: Monthly Review Press.

Coase, Ronald. 1937. "The Nature of the Firm." *Economica* 4 (Nov.):386–405.

Cochran, Bert. 1977. *Labor and Communism: The Conflict That Shaped American Unions.* Princeton, N.J.: Princeton University Press.

Cochran, Thomas. 1948. *The Pabst Brewing Company.* London: Oxford University Press.

Cochran, Thomas, and Miller, William. 1961. *The Age of Enterprise: A Social History of Industrial America.* New York: Harper and Row.

Cole, Arthur H. 1926. *The American Wool Manufacture.* Cambridge, Mass.: Harvard University Press.

Cole, Arthur H., and Williamson, Harold. 1941. *The American Carpet Manufacture.* Cambridge, Mass.: Harvard University Press.

Cole, Donald. 1963. *Immigrant City: Lawrence, Massachusetts, 1845–1921.* Chapel Hill: University of North Carolina Press.

Commons, John R. 1924. *Races and Immigrants in America.* 2nd edition. New York: Macmillan. (Originally published in 1907.)

Commons, John R. et al. 1918. *History of Labor in the United States.* Vols. I and II. New York: Macmillan.

1935. *History of Labor in the United States.* Vols. III and IV. New York: Macmillan.

Copeland, Melvin. 1912. *The Cotton Manufacturing Industry of the United States.* Cambridge, Mass.: Harvard University Press.

Coxe, Tench. 1965. *A View of the United States.* New York: A. M. Kelley. (Originally published in 1794.)

Creamer, Daniel; Dobrovolsky, Sergei P.; and Borenstein, Israel. 1960. *Capital in Manufacturing and Mining: Its Formation and Financing.* Princeton, N.J.: Princeton University Press.

Cronin, James E. 1979. *Industrial Conflict in Modern Britain.* London: Croom Helm.

1980. "Stages, Cycles, and Insurgencies: The Economics of Unrest." In *Processes of the World-System,* edited by T. Hopkins and I. Wallerstein. Beverly Hills, Calif.: Sage Publications.

Dale, E., and Meloy, C. 1969. "Hamilton MacFarland Barksdale and the Du Pont Contributions to Systematic Management." In *The History of American Management,* edited by H. P. Baughman. Englewood Cliffs, N.J.: Prentice-Hall.

Daugherty, Carroll. 1951. "Changing Status of Labor." In *The Growth of the American Economy,* edited by Harold F. Williamson. 2nd edition. Englewood Cliffs, N.J.: Prentice-Hall.

David, Paul. 1967. "The Growth of Real Product in the United States Before 1840: New Evidence, Controlled Conjecture." *Journal of Economic History* 27 (June):151–197.

Davies, Margery. 1975. "Woman's Place Is at the Typewriter: The Feminization of the Clerical Labor Force." In *Labor Market Segmentation,* edited by Richard C. Edwards, Michael Reich, and David M. Gordon. Lexington, Mass.: Lexington Books.

Davis, Lance, et al. 1972. *American Economic Growth: An Economist's History of the United States*. New York: Harper and Row.

Davis, Lance, and North, Douglass C. 1973. *Institutional Change and American Economic Growth*. Cambridge University Press.

Davis, Mike. 1980. "Why the U.S. Working Class Is Different." *New Left Review 123* (Sept.-Oct.):3–44.

Dawley, Alan. 1976. *Class and Community: The Industrial Revolution in Lynn*. Cambridge, Mass.: Harvard University Press.

de Kadt, Maarten. 1976. "The Development of Management Structures: The Problem of the Control of Workers in Large Corporations." Unpublished doctoral dissertation, New School for Social Research, New York City.

Delehanty, George E. 1968. *Nonproduction Workers in Manufacturing*. Amsterdam: North-Holland Publishing.

Derber, Milton. 1975. "The New Deal and Labor." In *The New Deal*, edited by John Braeman. Columbus: Ohio State University Press.

Dobb, Maurice. 1963. *Studies in the Development of Capitalism*. New York: International Publishers.

Doeringer, Peter B., and Piore, Michael J. 1971. *Internal Labor Markets and Manpower Analysis*. Lexington, Mass.: Lexington Books.

Douglas, Paul H. 1921. *American Apprenticeship and Industrial Education*. New York: Columbia University Press.

———— 1923. "Analysis of Strike Statistics, 1881–1921." *Journal of American Statistical Association 18* (Sept.):866–877.

Douty, Harold M. 1960. "Collective Bargaining Coverage in Factory Employment, 1958." *Monthly Labor Review 83* (Apr.):345–350.

Dublin, Thomas. 1979. *Women at Work: The Transformation of Work and Community in Lowell, Massachusetts, 1826–1860*. New York: Columbia University Press.

Dubofsky, Melvyn. 1971. *We Shall Be All: A History of the Industrial Workers of the World*. Chicago: Quadrangle Books.

Dunlop, John T. 1958. *Industrial Relations Systems*. New York: Holt.

Dunn, Robert W. 1927a. *The Americanization of Labor: The Employers' Offensive Against the Trade Unions*. New York: International Publishers.

———— 1927b. *Company Unions*. New York: Vanguard Press.

Dupriez, Leon. 1947. *Des Mouvements économiques généraux*. Vol. II. Louvain: Institut de Recherches Économiques et Sociales.

Easterlin, Richard. 1961. "Regional Income Trends, 1840–1950." In *American Economic History*, edited by Seymour Harris. New York: McGraw-Hill.

Eastman, Crystal. 1910. *Work-Accidents and the Law*. New York: Charities Publication Committee.

Eckler, A. Ross, and Zlotnick, Jack. 1949. "Immigration and the Labor Force." *Reappraising Our Immigration Policy*. Special volume of *Annals of the American Academy of Political And Social Science. 262* (Mar.):92–107.

Edwards, Alba. 1943. *Comparative Occupational Statistics for the United States, 1870 to 1940*. Washington, D.C.: GPO.

Edwards, Richard C. 1970. "Economic Sophistication in Nineteenth-Century Tariff Debates." *Journal of Economic History 30* (Dec.):802–838.

———— 1975a. "Stages in Corporate Stability and the Risks of Corporate Failure." *Journal of Economic History 35* (June):428–457.

———— 1975b. "The Social Relations of Production in the Firm and Labor Market

Structure." In *Labor Market Segmentation,* edited by Richard C. Edwards, Michael Reich, and David M. Gordon. Lexington, Mass.: Lexington Books.

1979. *Contested Terrain: The Transformation of the Workplace in the Twentieth Century.* New York: Basic Books.

Edwards, Richard C.; Reich, Michael; and Gordon, David M. (eds.). 1975. *Labor Market Segmentation.* Lexington, Mass.: Lexington Books.

Ehrenreich, Barbara, and Ehrenreich, John. 1972. *The American Health Empire: Power, Profits and Politics.* New York: Vintage.

Ehrlich, Richard L. 1974. "Immigrant Strikebreaking Activity: A Sampling of Opinion Expressed in the National Labor Tribune, 1878-1885." *Labor History 15*(Fall):528-542.

Eilbert, Henry. 1959. "The Development of Personnel Management in the United States." *Business History Review 33* (Autumn):345-364.

Elbaum, Bernard. 1982. "Labor and Uneven Development: Unions, Industrial Organization, and Wage Structure in the British and U.S. Iron and Steel Industry." Unpublished doctoral dissertation, Harvard University, Cambridge, Mass.

Erickson, Charlotte. 1957. *American Industry and the European Immigrant, 1860-1885.* Cambridge, Mass.: Harvard University Press.

Fabricant, Solomon. 1942. *Employment in Manufacturing, 1899-1939.* New York: National Bureau of Economic Research.

Faunce, William. 1958. "Automation in the Automobile Industry." *American Sociological Review 23*(Aug.):401-407.

Feldman, Herman. 1925. *The Regularization of Employment: A Study in the Prevention of Unemployment.* New York: Harper.

Fels, Rendigs. 1959. *American Business Cycles, 1865-1897.* Chapel Hill: University of North Carolina Press.

Flaherty, Sean E. 1981. "The Nature and Causes of Strikes During the Term of an Agreement: An Empirical Analysis." Unpublished doctoral dissertation. University of California, Berkeley.

Folbre, Nancy. 1979. "Patriarchy and Capitalism in New England, 1620-1900." Unpublished doctoral dissertation. University of Massachusetts, Amherst.

Foner, Philip. 1947-1972. *History of the Labor Movement in the United States.* Vol. 1, 1947; Vol. 2, 1955; Vol. 3, 1964; Vol. 4, 1972. New York: International Publishers.

Foner, Philip (ed.). 1978. *Factory Girls.* Springfield: University of Illinois Press.

Ford, Henry. 1929. "Mass Production." *Encyclopaedia Britannica,* ed. 14, vol. 15:38-41.

Frank, Andre Gunder. 1980. *Crisis: In the World Economy.* New York: Holmes and Meier.

Freedley, Edwin T. 1858. *Philadephia and Its Manufactures.* Philadelphia: Edward Young.

Freeman, Richard B. 1976. *The Over-Educated American.* New York: Academic Press.

Freeman, Richard B., and Medoff, James. 1979a. "New Estimates of Private Sector Unionism in the United States." *Industrial and Labor Relations Review 32*(Jan.):143-174.

1979b. "The Two Faces of Unionism." *Public Interest 57*(Fall):69-93.

Bibliography

Fröbel, Folker; Heinrichs, Jurgen; and Kreye, Otto. 1979. *The New International Division of Labour*. London: Cambridge University Press.

Galbraith, John Kenneth. 1967. *The New Industrial State*. Boston: Houghton Mifflin.

1975. *Money*. Boston: Houghton Mifflin.

Gallman, Robert. 1960. "Commodity Output, 1839–1899." In *Trends in the American Economy in the Nineteenth Century*. Studies in Income and Wealth No. 24. Princeton: National Bureau of Economic Research.

1966. "Gross National Production in the United States, 1834–1909." In *Output, Employment and Productivity in the United States After 1800*. Studies in Income and Wealth No. 30. New York: National Bureau of Economic Research.

1975. "The Agricultural Sector and the Pace of Economic Growth: The U.S. Experience in the 19th Century." In *Essays in Nineteenth-Century History*, edited by David Klingaman and Richard Vedder. Athens: Ohio University Press.

Garraty, John. 1968. *The New Commonwealth, 1877–1890*. New York: Harper and Row.

Garvy, George. 1943. "Kondratieff's Theory of Long Cycles." *Review of Economics and Statistics* 25 (Nov.):203–220.

Geller, Jules. 1979. "Forms of Capitalist Control Over the Labor Process." *Monthly Review* 31 (Dec.):39–46.

Giedion, Siegfried. 1948. *Mechanization Takes Command: A Contribution to Anonymous History*. New York: Norton.

Ginger, Ray. 1949. *Eugene V. Debs: A Biography*. New Brunswick, N.J.: Rutgers University Press.

Gintis, Herbert. 1976. "The Nature of Labor Exchange and the Theory of Capitalist Production." *Review of Radical Political Economics* 8 (Summer):36–54.

1980. "Communication and Politics: Marxism and the 'Problem' of Liberal Democracy." *Socialist Review* 10 (Mar.–June):189–232.

Gitelman, Howard M. 1967. "The Waltham System and the Coming of the Irish." *Labor History* 8 (Fall):227–253.

Gordon, David M. 1972a. *Theories of Poverty and Underemployment*. Lexington, Mass.: Lexington Books.

1972b. "From Steam Whistles to Coffee Breaks." *Dissent* 19 (Winter):197–210.

1976. "Capitalist Efficiency and Socialist Efficiency." *Monthly Review* 24 (July–Aug.):19–39.

1978a. "Up and Down the Long Roller Coaster." *Capitalism in Crisis*, edited by the Union for Radical Political Economics. New York: Union for Radical Political Economics.

1978b. "Capitalist Development and the History of American Cities." In *Marxism and the Metropolis*, edited by William Tabb and Larry Sawers. New York: Oxford University Press.

1980. "Stages of Accumulation and Long Economic Cycles." In *Processes of the World System*, edited by Terence Hopkins and Immanuel Wallerstein. Beverly Hills, Calif.: Sage Publications.

1981a. "Capital-Labor Conflict and the Productivity Slowdown." *American Economic Review, Papers and Proceedings* 71 (May):30–35.

Bibliography

1981b. "The Best Defense Is a Good Defense: Toward a Marxist Theory of Labor Union Structure and Behavior." In *New Directions in Labor Economics,* edited by Michael Carter and William Leahy. South Bend, Ind.: Notre Dame University Press.

1982. "Segmentation by the Numbers: Empirical Applications of the Theory of Labor Segmentation." Unpublished paper. New School for Social Research, New York City.

Gordon, R. A. 1974. *Economic Instability and Growth: The American Record.* New York: Harper and Row.

Gordon, Robert J. 1969. "$45 Billion of U.S. Private Investment Has Been Mislaid." *American Economic Review* 59(June):221-237.

1981. *Macroeconomics.* Boston: Little, Brown.

Gough, Ian. 1979. *The Political Economy of the Welfare State.* London: Macmillan.

Gramsci, Antonio. 1971. *The Prison Notebooks.* New York: International Publishers.

Green, James R. 1980. *The World of the Worker: Labor in Twentieth-Century America.* New York: Hill and Wang.

Green, Marguerite. 1956. *The National Civic Federation and the American Labor Movement, 1900-1925.* Washington, D.C.: Catholic University Press.

Greenbaum, Joan M. 1979. *In the Name of Efficiency: Management Theory and Shopfloor Practice in Data-Processing Work.* Philadelphia: Temple University Press.

Greene, Victor R. 1968. *The Slavic Community on Strike: Immigrant Labor in Pennsylvania Anthracite.* South Bend, Ind.: Notre Dame University Press.

Greer, Edward. 1979. *Big Steel: Black Politics and Corporate Power in Gary, Indiana.* New York: Monthly Review Press.

Griffin, John I. 1939. *Strikes: A Study in Quantitative Economics.* New York: Columbia University Press.

Grob, Gerald. 1964. *Workers and Utopia: A Study of Ideological Conflict in the American Labor Movement, 1865-1900.* Evanston, Ill.: Northwestern University Press.

Gutman, Herbert. 1968. "The Negro and the United Mine Workers of America." In *The Negro and the American Labor Movement,* edited by Julius Jacobson. New York: Anchor.

1970. "The Workers' Search for Power." In *The Gilded Age.* Revised edition, edited by H. Wayne Morgan. Syracuse: Syracuse University Press.

1973. "Work, Culture, and Society in Industrializing America, 1815-1919." *American Historical Review* 78(June):531-588.

1976. *Work, Culture, and Society in Industrializing America.* New York: Knopf.

Handlin, Oscar. 1970. "Boston's Immigrants: The Economic Adjustment." In *The City in American Life,* edited by Paul Kramer and Frederick Holborn. New York: Putnam.

Hansen, Alvin H. 1941. *Fiscal Policy and Business Cycles.* New York: Norton.

Harris, Donald J. 1978. *Capital Accumulation and Income Distribution.* Stanford, Calif.: Stanford University Press.

Harrison, Bennett. 1972a. *Education, Training and the Urban Ghetto.* Baltimore: Johns Hopkins Press.

1972b. "Education and Underemployment in the Urban Ghetto." *American Economic Review* 62(Dec.):796-812.

Hartman, Raymond S., and Wheeler, David R. 1979. "Schumpeterian Waves of Innovation and Infrastructure Development in Great Britain and the United States: The Kondratieff Cycle Revisited." In *Research in Economic History,* edited by P. Uselding. Vol. 4. Greenwich, Conn.: JAI Press.

Hartmann, Heidi. 1976. "Capitalism, Patriarchy and Job Segregation by Sex." *Signs 1* (Spring):137-169.

Hays, Samuel P. 1957. *The Response to Industrialism, 1885-1914.* Chicago: University of Chicago Press.

Hazard, Blanche. 1921. *The Organization of the Boot and Shoe Industry in Massachusetts before 1875.* Cambridge, Mass.: Harvard University Press.

Hershberg, Theodore; Cox, Harold E.; Light, Dale B., Jr.; and Greenfield, Richard R. 1981. "The 'Journey-to-Work': An Empirical Investigation of Work, Residence and Transportation, Philadelphia, 1850 and 1880." In *Philadelphia: Work, Space, Family, and Group Experience in the 19th Century,* edited by Theodore Hershberg. New York: Oxford University Press.

Hessen, Robert. 1974. "The Bethlehem Steel Strike of 1910." *Labor History 15* (Winter):3-18.

Hidy, Ralph W., and Hidy, Muriel E. 1955. *Pioneering in Big Business, 1882-1911.* New York: Harper and Row.

Higgs, Robert. 1980. *Competition and Coercion: Blacks in the American Economy, 1865-1914.* Chicago: University of Chicago Press.

Hill, Joseph A. 1929. *Women in Gainful Occupations: 1870-1920.* Census Monographs IX. Washington, D.C.: GPO.

Hirsch, Susan E. 1978. *Roots of the American Working Class: The Industrialization of the Crafts in Newark, 1800-1860.* Philadelphia: University of Pennsylvania Press.

Historical Statistics. See U.S. Bureau of the Census.

Hobsbawm, Eric. 1976. "The Crisis of Capitalism in Historical Perspective." *Socialist Revolution 6* (Oct.-Dec.):77-96.

Hoffmann, Charles. 1956. "The Depression of the Nineties." *Journal of Economic History 16* (June):137-164.

Howell, David. 1982. "Industry Structure, Job Skills, and the Industry Wage Structure." Unpublished doctoral dissertation, New School for Social Research. New York.

Hurvitz, Haggai. 1977. "Ideology and Industrial Conflict: President Wilson's First Industrial Conference of October 1919." *Labor History 18* (Fall):509-524.

Hutchins, Grace. 1934. *Women Who Work.* New York: International Publishers.

Hutchinson, E. P. 1956. *Immigrants and Their Children, 1850-1950.* New York: John Wiley.

Hyman, Richard. 1975. *Industrial Relations: A Marxist Introduction.* London: Macmillan.

Hymer, Stephen. 1972. "The Evolution of the Corporation." In *The Capitalist System,* edited by Richard C. Edwards, Michael Reich, and Thomas E. Weisskopf. Englewood Cliffs, N.J.: Prentice-Hall.

Jacoby, Sanford. 1981. "The Origins of Internal Labor Markets in American Manufacturing Firms, 1910-1940." Unpublished doctoral dissertation, University of California, Berkeley.

Jenks, Leland H. 1960. "Early Phases of the Management Movement." *Administrative Science Quarterly 5* (Dec.):421-447.

Bibliography

Jensen, Vernon. 1950. *Heritage of Conflict: Labor Relations in the Nonferrous Metals Industry to 1930.* Ithaca, N.Y.: Cornell University Press.

Jerome, Harry. 1934. *Mechanization in Industry.* New York: National Bureau of Economic Research.

Jeszeck, Charles A. 1981. "Plant Dispersion and Collective Bargaining in the Rubber Tire Industry." Unpublished doctoral dissertation, University of California, Berkeley.

Joffe, Jerome. 1975. "Job Ladders and Job Structures: A Study of Labor Stratification within Maintenance and Repair Occupations in New York City." Unpublished doctoral dissertation, New School for Social Research. New York City.

Johnson, George. 1981. "Changes Over Time in the Union/Non-Union Wage Differential." Unpublished paper, University of Michigan, Ann Arbor.

Jones, Edward D. 1925. *The Administration of Industrial Enterprises.* 2nd edition. New York: Longmans, Green. (Originally published in 1916.)

Josephson, Hannah. 1949. *The Golden Threads: New England Mill Girls and Magnates.* New York: Duell, Sloan and Pearce.

Kahn, Lawrence M. 1975. "Unions and Labor Market Segmentation." Unpublished doctoral dissertation, University of California, Berkeley.

Katzman, David M. 1978. *Seven Days a Week: Women and Domestic Service in Industrializing America.* New York: Oxford University Press.

Keat, Paul G. 1959. "Changes in Occupational Wage Structure, 1900–1956." Unpublished doctoral dissertation, University of Chicago.

Kendrick, John W. 1961. *Productivity Trends in the United States.* Princeton, N.J.: Princeton University Press.

Kendrick, John W., and Grossman, Elliot S. 1980. *Productivity in the United States: Trends and Cycles.* Baltimore: Johns Hopkins University Press.

Kerr, Clark. 1977. *Labor Markets and Wage Determination: The Balkanization of Labor Markets and Other Essays.* Berkeley: University of California Press.

Kerr, Clark, and Siegel, Arthur. 1969. "The Inter-Industry Propensity to Strike." In *Collective Bargaining,* edited by Allan Flanders. Baltimore: Penguin.

Kerr, Clark, et al. 1960. *Industrialism and Industrial Man.* Cambridge, Mass.: Harvard University Press.

Kerr, William O. 1979. "The Effects of Unionism in a Dual Labor Market." Unpublished doctoral dissertation, New School for Social Research, New York.

Kindleberger, Charles P. 1974. *The World in Depression, 1929–1939.* Berkeley: University of California Press.

Kipnis, Ira. 1952. *The American Socialist Movement, 1897–1912.* New York: Columbia University Press.

Kirkland, Edward C. 1964. *Dream and Thought in the Business Community, 1860–1900.* Chicago: Quadrangle Books.

   1967. *Industry Comes of Age: Business, Labor, and Public Policy, 1860–1897.* Chicago: Quadrangle Books.

Klaczynska, Barbara. 1976. "Why Women Work: A Comparison of Various Groups – Philadelphia, 1910–1930." *Labor History* 17(Winter):73–87.

Kleinknecht, Alfred. 1981. "Innovation, Accumulation and Crisis." *Review* 4(Spring):683–712.

Kolko, Gabriel. 1963. *The Triumph of Conservatism: A Reinterpretation of American History, 1900–1916.* Glencoe, Ill.: Free Press.

Bibliography

Korman, Gerd. 1967. *Industrialization, Immigrants, and Americanizers: The View from Milwaukee, 1866–1921*. Madison: State Historical Society of Wisconsin.

Korstad, Bob. 1980. "Those Who Were Not Afraid: Winston-Salem, 1943." In *Working Lives*, edited by Marc S. Miller. New York: Pantheon.

Kotz, David. 1978. *Bank Control of Large Corporations in the United States*. Berkeley: University of California Press.

Kraft, Philip. 1977. *Programmers and Managers: The Routinization of Computer Programming in the United States*. New York: Heidelberg Science Library; Springer-Verlag.

Kreckl, Reinhard. 1979. "Unequal Opportunity Structure and Labour Market Segmentation." Unpublished manuscript, Universität Erlangen-Nürnberg.

Kuhlman, Charles. 1929. *The Development of the Flour-Milling Industry in the United States*. Boston: Houghton Mifflin.

Kuznets, Simon. 1961a. *Capital in the American Economy: Its Formation and Financing*. New York: National Bureau of Economic Research.

    1961b. "Quantitative Aspects of the Economic Growth of Nations: VI. Long-Term Trends in Capital Formation Proportions." *Economic Development and Cultural Change*, Part II, 9(July):1–124.

Laclau, Ernesto. 1977. *Politics and Ideology in Marxist Theory*. London: New Left Books.

Laslett, John H. M. 1970. *Labor and the Left: A Study of Socialist and Radical Influences in the American Labor Movement, 1881–1924*. New York: Basic Books.

Laslett, John H. M., and Lipset, Seymour Martin (eds.). 1974. *Failure of a Dream? Essays in the History of American Socialism*. New York: Basic Books.

Lauck, W. Jett. 1929. *The New Industrial Revolution and Wages*. New York: Funk and Wagnalls.

Lauck, W. Jett, and Sydenstricker, Edgar. 1917. *Conditions of Labor in American Industries*. New York: Funk and Wagnalls.

Laurie, Bruce. 1980. *Working People of Philadelphia, 1800–1850*. Philadelphia: Temple University Press.

Laurie, Bruce, and Schmitz, Mark. 1981. "Manufacture and Productivity: The Making of an Industrial Base, Philadelphia, 1850–1880." In *Philadelphia: Work, Space, Family, and Group Experience in the 19th Century*, edited by Theodore Hershberg. New York: Oxford University Press.

Laurie, Bruce; Hershberg, Theodore; and Alter, George. 1977. "Immigrants and Industry: The Philadelphia Experience, 1850–1880." In *Immigrants in Industrial America, 1850–1920*, edited by Richard Ehrlich. Charlottesville: University of Virginia Press.

Lazonick, William. 1980. "Industrial Relations, Work Organization and Technological Change: U.S. and British Cotton Spinning." Harvard Institute of Economic Research, Discussion Paper No. 774, July.

Lebergott, Stanley. 1964. *Manpower in Economic Growth: The U.S. Experience*. New York: McGraw-Hill.

    1972. "The American Labor Force." In *American Economic Growth*, edited by Lance Davis et al. New York: Harper and Row.

Lee, Susan Previant, and Passell, Peter. 1979. *A New Economic View of American History*. New York: Norton.

Bibliography

Leiserson, William M. 1931. "The Economics of Restriction of Output." In Stanley B. Mathewson (ed.), *Restriction of Output Among Unorganized Workers*. New York: Viking Press.

Lenin, V. I. 1934. *Imperialism: The Highest Stage of Capitalism*. New York: International Publishers. (Originally published in 1917.)

Leone, William C. 1967. *Production Automation and Numerical Control*. New York: Ronald Press.

Lester, Richard A. 1958. *As Unions Mature: An Analysis of the Evolution of American Unionism*. Princeton, N.J.: Princeton University Press.

Lester, Richard A., and Robie, Edward A. 1946. *Wages under National and Regional Collective Bargaining: Experience in Seven Industries*. Princeton, N.J.: Princeton University Press.

Lichtenstein, Nelson. 1975. "Defending the No-Strike Pledge: CIO Politics during World War II." *Radical America* 9 (July–Oct.):49–76.

——— 1980. "Auto Worker Militancy and the Structure of Factory Life, 1935–1955." *Journal of American History* 67 (Sept.):335–353.

Lindert, Peter H., and Williamson, Jeffrey G. 1977. "Three Centuries of American Inequality." In *Research in Economic History*, edited by P. Uselding. Vol. 1, Greenwich, Conn.: JAI Press.

Lockwood, David. 1958. *The Black-Coated Worker*. New York: Oxford University Press.

Lohr, Steve. 1981. "Overhauling America's Business Management." *New York Times Magazine*, January 4. pp. 14–174.

Long, Clarence D. 1960. *Wages and Earnings in the United States, 1860–1890*. Princeton, N.J.: Princeton University Press.

Lowell Offering. Lowell, Mass., vols. 1–5, 1840–1845.

McGouldrick, Paul. 1968. *New England Textiles in the Nineteenth Century*. Cambridge, Mass.: Harvard University Press.

Maddison, Angus. 1977. "Phases of Capitalist Development." *Banca Nazionale del Lavoro Quarterly Review* 121 (June):103–137.

Maltese, Francesca. 1975. "Notes for a Study of the Automobile Industry." In *Labor Market Segmentation*, edited by Richard C. Edwards, Michael Reich, and David M. Gordon. Lexington, Mass.: Lexington Books.

Mandel, Ernest. 1975. *Late Capitalism*. London: New Left Books.

——— 1977. *The Second Slump*. London: New Left Books.

——— 1980. *Long Waves of Capitalist Development*. Cambridge University Press.

Mandle, Jay. 1978. *The Roots of Southern Black Poverty*. Durham, N.C.: Duke University Press.

Mares, William, and Simmons, John. 1982. *Working at Democracy*. New York: Simon and Schuster.

Marglin, Stephen A. 1974. "What Do Bosses Do? The Origins and Functions of Hierarchy in Capitalist Production." *Review of Radical Political Economics* 6 (Summer):60–112.

——— In press. *Growth, Distribution, and Prices: Neoclassical, Neo-Marxian, and Neo-Keynesian Approaches*. Cambridge, Mass.: Harvard University Press.

Martineau, Harriet. 1962. *Society in America*. 2 vols. New York: Anchor. (Originally published in 1837.)

Mathewson, Stanley B. 1931. *Restriction of Output among Unorganized Workers*. New York: Viking Press.

Medoff, James L. 1971. "Immigration, the Wage Differential, and the Proletariat from 1870 to 1914." Unpublished paper, Harvard University, Cambridge, Mass.

Medoff, James L., and Abraham, Katharine G. 1979. "Can Productive Capacity Differentials Really Explain the Earnings Differentials Associated with Demographic Characteristics? The Case of Experience." Harvard Institute of Economic Research. Discussion Paper 705.

——— 1980. "Experience, Performance, and Earnings." *Quarterly Journal of Economics* 95 (Dec.):703–36.

Meyer, Stephen. 1977. "Mass Production and Human Efficiency: The Ford Motor Company, 1908–1921." Unpublished doctoral dissertation, Rutgers University, New Brunswick, N.J.

Millis, Harry A., and Montgomery, Royal E. 1938. *The Economics of Labor.* Vol. I, *Labor's Progress and Some Basic Labor Problems.* New York: McGraw-Hill.

——— 1945. *The Economics of Labor.* Vol. III, *Organized Labor.* New York: McGraw-Hill.

Mills, C. Wright. 1951. *White Collar.* New York: Oxford University Press.

Mills, Frederick C. 1932. *Economic Tendencies in the United States: Aspects of Pre-War and Post-War Changes.* New York: National Bureau of Economic Research.

Mitchell, Wesley C. 1913. *Business Cycles.* Berkeley: University of California Press.

Modell, John. 1968. "A Regional Approach to Urban Growth." Unpublished paper, University of Minnesota, Minneapolis.

——— 1971. "The Peopling of a Working Class Ward: Reading, Pennsylvania, 1850." *Journal of Social History* 5 (Fall):71–95.

Montgomery, David. 1967. *Beyond Equality: Labor and the Radical Republicans, 1862–1872.* New York: Knopf.

——— 1968. "The Working Classes of the Pre-Industrial American City, 1780–1830." *Labor History* 9 (Winter):3–22.

——— 1974. "The 'New Unionism' and the Transformation of Workers' Consciousness in America, 1909–1922." *Journal of Social History* 7 (Fall):509–29.

——— 1976. "Workers' Control of Machine Production in the Nineteenth Century." *Labor History* 17 (Fall):486–509.

——— 1979. *Workers' Control in America: Studies in the History of Work, Technology, and Labor Struggles.* Cambridge University Press.

——— 1980. "To Study the People: the American Working Class." *Labor History* 21 (Fall):485–512.

Moody, John. 1904. *The Truth about the Trusts.* New York: Moody Publishing.

Morishima, M., and Saito, M. 1968. "An Economic Test of Hick's Theory of Biased Induced Inventions." In *Value, Capital, and Growth,* edited by J. Wolfe. Chicago: Aldine.

Morris, Richard. 1946. *Government and Labor in Early America.* New York: Columbia University Press.

Naples, Michele I. 1981. "Labor Militánce and the End of the Postwar Truce." *American Economic Review, Papers and Proceedings* 71 (May):36–41.

——— 1982. "Erosion of the Postwar Truce: Worker Militance and Labor Productivity." Unpublished doctoral dissertation, University of Massachusetts, Amherst.

National Civic Federation Archives, Ralph M. Easley Papers. n.d. New York City Public Library Archives, New York.

National Industrial Conference Board. 1923. *A Graphic Analysis of the Census of Manufactures of the United States, 1849–1919.* New York: National Industrial Conference Board.

    1929. *Industrial Relations in Small Plants.* New York: National Industrial Conference Board.

    1930. *Systems of Wage Payment.* New York: National Industrial Converence Board.

    1933. *Surveys of Wages and Working Conditions.* New York: National Industrial Conference Board.

Navin, Thomas, and Sears, Marion. 1955. "The Rise of a Market for Securities." *Business History Review* 29(June):105–138.

Nelson, Daniel. 1974. "The New Factory System and the Unions: The National Cash Register Dispute of 1901." *Labor History* 15(Spring):163–178.

    1975. *Managers and Workers: Origins of the New Factory System in the United States, 1880–1920.* Madison: University of Wisconsin Press.

Nelson, Daniel, and Campbell, Stuart. 1972. "Taylorism versus Welfare Work in American Industry: H. L. Gantt and the Bancrofts." *Business History Review* 46(Spring):1–16.

Nelson, Ralph L. 1959. *Merger Movements in American Industry, 1895–1956.* Princeton, N.J.: Princeton University Press.

Nevins, Allen. 1954. *Ford: The Times, the Man, the Company.* New York: Scribner.

Noble, David. 1977. *America by Design: Science, Technology, and the Rise of Corporate Capitalism.* New York: Knopf.

North, Douglass C. 1961. *The Economic Growth of the United States, 1790–1860.* Englewood Cliffs, N.J.: Prentice-Hall.

    1966. *Growth and Welfare in the American Past: A New Economic History.* Englewood Cliffs, N.J.: Prentice-Hall.

North, Douglass C., and Thomas, Robert Paul. 1973. *The Rise of the Western World.* Cambridge University Press.

Ober, Harry. 1948. "Occupational Wage Differentials, 1907–1947." *Monthly Labor Review* 67(Aug.):127–134.

Organization for Economic Cooperation and Development. Various years. *Main Economic Indicators: Historical Statistics.* Geneva: OECD.

Oster, Gerry. 1979. "A Factor-Analytic Test of the Theory of the Dual Economy." *Review of Economics and Statistics* 62(Mar.):33–39.

Ozanne, Robert. 1967. *A Century of Labor-Management Relations at McCormick and International Harvester.* Madison: University of Wisconsin Press.

Palmer, Bryan. 1975. "Class, Conception and Conflict: The Thrust for Efficiency, Managerial View of Labor and the Working Class Rebellion, 1903–1922." *Review of Radical Political Economics* 7(Summer):31–49.

Panico, Carlo. 1980. "Marx's Analysis of the Relationship Between the Rate of Interest and the Rate of Profits." *Cambridge Journal of Economics* 4(Dec.):363–378.

Passer, Harold G. 1952. "The Development of Large-Scale Organization: Electrical Manufacturing Around 1900." *Journal of Economic History* 12(Fall):378–395.

Perlman, Mark. 1961. *The Machinists: A New Study in American Trade Unionism.* Cambridge, Mass.: Harvard University Press.

    1968. "Labor in Eclipse." In *Change and Continuity in Twentieth-Century*

America: The 1920s, edited by John Braeman, Robert H. Bremner, and David Brody. Columbus: Ohio State University Press.

Perlman, Selig. 1922. *History of Trade Unionism in the United States.* New York: Macmillan.

Peterson, Florence, 1938. *Strikes in the United States, 1880–1936.* U.S. Bureau of Labor Statistics Bulletin No. 651. Washington, D.C.: GPO.

Piore, Michael J. 1975. "Notes for a Theory of Labor Market Stratification." In *Labor Market Segmentation,* edited by Richard C. Edwards, Michael Reich, and David M. Gordon. Lexington, Mass.: Lexington Books.

⎯⎯⎯ 1979a. *Birds of Passage: Migrant Labor and Industrial Societies.* Cambridge University Press.

⎯⎯⎯ (ed.). 1979b. *Inflation and Unemployment: Institutionalist and Structuralist Views.* White Plains, N.Y.: M. E. Sharpe.

Piven, Frances Fox, and Cloward, Richard A. 1977. *Poor People's Movements: Why They Succeed, How they Fail.* New York: Pantheon Books.

Plotke, David. 1980. "The United States in Transition: Toward a New Order?" *Socialist Review 10*(Nov.–Dec.):71–123.

⎯⎯⎯ 1981. "The Politics of Transition: The United States in Transition, II." *Socialist Review 11*(Jan.–Feb.):21–72.

Pope, Jesse E. 1905. *The Clothing Industry in New York.* Columbia: University of Missouri Press.

Preston, William. 1963. *Aliens and Dissenters: Federal Suppression of Radicals, 1903–1933.* Cambridge, Mass.: Harvard University Press.

Quality of Work Life. 1979. Institute for Social Research, University of Michigan, Ann Arbor.

Radical History Review. 1978–1979. "Marxism and History: The British Contribution." Special Issue (Winter).

Ransom, Roger, and Sutch, Richard, 1977. *One Kind of Freedom: The Economic Consequences of Emancipation.* Cambridge University Press.

Rees, Albert G. 1962. *The Economics of Trade Unions.* Chicago: University of Chicago Press.

Reich, Michael. 1978. "The Development of the Wage Labor Force." In *The Capitalist System,* by Richard C. Edwards, Michael Reich, and Thomas E. Weisskopf. Revised edition. Englewood Cliffs, N.J.: Prentice-Hall.

⎯⎯⎯ 1981a. *Racial Inequality: A Political-Economic Analysis.* Princeton, N.J.: Princeton University Press.

⎯⎯⎯ 1981b. "Labor Market Segmentation: Time Series Hypotheses and Evidence." Unpublished paper, University of California, Berkeley.

Reich, Michael, and Edwards, Richard C. 1978. "Class Conflict and Political Parties in the United States." *Socialist Review 9*(May–June):55–74.

Reich, Michael, and Devine, James. 1981. "The Microeconomics of Conflict and Hierarchy in Capitalist Production." *Review of Radical Political Economics 12*(Winter):27–45.

Reich, Michael; Gordon, David M.; and Edwards, Richard C. 1973. "A Theory of Labor Market Segmentation." *American Economic Review 63*(May):359–365.

Reid, Joseph. 1973. "Sharecropping as an Understandable Market Response: The Post-Bellum South." *Journal of Economic History 33*(Mar.):106–130.

Reitell, Charles. 1964. "Machinery and Its Effect Upon Workers in the Automobile Industry." In *Giant Enterprise: Ford, General Motors, and the Au-*

tomobile Industry, edited by Alfred D. Chandler. New York: Harcourt, Brace and World.

Riegel, John W. 1942. *Management, Labor, and Technological Change.* Ann Arbor: University of Michigan Press.

Ripley, William. 1915. *Railroads: Finance and Organization.* London: Longmans, Green.

Roemer, John E. 1981. *Analytical Foundations of Marxian Economics.* Cambridge University Press.

Roethlisberger, Fritz, and Dickson, William. 1969. *Management and the Worker.* Cambridge, Mass.: Harvard University Press.

Rosenberg, Nathan. 1972. *Technology and the American Economy.* New York: Harper and Row.

Rosenberg, Sam. 1979. "A Survey of Empirical Work on Labor Market Segmentation." Working Paper no. 138, Department of Economics, University of California, Davis.

Rosenberg, Sam, and Weisskopf, Thomas E. 1981. "A Conflict Theory Approach to Inflation in the Postwar U.S. Economy." *American Economic Review Papers and Proceedings 71* (May):42–47.

Rostow, Walt W. 1978. *The World Economy: History and Prospect.* Austin: University of Texas Press.

Rubery, Jill. 1978. "Structured Labour Markets, Worker Organisation, and Low Pay." *Cambridge Journal of Economics 2* (Mar.):17–36.

Rumberger, Russell W. 1981a. "The Changing Skill Requirements of Jobs in the U.S. Economy." *Industrial and Labor Relations Review 34* (July):578–590.

1981b. *Overeducation in the U.S. Labor Market.* New York: Praeger.

Rumberger, Russell W., and Carnoy, Martin. 1980. "Segmentation in the U.S. Labor Market: Its Effects on Mobility and Earnings of Whites and Blacks." *Cambridge Journal of Economics 4* (June):117–132.

Russell, Jack. 1978. "The Coming of the Line: The Ford Highland Park Plant, 1910–1914." *Radical America 12* (May–June):28–46.

Ryan, Paul. 1980. "Empirical Analysis of Labor Market Segmentation." Paper presented at the Second Conference of the International Working Party on Labor Market Segmentation. Berlin.

Schumpeter, Joseph. 1939. *Business Cycles: A Theoretical, Historical and Statistical Analysis of the Capitalist Process.* 2 vols. New York: McGraw-Hill.

Shannon, David. 1945. "Post-Mortem on the Labor Safety-Valve Thesis." *Agricultural History 19* (Jan.):31–38.

Shergold, Peter R. 1977. "Wage Differentials Based on Skill in the United States, 1899–1914: A Case Study." *Labor History 18* (Fall):485–508.

Shlakman, Vera. 1934. *Chicopee: The Economic History of a Factory Town.* Northampton, Mass.: Smith College.

Slichter, Sumner H. 1919. *The Turnover of Factory Labor.* New York: D. Appleton.

1920. "The Scope and Nature of the Labor Turnover Problem." *Quarterly Journal of Economics 34* (Feb.):329–345.

1928. *Modern Economic Society.* New York: Holt.

1941. *Union Policies and Industrial Management.* Washington, D.C.: Brookings Institution.

Smith, Elliott Dunlap. 1939. *Technology and Labor: A Study of the Human Problems of Labor Saving.* New Haven, Conn.: Yale University Press.

Bibliography

Sogge, Tillman M. 1933. "Industrial Classes in the United States in 1930." *Journal of the American Statistical Association* 28(June):199–203.

Soule, George. 1947. *Prosperity Decade: From War to Depression, 1917–1929.* New York: Rinehart and Co.

Spengler, J. J. 1958. "Effects Produced in Receiving Countries by Pre-1939 Immigration." In *Economics of International Migration,* edited by Brinley Thomas. London: Macmillan.

Staines, Graham L. 1979. "Is Worker Dissatisfaction Rising?" *Challenge* 22(May–June):38–45.

Stone, Katherine. 1975. "The Origins of Job Structures in the Steel Industry." In *Labor Market Segmentation,* edited by Richard C. Edwards, Michael Reich, and David M. Gordon. Lexington, Mass.: Lexington Books.

Tabb, William, and Sawers, Larry (eds.). 1978. *Marxism and the Metropolis.* New York: Oxford University Press.

Taylor, Frederick Winslow. 1911. *The Principles of Scientific Management.* New York: Norton.

Taylor, George R. 1964. "American Economic Growth before 1840: An Exploratory Essay." *Journal of Economic History* 24(Dec.):427–444.

Taylor, Graham R. 1915. *Satellite Cities: A Study of Industrial Suburbs.* New York: Arno Press.

Temin, Peter. 1972. "Manufacturing." In *American Economic Growth,* by Lance Davis et al. New York: Harper and Row.

Thernstrom, Stephan, and Knights, Peter R. 1970. *Men in Motion: Some Data and Speculation About Urban Population Mobility in Nineteenth-Century America.* Los Angeles: Institute of Government and Public Affairs. University of California, Los Angeles.

Thistlewaite, Frank. 1958. "The Atlantic Migration of the Pottery Industry." *Economic History Review* 11(Dec.):264–278.

———. 1960. "Migration from Europe Overseas in the Nineteenth and Twentieth Centuries." In *Rapports* V, International Committee of Historical Sciences. Uppsala: Almquist and Wiksell.

Thomas, Brinley. 1954. *Migration and Economic Growth.* Cambridge University Press.

Thompson, Alexander M. 1979. "Capital Accumulation in U.S. Coal: A Case Study of Labor, Technology, and Competition." Unpublished doctoral dissertation. Stanford University, Stanford, Calif.

Thompson, C. Bertrand. 1915. "Scientific Management in Practice." *Quarterly Journal of Economics* 29(Feb.):262–307.

Thompson, E. P. 1979. *The Poverty of Theory and Other Essays.* New York: Monthly Review Press.

Tryon, Rolla M. 1917. *Household Manufactures in the United States, 1640–1860.* Chicago: University of Chicago Press.

Tuttle, William M., Jr. 1969. "Labor Conflict and Racial Violence in Chicago, 1894–1919." *Labor History* 10(Summer):408–432.

Ulman, Lloyd. 1955. *The Rise of the National Trade Union.* Cambridge, Mass.: Harvard University Press.

U.S. Bureau of the Census. 1903. *Census of Manufactures, 1900,* vol. I. Washington, D.C.: GPO.

———. 1975. *Historical Statistics of the United States, Colonial Times to 1970.* Washington, D.C.: GPO.

———. Various years. *Census of Manufacturing.* Washington, D.C.: GPO.

Bibliography

U.S. Department of Commerce. Various years. *Statistical Abstract of the United States.* Washington, D.C.: GPO.

U.S. Department of the Interior. 1871. *Ninth Census of the United States.* Vol. III, *The Statistics of Wealth and Industry.* Washington, D.C.: GPO.

U.S. Department of Labor, Bureau of Labor Statistics. 1979. *Handbook of Labor Statistics, 1978.* Washington, D.C.: GPO.

1980. *Employment and Earnings.* Washington, D.C.: GPO.

U.S. Department of State. 1841. *Compendium of the Enumeration of the Inhabitants and Statistics of the United States.* Washington, D.C.: GPO.

U.S. Immigration Commission. 1911a. *Abstracts of Reports of the Immigration Commission,* vol. I. Washington, D.C.: GPO.

1911b. *Statistical Review of Immigration, 1820–1910.* Washington, D.C.: GPO.

U.S. Industrial Commission. 1901. *Report.* 17 vols. Washington, D.C.: GPO.

U.S. President. 1972. *Report on Occupational Safety and Health.* Washington, D.C.: GPO.

U.S. President. 1980a. *Economic Report of the President 1980.* Washington, D.C.: GPO.

1980b. *Employment and Training Report of the President 1980.* Washington, D.C.: GPO.

Varaiya, Pravin, and Wiseman, Michael. 1980. "Reindustrialization and the Outlook for Declining Areas." Unpublished paper, University of California, Berkeley.

Vaughan, Roger J. 1979. *State Taxation and Economic Development.* Washington, D.C.: Council of State Planning Agencies.

Voice of Industry. Lowell, Mass., 1845–1848.

Wachtel, Howard. 1975. "Class Consciousness and Stratification in the Labor Process." In *Labor Market Segmentation,* edited by Richard C. Edwards, Michael Reich, and David M. Gordon. Lexington, Mass.: Lexington.

Wachtel, Howard, and Betsey, Charles. 1972. "Employment at Low Wages." *Review of Economics and Statistics* 54 (May):121–129.

Wachter, Michael. 1974. "Primary and Secondary Labor Markets: A Critique of the Dual Approach." *Brookings Papers on Economic Activity* 3:637–680.

Wakstein, Allen M. 1969. "The National Association of Manufacturers and Labor Relations in the 1920s." *Labor History 10* (Summer):375–407.

Ware, Caroline. 1931. *The Early New England Cotton Manufacture: A Study in Industrial Beginnings.* Boston: Houghton Mifflin.

Ware, Norman. 1935. *Labor in Modern Industrial Society.* New York: Russell and Russell.

1959. *The Labor Movement in the United States, 1860–1895.* Gloucester, Mass.: Peter Smith.

1964. *The Industrial Worker, 1840–1860.* Chicago: Quadrangle Books. (Originally published in 1924.)

Weinstein, James. 1967. *The Decline of Socialism in America, 1912–1925.* New York: Monthly Review Press.

1968. *The Corporate Ideal in the Liberal State, 1900–1918.* Boston: Beacon Press.

Weir, Stan. 1977. "Informal Work Groups and Management Practice." Unpublished paper, University of California, Los Angeles.

Weiss, Rona. 1976. "Transition in the Early American Economy: The Randolph Boot and Shoe Industry: A Case in Point." Unpublished paper, University of Massachusetts, Amherst.

Bibliography

Weisskopf, Thomas E. 1978. "Marxist Perspectives on Cyclical Crisis." In *U.S. Capitalism in Crisis,* edited by the Union for Radical Political Economics. New York: Union for Radical Political Economics.

1981. "The Current Economic Crisis in Historical Perspective." *Socialist Review 11*(May–June):9–53.

Wells, David. 1895. *Recent Economic Changes.* New York: Appleton.

Wilcock, Richard C. 1961. "Industrial Management's Policies toward 'Unionism'." In *Labor and the New Deal,* edited by Milton Derber and Edwin Young. Madison: University of Wisconsin Press.

Wilkinson, Frank. In press. *The Dynamics of Labor Market Segmentation.* New York: Academic Press.

Williams, William A. 1962. *The Contours of American History.* New York: Knopf.

Williamson, Harold F. (ed.). 1951. *The Growth of the American Economy.* 2nd edition. N.J.: Prentice-Hall, Englewood Cliffs.

Williamson, Jeffrey G., and Lindert, Peter H. 1980. *American Inequality: A Macroeconomic History.* New York: Academic Press.

Wolman, Leo. 1936. *Ebb and Flow in Trade Unionism.* New York: National Bureau of Economic Research.

1952. "Concentration of Union Membership." *Proceedings of the Fifth Annual Meeting of the Industrial Relations Research Association 5.* Madison, Wis.: Industrial Relations Research Association (Dec.):214–219.

Woodward, C. Vann. 1951. *Origins of the New South, 1877–1913.* Baton Rouge: Louisiana University Press.

Worthman, Paul B. 1969. "Black Workers and Labor Unions in Birmingham, Alabama, 1897–1904." *Labor History 10*(Summer):375–407.

Woytinsky, W. S. 1953. *Employment and Wages in the United States.* New York: Twentieth Century Fund.

Wright, Carroll D. 1895. *The Industrial Evolution of the United States.* New York: Flood & Vincent.

1905. "Influence of Trade Unions on Immigrants." U.S. Department of Labor, Bulletin No. 56, January.

Wright, Erik Olin. 1978. *Class, Crisis and the State.* London: New Left Books.

Young, Michael. 1954. *The Rise of the Meritocracy.* Baltimore: Penguin Books.

Zevin, Robert. 1972. "The Growth of Cotton Production after 1815." In *The Reinterpretation of American Economic History,* edited by Robert Fogel and Stanley Engerman. New York: Harper and Row.

Zimbalist, Andrew (ed.). 1979. *Case Studies on the Labor Process.* New York: Monthly Review Press.

Index

Abbott, Edith, 71
accidents, industrial
  and homogenization of labor, 148
  and segmentation of labor, 217
accumulation, *see* capital accumulation; social structure of accumulation
Adams, Henry, 102
Aid for Dependent Children, 209
Almy and Brown, 65, 71
Amalgamated Clothing Workers of America, 158
American Federation of Labor, 144, 177
American Railway Union, 126
American Tobacco Co., 110
antitrust, and corporate consolidation, 107, 110, 111
antiunionism, 142, 143-4, 219
assembly line, and mass production, 131-3

Bagley, Sarah, 72
balkanization of labor markets, 7
big business, monopoly capital and challenge to, 106-12
blacks
  and homogenization of labor, 152-3
  in core firms vs. periphery, 190-2
  job segregation, 174
  outmigration from South, 153
  and segmentation of labor by race, 206-10
  as strikebreakers, 152-3
  wage labor, 56
Boot and Shoe Workers Union, 144-5
Boston Associates, 65, 69

boundaries, social structure of accumulation, 24-5
Braverman, Harry, 6
Brecher, Jeremy, 97
Bretton Woods monetary system, 167, 170
Brown, Moses, 57, 58, 59
building trades, business unionism, 145
bureaucratic control, post-WWII, 187
Burlington Mills, 189-190
Business Roundtable, 219
business unionism, 144-5

capital accumulation
  and collective working-class activity, 20
  and concentration of control and ownership, 19
  and economic recovery, 102-3
  and environment, 23-4
  and labor process, 20
  and macrodynamics, 27
  and spread of wage labor, 19-20
  steps, 23
  and untransformed labor, 79
capitalism
  dynamics of development, 18-22
  stages: and long swings, 22-39; and social structure of accumulation, 9-10, 32
capitalist economy, *see* economy; long swings; world economy
capitalist organization, and crafts, 64-6
capitalists, rising from ranks of craftsmen, 65
Carnegie, Andrew, 59, 106

282

children
  initial proletarianization, 67–73
  replacement by women in labor
    force, 121
Clark, Victor, 66, 69, 115
class conflict, and homogenization of
  labor, 121–7
clothing industry, industrial union,
  158–9
Cole, Arthur, 85–6
Communist Party, 184
competition, and corporate consolidation, 106–7
Congress of Industrial Organizations, 169, 177
consolidation, corporate, 106–7
  and firm size, 108–9
consolidation period
  homogenization of labor, 127–62
  initial proletarianization of labor,
    79–94
  innovations necessary for, 11–13
  in labor process and labor markets,
    10–11
  segmentation of labor, 184–92
contracting, inside, 91–2
core firms vs. periphery, 190–2
  blacks in, 208–9
  divergence, 192–200
  secondary labor processes in,
    200–2
corporations, large, and capital accumulation, 19
crafts, demise of, 59
craftsmen, initial proletarianization,
  64–7
craft system of organizing labor process, 92
craft unionism, and homogenization
  of labor, 159–60

Dawley, Alan, 63
Debs, Eugene, 126
decay
  homogenization of labor, 162–4
  initial proletarianization, 53–4,
    94–9
  in labor process and labor markets,
    11
  segmentation of labor, 215–26

decentralization of factories, and
  homogenization of labor, 138–9
drive system, and homogenization of
  labor, 14–15, 128–35
dues checkoff, 184
Du Pont Co., 110

earnings, of primary workers, 222
  see also wages
Eastman Kodak, 180
economy
  expansion and contraction, 28–9,
    45
  growth in 1920s, 104–5
  turn of century, 102–3
  see also Great Depression; long
    swings; world economy
employers' offensive, against unions,
  143–4
employment
  immigrants, 93
  and output, 80–2
  see also labor; labor market; unem-
    ployment
Employment Act (1946), 169
environment, and capital accumulation, 23–4
exogenous forces, and social structure of accumulation, 31
expansion, *see* economy; long swings;
  world economy
exploration
  and homogenization of labor,
    113–27
  and initial proletarianization of
    labor, 56–78
  in labor process and labor markets,
    10
  and segmentation of labor, 171–6

factories
  control of labor process in, 58–9
  decentralization, and homogeniza-
    tion of labor, 138–9
  families as labor in, 68
  females, *see* women
Folbre, Nancy, 71
Fordism, 131–3, 145–6
Ford Motor Co., 132–3, 174, 180

union(s)
  corporate debate on future of, 221
  employer offensive against, 143–4
  membership early 1900s, 154–5;
    and success of workers' protest,
    153–4
  membership 1930s, 177
  and worker unrest, 122–6
union contracts
  management prerogatives clauses,
    188
  productivity bargaining, 188
unionism, business, 144–5
unionization, in core vs. periphery
    firms, 199
United Auto Workers, 184, 188
United Brotherhood of Carpenters
    and Joiners, 144
United Mine Workers, 144, 157–8,
    184, 188
U.S. Rubber Co., 174, 180
U.S. Steel Corp., 110, 111
untransformed labor, and capital ac-
    cumulation, 79

value added per production worker,
    in core vs. periphery firms,
    193–6
vocational training, 1920s, 174
Voice of Industry, 78

wage labor
  and capital accumulation, 19–20
  development of system, 13–14
  in pre-capitalist society, 54–5
  and stagnation, late 1800s, 53
  Yankee farm girl experiment, 53,
    68, 70–2
wages
  in core vs. periphery firms, 193–7
  and homogenization of labor,
    119–20, 149–50
  incentive schemes, 140–1
  of primary workers, 222
Wagner Act, 169
Waltham System, 69
Waltham Watch Co., 92
Ware, Caroline, 68
Ware, Norma, 66–7, 70, 90

War Labor Board, 183
war millionaires, 1860s, 52
War Time Labor Disputes Act, 183
welfare payments, and segmentation
    of labor by race, 209
Wells, David, 102, 116, 118
Western Electric Co., Hawthorne ex-
    periments, 173
Western Federation of Miners, 161
Westinghouse Corp., 108, 180
white-collar work, segmentation by
    sex in, 205
wildcat strikes, WWII, 183
Williamson, Harold, 85–6
women
  employment, and structure of
    labor market, 93–4
  initial proletarianization, 67–73
  and labor market homogenization,
    120–1
  occupational segregation, 150–2,
    174
  and segmentation of labor, 204–6
workers' protest
  and strike activity, 155–7
  and union membership, 153–4
working class
  collective activity, and capital ac-
    cumulation, 20
  power, and social structure of ac-
    cumulation, 169
working-class divisions
  and balkanization of labor mar-
    kets, 7–8
  and growing homogeneity, 6
  and new social history, 6–7
  and postindustrial tendencies, 5
workplace, capitalist, 87–8
world economy
  in 1820s–1890s, 49–54
  1870s to WWII, 101–12
  since 1920, 166–70
  output declines, 46
world trade, over long swing, 46
World War II, and segmentation of
    labor, 182–4

Yankee farm girls
  in labor force, 53, 68, 70–2
  replaced by Irish immigrants, 75–6

288